Why We Lost the Sex Wars

Why We Lost the Sex Wars

SEXUAL FREEDOM IN THE #METOO ERA

Lorna N. Bracewell

UNIVERSITY OF MINNESOTA PRESS
Minneapolis
London

Published by the University of Minnesota Press
111 Third Avenue South, Suite 290
Minneapolis, MN 55401-2520
http://www.upress.umn.edu

ISBN 978-1-5179-0673-3 (hc)
ISBN 978-1-5179-0674-0 (pb)

Library of Congress record available at https://lccn.loc.gov/2020048342

Printed in the United States of America on acid-free paper

The University of Minnesota is an equal-opportunity educator and employer.

29 28 27 26 25 24 23 22 21   10 9 8 7 6 5 4 3 2 1

Contents

Introduction

RETHINKING THE SEX WARS

On October 5, 2017, the *New York Times* reported that movie mogul Harvey Weinstein had used his position as one of the most powerful producers in Hollywood to pressure (and in some cases coerce) women into engaging in unwanted sexual acts (Kantor and Twohey 2017). A few days later, both the *New York Times* and the *New Yorker* published follow-up stories further exposing Weinstein's career of sexual abuse, which spanned five decades and targeted dozens of women, including some of the best-known actresses in the world (Farrow 2017; Kantor and Abrams 2017). In the following days, more and more witnesses stepped forward to break the decades-long silence regarding Weinstein's predatory behavior. On the afternoon of October 15, 2017, this outpouring of accusations against one man burgeoned into a global mass-mediated speak-out against sexual harassment and assault. Inspired by a tweet from actress Alyssa Milano, which was inspired in turn by a campaign launched over a decade earlier by activist Tarana Burke, millions of people began sharing their own stories of sexual abuse on social media using the hashtag #MeToo.[1] Since the hashtag first went viral, a number of astonishing shifts have taken place. As of January 2019, over two hundred high-profile celebrities, politicians, and business leaders have been publicly accused of sexual misconduct and, in many cases, met with serious consequences.[2] Formal complaints of sexual harassment to the federal Equal Employment Opportunity Commission increased in 2018 by nearly 14 percent over previous years.[3] While 2019 saw a 1.2 percent year-over-year decrease in sexual harassment complaints to the EEOC, the 7,514 sexual harassment charges filed that year still represent an increase over the five years preceding the start of the #MeToo movement. State legislatures and the notoriously gridlocked U.S. Congress have even taken up a variety of #MeToo-inspired legislation, including laws limiting the use of nondisclosure agreements, improving the testing of rape kits, and extending the statute of limitations for victims of sexual assault to file civil lawsuits against their abusers.[4] Perhaps most significantly, countless survivors have come forward and spoken out publicly about their experiences of sexual harassment and assault for the first time, reaching audiences of unprecedented size via social media.[5]

Almost as quickly as this #MeToo moment coalesced, a backlash against it emerged. At the forefront of this backlash were conservatives who, just days after Milano's inaugural #MeToo tweet, publicly denounced the movement as "mass hysteria," "trial-by-mob," and an affront to "due process" (Hernroth-Roghtstein 2017). In the following weeks, conservatives refined their critique, adding a dose of sex and gender traditionalism to this classical liberal brew. In outlets like the *National Review* and the *Weekly Standard,* expressions of concern for the rights of the accused mingled with tirades against "contemporary feminism," "consent morality," and what columnist Mona Charen called "our unbuttoned age" (Wilhelm 2018; Charen 2018; French 2018). Feminist meddling with traditional gender roles and sexual morality was the cause of sexual harassment, not its cure, and as long as #MeToo remained tethered to feminist goals like social equality and sexual autonomy for women, #MeToo's conservative critics insisted, the movement was doomed to fail.

While conservatives were at the vanguard of the #MeToo backlash, criticism of the movement has also emanated from more progressive ideological quarters. For example, just one month after #MeToo first went viral, journalist and socialist Barbara Ehrenreich chastised the movement on Twitter for its bourgeois bias. "Our current sex harassment discussion is woefully class-skewed," Ehrenreich wrote. "Too much about actresses and not enough about hotel housekeepers." Other progressives, like philosopher Yolanda Wilson (2018) and journalist Gillian B. White, have openly questioned #MeToo's ability to address the distinctive forms of racialized sexual harassment experienced by nonwhite women. As White (2017) observes, "believability, sympathy, and public rage are reserved

only for certain women. And those women are rarely women of color."
#MeToo has also faced criticism from the academic left for what cultural
studies professor Lisa Duggan characterizes as its neoliberalism, meaning
its tendency to frame sexual harassment as an individual, as opposed to a
structural, problem that should be handled on a case-by-case basis through
the instigation of public scandal and corporate practices of accountability
such as internal investigation and firing.[6]

While this small contingent has called attention to #MeToo's limitations as intersectional feminist praxis, a far more prominent chorus of
progressive voices has offered what might best be described as a sex-
positive critique of the #MeToo movement. This genre of progressive
critique made its debut in early 2018, when a group of artists affiliated
with the cultural left, including actress Catherine Deneuve, director
Michael Haneke, and writer Catherine Millet, issued public statements
expressing concern that the #MeToo movement was careening off course,
mutating from a righteous campaign against sexual harassment into a "crusade against any form of eroticism" and a "new puritanism" (Safronova
2018). Within a matter of weeks, self-identified feminists like Margaret
Atwood, Daphne Merkin, and Bari Weiss joined the ranks of this sex-
positive chorus, warning that the #MeToo movement was "stripping sex
of eros," undercutting women's "agency," and transporting us "back to
a more sexually restrictive era" of "smelling salts and fainting couches"
(Merkin 2018; Atwood 2018; Weiss 2018).

Although they could not differ more with respect to their sexual
ethics (an effusive *laissez faire et laissez passer* eroticism versus a compen-
dium, almost perverse in its thoroughness, of sexual "thou shalt nots"),
#MeToo's sex-positive critics share with conservatives a concern that
the #MeToo movement is riding roughshod over due process rights and
civil liberties. Bari Weiss (2018) has laid out the progressive version of
this critique in an op-ed for the *New York Times*. According to Weiss,
#MeToo promotes a "'believe all women' vision of feminism" that de-
mands "unthinking belief" of every allegation of harassment and abuse
and leaves those accused without recourse or defense. Dismissing this
"ideological orthodoxy" as "condescending" and "pedantic," Weiss asserts
that "facts serve feminists far better than faith" and that "due process is

better than mob rule." Margaret Atwood has expressed a similar sentiment in an op-ed addressing #MeToo for the *Globe and Mail*. Cautioning that "understandable and temporary vigilante justice can morph into a culturally solidified lynch mob habit," Atwood (2018) likens the #MeToo movement to the Cosa Nostra, another "extralegal power structure" that "began as a resistance to political tyranny" but devolved into arbitrary and unaccountable thuggery.

This convergence of conservatives and sex-positive progressives on the question of #MeToo's relationship to due process rights and civil liberties is telling; it points toward a deep commonality uniting segments of the progressive left with the conservative right in our present political moment. What these seemingly disparate political forces have in common is a deep attachment to the core tenets of classical liberalism, particularly the belief that individual liberty is of paramount concern, taking precedence over goals like dismantling entrenched structural inequalities of race, gender, class, and sexuality. Sex-positive progressives' commitment to individual liberty is, of course, more thoroughgoing than that of conservatives, extending as it does deep into the so-called private sphere to stake out an expansive sphere for personal sexual choice. Nevertheless, the basic ideological posture of conservatives and sex-positive progressives vis-à-vis #MeToo is the same: Potent collective challenges to normalized and institutionally entrenched practices of sexual oppression and domination threaten individual liberty, and the only legitimate recourse available to those aggrieved by sexual harassment, sexual assault, or other sexual injustice is liberalism's signature cocktail of individual rights, formal equality, limited government, and the rule of law.[7]

This overlap between two otherwise vigorously opposed adversaries in the arena of sexual politics has been largely overlooked in the abundant commentary on the #MeToo movement. I note it here to raise the following question: How did such a narrow set of political possibilities for resisting the wielding of sex as an instrument of domination come to be embraced across so broad a swath of the political spectrum in the contemporary United States? Or, to put the same question more directly, how did sexual-political possibilities not tethered to liberal notions of individual rights, civil liberties, due process, and personal privacy come to be as anathema to sex-positive progressives and feminists as they are to traditionalists and conservatives? A core aim of this book is to answer this question—to render the pride of place liberalism has within the landscape of contemporary sexual politics more legible and also, I hope, more vexing, contingent, and amenable to change. To do this, I will offer a version of what Michel Foucault calls a "history of the present," tracing the descent of our current homochromous and claustrophobic sexual politics[8] back through the political struggles and conceptual transformations of the feminist sex wars (1977, 31).[9]

THE CATFIGHT NARRATIVE

The feminist sex wars, also known as the lesbian sex wars, the feminist sexuality debates, and, most reductively, the porn wars, were a series of conflicts over matters pertaining to sex and sexuality that embroiled the feminist movement primarily in the United States, but also, to a lesser extent, Australia, Canada, and England, from the mid-1970s to the early 1990s. Over the course of these conflicts, feminists staked out a variety of positions on a number of issues, including pornography, sadomasochism, butch–femme identities and practices, intergenerational sex, commercial sex, lesbianism, heterosexuality, the eroticization of race and ethnicity, the nature and limits of law, the First Amendment's free speech guarantee, the wisdom and sufficiency of state-centered politics, the boundaries of the category of woman, and the meaning of sexual freedom. However, despite the wide-ranging character of these debates, the sex wars tend to be remembered as a straightforward clash between sex-negative feminists concerned primarily with sexual danger on one side and sex-positive feminists concerned primarily with sexual pleasure on the other.

I call this simplistic framing of the history of the sex wars the catfight narrative because it portrays the sex wars along the lines of a stereotypical catfight: a straightforward, two-sided, and wholly internecine squabble among women. The origins of the catfight narrative are not difficult to trace. On April 24, 1982, about eight hundred scholars, students, artists, and activists convened at Barnard College for a conference titled "The Scholar and the Feminist 9: Towards a Politics of Sexuality." According to Carole Vance, the academic coordinator for the conference, the conference's aim was to "refocus" the "feminist agenda on sexuality" by addressing "women's sexual pleasure, choice, and autonomy, acknowledging that sexuality is simultaneously a domain of restriction, repression, and danger as well as a domain of exploration, pleasure, and agency" (1993a, 294; 1984, 443). Judith Butler (1982), who attended the conference as a graduate student[10] and reviewed its controversial program, *A Diary of a Conference on Sexuality,* states the conference's aim more directly: "The clear purpose of the *Diary*—and of the Barnard conference—is to dislodge the anti-pornography movement as the one and only feminist discourse on sex" and "counterbalance the anti-pornography perspective on sexuality with an exploration into women's sexual agency and autonomy."

Not all those who attended the Barnard conference embraced this aim. In fact, on the morning of the conference, just outside the gates of Barnard Hall, a group of self-identified radical and lesbian feminists formed a picket line. Sporting T-shirts that read "For a Feminist Sexuality" on the front and "Against S&M" on the back, the protestors distributed a two-page leaflet accusing the conference and its organizers of endorsing "sexual institutions and values that oppress all women," including "pornography," "butch–femme sex roles," "sadomasochism," "violence against women," and the sexual abuse of children.[11] Although the leaflet was signed "the Coalition for a Feminist Sexuality and Against Sadomasochism (Women Against Violence Against Women; Women Against Pornography; New York Radical Feminists)," it was soon discovered to have been the almost exclusive handiwork of Women Against Pornography (WAP), at the time the leading antipornography feminist organization in the United States.[12]

In the weeks after this dramatic clash at the gates of Barnard Hall, the battle between supporters of the Barnard conference and their feminist detractors continued in the pages of some of the foremost feminist and gay and lesbian periodicals of the day. For example, in an open letter reprinted in the *Body Politic,* Barnard conference organizers accused the antipornography feminist protesters of flouting "the basic principles of a democratic radical movement," embracing "authoritarianism," and feeding an antifeminist "backlash" (Body Politic 1982, 16). Not to be outdone, in a pamphlet reproduced in the back matter of the journal *Feminist Studies,* antipornography feminists accused the Barnard conference's organizers of promoting "sexual fascism," "patriarchal sexuality," and "crimes of sexual violence against women" (Vance et al. 1983, 180). The fallout from the Barnard conference proved so intense that, in a reflection essay published thirty years later, Gayle Rubin notes that, far from feeling privileged to have been a firsthand witness to such a significant part of feminist history, she feels "traumatized" and "nurse[s] the horror of having been there" (2011a, 195). Due, no doubt, to their sorocidal ferocity, the conflicts surrounding the Barnard conference have been seared indelibly into feminism's collective memory, coming to serve as a symbolic shorthand for the sex wars and providing the foundation of the catfight narrative.

Examples of the catfight narrative abound. One of the earliest can be found in Ann Ferguson's "Sex War: The Debate between Radical and Libertarian Feminists," published in a 1984 special issue of *Signs* devoted to "the feminist sexuality debates." Ferguson describes "an increasing polarization of American feminists into two camps on issues of feminist sexual morality" (106). "The first camp," according to Ferguson, "holds that sexuality in a male-dominant society involves *danger*—that is, that sexual practices perpetuate violence against women" (106). "The opposing camp," Ferguson continues, holds that "the key feature of sexuality is the potentially liberating aspects of the exchange of pleasure between consenting partners" (106). Here, in the influential article that gave the sex wars their name,[13] we have the basic structure of the catfight narrative: two feminist camps, described in the language of pleasure and danger lifted directly from the Barnard conference's concept paper,[14] squared off against each other with no intimation that others may have been party to these debates.

Since the publication of Ferguson's article, many other prominent accounts of the sex wars have reproduced this Barnard-centric catfight narrative. For example, historian Ruth Rosen describes what she calls "the pornography wars" as "debates over pornography" that "polarized the women's movement" and "turned on whether sex represented more of a danger than a pleasure" (2000, 191, 193, 416). Similarly, Christine Stansell presents the sex wars as a "bitter and irreconcilable" "division between antipornography crusaders and their opponents, the 'pro-sex' radicals"

(2010, 346). "Each side accused the other of advocating ideas that would destroy feminism," Stansell elaborates, with "pro-sex feminists decr[ying] the self-righteous morality of the antipornography forces and its animus to free speech" and antipornography feminists "accus[ing] their critics of being brainwashed by patriarchal sexuality and ignoring the deadly injuries pornography inflicted on millions of voiceless women" (346).

A particularly extreme example of the catfight narrative can be found in Jane F. Gerhard's *Desiring Revolution: Second-Wave Feminism and the Rewriting of American Sexual Thought, 1920 to 1982* (2001). Here Gerhard writes of the sex wars as though they are entirely reducible to the events of the Barnard conference. For example, in the book's concluding chapter, "Negotiating Legacies in the Feminist Sex Wars, 1982," the only place in which Gerhard shows the legacies of feminist sexual thought being negotiated is in the proceedings of the Barnard conference. More recently, the catfight narrative has made an appearance in the preface to *Last Days at Hot Slit* (2019), an anthology of the fiction and nonfiction writings of leading antipornography feminist theorist and activist Andrea Dworkin. While Dworkin is widely viewed by contemporary feminists as "the censorial demagogue to shoot down," the anthology's coeditor, Johanna Fateman, writes, "Nearly four decades after the historic Barnard Conference on Sexuality, which drew the battle lines of the feminist sex wars—pro-sex feminists staking out territory for the investigation of pleasure, while Women Against Pornography protested outside . . . we hope it's possible to consider what was lost in the fray" (2019, 12). Fateman's intention with this anthology is clearly to elevate Dworkin above the fray of the sex wars and enable readers to consider her work in fresh and broader contexts. Unfortunately, by reproducing the reductive catfight-narrative version of the history of the sex wars right in the collection's preface, she all but dooms this worthy project from the start.

Of all the scholars who have taken the sex wars as an object of inquiry, Carolyn Bronstein has perhaps done the most to challenge the narrow parameters of the catfight narrative. In her 2011 rigorously researched history of the first decade of antipornography feminist organizing in the United States, *Battling Pornography: The American Feminist Antipornography Movement, 1976–1986,* Bronstein recounts a dramatic sex wars confrontation that did not take place at Barnard College and that did not involve feminism's "pleasure" and "danger" factions. The clash Bronstein describes occurred between antipornography feminists and nonfeminist civil libertarian attorneys at a colloquium at the New York University School of Law in 1978. According to Bronstein, the central conflict at this colloquium was between "classical liberalism," represented by the civil libertarians, and "a communitarian social position," represented by the antipornography feminists (181). While Bronstein's characterization of antipornography feminism as a variant of communitarianism here is just plain wrong, a point I will flesh out more fully in just a moment, her decision to highlight the schism between antipornography feminists and civil libertarians at this colloquium marks a significant step outside of the catfight narrative's restrictive frame. Unfortunately, Bronstein's discussion of this aspect of the sex wars is limited to this single event and is thus far from complete. Moreover, because her study is focused narrowly on antipornography feminist organizing, Bronstein fails to explore the complex relationships other feminist parties to the sex wars had with liberal activists and ideas. As a whole, then, *Battling Pornography* portrays the sex wars as a battle primarily between antipornography feminists and pro-sex feminists, largely reproducing the terms of the catfight narrative that it seemed, at one moment at least, poised to challenge.

As this brief survey of prominent examples suggests, reductive dualisms are a hallmark of the catfight narrative: pro-sex versus anti-sex, sex-positive versus sex-negative, anti-censorship versus pro-censorship, pleasure versus danger. As these examples also demonstrate, the catfight narrative tends to present the sex wars in such a way that an obvious moral or political lesson is implied: true feminism is always on the side of sex, pleasure, expression, and personal freedom; a feminist sexual politics articulated outside of this implicitly liberal sex-positive idiom—a feminist sexual politics that, for example, emphasizes the vulnerability of members of marginalized groups to sexual oppression and exploitation in a society deeply stratified by hierarchies of race, gender, sex, and class—is nothing but antisex prudery that bolsters conservative notions of sex as inherently degrading and women as inherently vulnerable.

Nowhere is the political lesson implicit in the catfight narrative made more explicit than in journalist Masha Gessen's "Sex, Consent, and the Dangers of 'Misplaced Scale'" (2017). In this short essay, published just over a month after Alyssa Milano's inaugural #MeToo tweet, Gessen surveys the fissures on the feminist left opened up by the rise of the #MeToo movement and draws a line between what they call "our present moment of sexual renegotiation" and the feminist sex wars. During the sex wars, Gessen writes, "the women's movement had split into two camps: a less audible and less visible sexual liberationist wing and a dominant wing that was highly, militantly suspicious of sex." In Gessen's view, these sex wars–era battle lines have reemerged in the #MeToo moment, with the #MeToo movement representing a revival of feminism's sex-skeptical wing and #MeToo's sex-positive critics, including Gessen themself, representing the resurgent "sexual liberationist wing." That Gessen sees themself as fighting in a kind of Barnard conference reenactment is confirmed by the fact that they draw on one of the most influential texts to come out of that conference, Gayle Rubin's "Thinking Sex: Notes for a Radical Theory of the Politics of Sexuality" (1984), to frame #MeToo as a movement steeped in conservative ideas about the inherent sinfulness of sex and the weakness and vulnerability of women. By imposing the reductive dualisms of the catfight narrative directly onto the contemporary feminist debate surrounding #MeToo, Gessen signals that in their view, not much has changed since the sex wars. Feminism remains divided into the same two camps, with one undoubtedly feminist camp fighting on the side of sex, pleasure, expression, and personal freedom, and the other feminist-in-name-only camp unwittingly promoting an agenda of conservative sexual authoritarianism that undermines women's autonomy and agency.

The lesson Gessen derives here from the history of the sex wars sheds important light on the question I posed earlier: Why has the sex-positive feminist left converged with the antifeminist right on a quintessentially liberal defense of individual rights, civil liberties, due process, and personal privacy in the #MeToo moment? As Gessen helps us see, the catfight narrative's rendition of the history of the sex wars is driving, at least in part, this improbable conjunction. According to the catfight narrative, during the sex wars, valiant feminist defenders of consensual pleasure, individual choice, and sexual expression confronted their censorious foes, exposing them for the prudish and paternalistic pseudo feminists they truly were. If the lesson of the catfight narrative is that a feminist sexual politics articulated outside of a liberal idiom of individual rights, expressive freedom, and personal privacy is no feminism at all, then #MeToo, with its emphasis on the structural vulnerability of members of marginalized groups to sexual oppression and exploitation in a context of grave inequalities of gender, race, wealth, and status, must be a kind of conservatism in disguise, and the only valid feminist response to this thinly veiled attack on pleasure, expression, freedom, and choice is an uncompromising assertion of an implicitly liberal sex positivity.

My guiding aim in this book is to explode the catfight narrative, and the narrow and debilitating feminist sexual politics it secretes. I hope to effect this explosion by rethinking the sex wars—that is, by excavating and then analyzing aspects of the sex wars that the Barnard-centric catfight narrative has occluded from view. This rethinking unfolds along two dimensions. The first dimension concerns the influential role played by liberalism and its associated concepts like limited government, the public and the private, the harm principle, and expressive freedom during the sex wars. While civil libertarian defenders of privacy, free speech, and personal liberty were not present at the Barnard conference, and therefore tend not to be cast as key protagonists in the catfight narrative's rendition of the sex wars, liberal jurists, philosophers, and activists, in fact, actively engaged in the sex wars in a variety of ways, profoundly transforming both liberal and feminist sexual politics along the way. *Why We Lost the Sex Wars* explores these transformative liberal engagements in detail, arguing that the sex wars were as much about negotiating the relationship of feminism to liberalism as they were about competition between rival feminist factions.

The second dimension along which the rethinking at the heart of *Why We Lost the Sex Wars* unfolds concerns the contributions made by feminists of color to the sex wars debates. While the catfight narrative suggests that the sex wars were a conflict between two predominantly white feminist camps from which the voices, experiences, and concerns of women of color were, by and large, absent, a careful examination of the historical record—including the proceedings of the Barnard conference itself—reveals a markedly different story. Black and so-called third world feminists, as many feminists of color identified themselves during this period, did not sit the sex wars out; nor did they simply side with one of the catfight narrative's leading white feminist factions. Rather, during the sex wars, including at the Barnard conference itself, Black and third world feminists articulated their own distinctive analyses of pornography, S&M, and other sex-related issues, challenging the terms in which white feminists were analyzing these issues at the time and exceeding and confounding reductive pro-sex/anti-sex categories.

Taken together, these two dimensions of *Why We Lost the Sex Wars* comprise an effort to shift contemporary thinking about the sex wars beyond Barnard—that is, beyond the internecine feminist conflict foregrounded by the catfight narrative and toward other conflicts, confrontations, and relationships that were integral to the sex wars and that continue to be of enduring significance for feminist sexual politics today.

BEYOND BARNARD

As described above, there is widespread agreement among scholars and more casual students of feminist history alike that the sex wars were a two-sided, internecine feminist conflict along the lines of the clash that occurred between rival feminist factions at the Barnard conference on sexuality in spring 1982. However, despite this broad-based agreement on the cogency of the catfight narrative, there is no shared consensus among scholars on what the sides in this catfight ought to be called. For example, in her influential 1984 *Signs* article, Ann Ferguson describes the sex wars as a conflict between "radical" and "libertarian" feminists.[15] However, since Ferguson's article first appeared, names for the sex wars' central combatants have proliferated. Anti-pornography and pro-sex feminists, pro-censorship and anti-censorship feminists, anti-sex and pro-sex feminists, and sex-negative and sex-positive feminists are among the most common (Bronstein 2011; Stansell 2010; Strossen 1993, 1995; Vance and Snitow 1984; Rubin 1983; Strub 2011; Fahs 2014). Others include anti-pornography and pro-pornography feminists, anti-pornography and anti-anti-pornography feminists, radical and sex radical feminists, sexism and sex feminists, dominance feminists and sex positivists, and radical feminists and sexual liberals (Vance 1993a; Rosen 2000; Chapkis 1997; Chancer 1998; Bazelon 2015; Leidholdt and Raymond 1990).

That simply naming the sex wars' central combatants has proven to be such a bewildering and controversial task is telling. Not only does it point to the extent to which many of the sex wars' constitutive conflicts remain unsettled, but it also raises serious doubts about attempts to portray the sex wars as a straightforward, two-sided catfight.[16] After all, if the sex wars were simple enough to lend themselves to some tidy dichotomous schema, then why is there such widespread disagreement about which tidy dichotomous schema is most appropriate to describe them? The answer, of course, is that the sex wars were not so simple, and any attempt to make them out to be not only obscures important events in feminist history but also diminishes our capacity to reckon with the potent currents in contemporary feminism that these events have, at least in part, produced.

It should be noted here that I am not the first scholar to lament the simplistic and inaccurate terms in which the sex wars are commonly represented.[17] Carole Vance, a feminist scholar who directly participated in the sex wars as the academic coordinator of the Barnard conference, has also criticized something very similar to what I am calling the catfight narrative. "The common conceptualization that the sex debates had two 'sides,'" Vance writes, "dichotomized by opposing positions (pro- or anti-pornography, or pro- or anti-sex, for example) is erroneous." Interestingly, Vance lays the blame for this erroneous conceptualization of the sex wars at the feet of the Barnard conference's antipornography feminist detractors. According to Vance, the Barnard conference was not a broadside against antipornography feminism as its critics alleged. "The purpose of the conference," Vance writes, "was unassailably balanced and inclusive: a feminist politics of sexuality must address both pleasure and danger" (1993a, 296). Unfortunately, Vance maintains, the Solomonic intent of the Barnard conference's organizers was lost on antipornography feminist activists who unfairly depicted the conference as "a mindless, hedonistic extravaganza doubling as an attack on feminism" (296). As Vance tells the story, these antipornography feminist polemics "gave birth to a 'phantom' conference" pitting "sexual perverts" against true feminists (295). This "phantom conference" narrative, Vance alleges, was widely disseminated by "hostile publications" like *off our backs,* giving rise to the widespread view of the sex wars as a two-sided sororicidal skirmish (295). While Vance's concern about reductive and dichotomizing portrayals of the sex wars is well placed, her effort to lay the blame for such portrayals at the feet of her antipornography feminist foes does more to perpetuate the catfight narrative than to contest it. If the sex wars are ever to be reckoned with in at least something close to their full nuance and complexity, then a counternarrative that looks beyond Barnard—that is, beyond the binaries of the catfight narrative—is in order.

The chapters that follow offer just such a counternarrative. The sex wars, I propose, are most accurately and generatively conceived of not as a two-sided catfight wholly internal to feminism itself, but rather as a dynamic and multidimensional series of conflicts, relationships, and exchanges between several different parties, only some of whom were feminists. If it makes sense to speak of a primary cleavage in my counternarrative of the sex wars—and I am not sure that it does—then that cleavage would not be between feminists as the catfight narrative has it, but between feminists and liberals of various stripes. On the feminist side in my counternarrative, the central players include antipornography feminists, sex-radical feminists, and Black and third world feminists, who, I argue, intervened strategically within both antipornography and sex-radical feminist discourses to center the sexual desires and concerns of women of color. On the liberal side in my counternarrative, the key players are non-, and in some cases even anti-, feminist civil libertarians, who fought pitched battles against both antipornography feminists and sex-radical feminists during the sex wars, as well as a group of more ideologically supple liberals who were receptive to antipornography feminist and sex-radical feminist arguments and developed ingenious and innovative ways to reconcile them with the core tenets of liberal theory. Before I expound on all of this more fully, a few remarks about terminology are in order.

First, I should clarify precisely what I mean by antipornography feminism. In the present work, I use that term to designate a set of positions and beliefs defended by feminists who, beginning in the mid-1970s, formulated a distinctively feminist conception and critique of pornography and worked in various ways to curtail the production, distribution, and display of materials that they deemed pornographic. As I noted in the preceding section, this set of positions and beliefs has been described by many names, including antisex feminism, sex-negative feminism, cultural feminism, dominance feminism, radical feminism, and procensorship feminism. I have settled on the term "antipornography feminism" for two reasons. First, unlike other descriptors like "cultural feminism" or "dominance feminism," "antipornography feminism" is specific and precise; it nicely captures the defining feature of this set of positions and beliefs: its critical orientation toward pornography. Second, the label "antipornography feminist" would have been, at the very least, tolerable to individuals who embraced this set of positions and beliefs during the sex wars. The same cannot be said of some other possible alternatives, like "sex-negative feminist," "antisex feminist," and "procensorship feminist," each of which was devised by opponents of antipornography feminism to malign and impugn, not identify and describe. The one exception here is "radical feminism." As the leaflet distributed by the antipornography feminist picketers at the Barnard conference indicates, many feminists engaged on behalf of the antipornography feminist cause considered their antipornography stance to be an outgrowth of their commitment to radical feminism. I eschew this particular descriptor because "radical feminism" was a deeply contested concept during the sex wars, and one is just as likely to find self-identified radical feminists among opponents and critics of antipornography feminism during this time as within the ranks of antipornography feminism itself.[18] For all of these reasons then, "antipornography feminism" is my term of choice in the present work.[19]

So, who were these antipornography feminists and what exactly were the positions and beliefs they embraced? During the sex wars, antipornography feminists counted among their ranks writers, scholars, and activists like Kathleen Barry, Susan Brownmiller, Patricia Hill Collins, Andrea Dworkin, Susan Griffin, Audre Lorde, Catharine MacKinnon, Robin Morgan, Adrienne Rich, Diana Russell, Gloria Steinem, and Alice Walker. What united these antipornography feminists was their shared belief that pornography was a linchpin of gender (and, in the case of Black and third world feminists aligned with antipornography feminism during the sex wars, like Collins, Lorde, and Walker, also racial) oppression. Antipornography feminists objected to pornography not on account of its sexual explicitness, which conservatives had long condemned, but on account of its pernicious political effects. By portraying women as "anonymous, panting playthings, adult toys, dehumanized objects to be used, abused, broken and discarded," antipornography feminists believed that pornography made rape, battering, sexual harassment, incest, child abuse, forced prostitution, and every other imaginable form of gender-based violence and subordination appear normal, natural, and even pleasurable for both perpetrators and victims (Brownmiller 1975, 394). Black and third world antipornography feminists also emphasized pornography's role in sustaining white supremacy. By representing nonwhite women and men as subhuman beasts, and by fusing sexual desirability and whiteness in the consciousness of pornography's consumers, both Black and white, Black and third world antipornography feminists believed pornography dehumanized people of color and subverted possibilities for intraracial intergender political solidarity between women and men of color. Thus, despite the single-minded focus on pornography that their name implies, antipornography feminists were in fact concerned with a bevy of issues. By curtailing the availability and visibility of pornography, antipornography feminists believed they could short-circuit oppressive systems and strike decisive blows against inequalities of gender and race.

The term "sex-radical feminism" also needs clarification. By "sex-radical feminism," I mean the set of positions and beliefs embraced by feminists who, also beginning in the mid-1970s, formulated a distinctly feminist vindication of sexual freedom and worked to end the stigmatization and marginalization of sexual minorities, including sadomasochists, fetishists, butch and femme lesbians, boy lovers, and sex workers, within the feminist community and beyond. Like antipornography feminism, this set of positions and beliefs has also been described by many names, including pro-sex feminism, sex-positive feminism, pro-porn feminism, and anticensorship feminism. As was the case with antipornography feminism, many of these names vastly oversimplify or willfully misrepresent the sexual politics of sex-radical feminism. In the present work, I follow Carole Vance, who has persuasively argued that the term "sex-radical feminism" does the least violence to this complex set of positions and beliefs (1993a, 297; 1984, 127).

So, who were these sex-radical feminists and what exactly was the distinctively feminist vindication of sexual freedom that they formulated? During the sex wars, sex-radical feminists like Pat (now Patrick) Califia, Lisa Duggan, Amber Hollibaugh, Nan Hunter, Cherríe Moraga, Mirtha Quintanales, Gayle Rubin, Ann Snitow, and Carole Vance argued that depriving women of sexual pleasure and autonomy was key to shoring up male dominance.[20] By cutting women off from sexual experiences that sex-radical feminists considered to be vital sources of power, identity, community, and resistance, sex-radical feminists believed that patriarchy ensured women's isolation, compliance, and resignation. Upending the complex system of stigmatization, medicalization, and criminalization that kept women (and many men) trapped within the bounds of monogamous, procreative, "vanilla" heterosexuality was thus key to sex-radical feminists' agenda for women's liberation. To this end, they vindicated a variety of unconventional, and in their minds subversive, sexual practices, including the production and consumption of pornography, especially pornography depicting nonnormative sexualities, the cultivation of diverse sexual counterpublics in which a broad range of sexual desires and identities could be articulated and enacted, nonmonogamy, sadomasochism, lesbian sexuality orchestrated around butch and femme roles, commercial sex, public sex, and even consensual intergenerational sex. As leading sex-radical feminists Deirdre English, Amber Hollibaugh, and Gayle Rubin once put it, the goal of sex-radical feminism was essentially to make good on the promise of the sexual revolution by bringing about a genuine "sexual liberation that is not sexist" or a "non-sexist sexual liberation" (1982, 41–42). Third world sex-radical feminists like Cherríe Moraga and Mirtha Quintanales pushed this expansive sex-radical feminist agenda even further, fighting for a sexual liberation that was also not racist. Pressing sex-radical feminism beyond the limited experiences of white women, third world sex-radical feminists imagined ways nonwhite women on the sexual margins might rebel against the sexual status quo not only of the hegemonic white/ Anglo culture but also of their own cultures of origin, while at the same time remaining connected to these home cultures and engaged in their vital struggles against cultural imperialism, economic exploitation, and racial oppression.

As my discussion of the catfight narrative above indicates, much has been made of the conflicts between antipornography and sex-radical feminists—so much, in fact, that these conflicts are frequently presented as coextensive with the sex wars themselves. And, of course, as the descriptions I have just offered indicate, antipornography feminists and sex-radical feminists disagreed on a great deal. For instance, they offered markedly different accounts of women's oppression, with antipornography feminists emphasizing the sexual objectification of women and the veritable onslaught of violence and discrimination it provokes, and sex-radical feminists emphasizing women's sexual deprivation and the resignation and isolation it engenders. Antipornography feminists and sex-radical feminists also pursued markedly different political programs, particularly where pornography was concerned. For antipornography feminists, objectifying and dehumanizing sexual representations were oppressively ubiquitous, and they set about devising means to curtail and resist their pernicious influence. For sex-radical feminists, in contrast, sexually explicit materials, particularly those depicting nonnormative sexual fantasies and practices, were marginalized to the point of invisibility, and they set about devising ways to enhance and promote their visibility and potentially liberating influence. Perhaps the most conspicuous difference dividing antipornography feminists from sex-radical feminists was the difference captured by Carole Vance in her evocative pleasure/danger pairing from the Barnard conference concept paper. As Vance perceptively observes, antipornography feminists and sex-radical feminists embraced radically divergent priorities where sexual freedom is concerned. For antipornography feminists, ending violence and oppression was the most pressing matter, and exploring diverse possibilities for sexual pleasure could wait until "after the revolution," so to speak.[21] In contrast, for sex-radical feminists, realizing to their fullest extent capacities for sexual pleasure was itself a potentially liberating praxis that could and should not await the arrival of some uncertain utopian future.[22]

I could, of course, go on cataloging the differences between antipornography feminists and sex-radical feminists; they are numerous, and they were the cause of prodigious strife within the women's movement for over two decades. However, rather than repeating what has already been sufficiently well established, I would like to undertake a different and potentially more generative task. Without denying the significance of the differences between antipornography feminists and sex-radical feminists or the severity of the rancor to which these differences have given rise, I would like to highlight some affinities between these bitter feminist rivals that the catfight narrative version of the history of the sex wars has for too long obscured.

The first affinity concerns antipornography feminists' and sex-radical feminists' views regarding gender and sexuality. While both frequently accused one another of propagating essentialist notions of gender and sexuality—of claiming that men were innately sexually aggressive, or that sexual desire was born of inexorable natural instincts or Freudian drives—both antipornography feminists and sex-radical feminists in fact eschewed such simplistic notions and embraced some version of a social constructivist thesis where gender and sexuality were concerned. This aspect of sex-radical feminism is most readily evident in the work of Gayle Rubin, who argues emphatically that "sexuality is not natural, not an unchanging, ahistorical item in the human repertoire of behavior" and defends what she calls a "constructivist alternative to sexual essentialism" rooted in the work of historians of sexuality like Jeffrey Weeks, Judith Walkowitz, and Michel Foucault (English, Hollibaugh, and Rubin 1982, 41; Vance 1984, 276). On the antipornography feminist side, Catharine MacKinnon embraces a similarly thoroughgoing constructivist view, arguing that "the condition of the sexes and the relevant definition of women as a group is . . . social down to the somatic level. Only incidentally, perhaps even consequentially, is it biological" (1989, 46).[23] Clearly, whatever their other faults and failings, neither antipornography nor sex-radical feminists were guilty of the facile essentialisms they both accused each other of.

In addition to their shared antiessentialism, antipornography feminists and sex-radical feminists also exhibited similarly critical orientations toward conventional, or what we might today call normative, heterosexuality. In the antipornography feminist view, heterosexuality was a political institution that ensured women's sexual, economic, creative, and reproductive capacities would be brought and remain under men's control. As Andrea Dworkin (1995) describes it, under cultural conditions of male supremacy, heterosexual intercourse is the "penultimate expression of male dominance," with rape being the ultimate expression.[24] A guiding aim of antipornography feminism was thus to dismantle the political institution of heterosexuality by depriving it of what antipornography feminists understood to be one of its most potent forms of propaganda: pornography.[25]

Sex-radical feminists offered a different but no less pointed critique of heterosexuality. In the sex-radical feminist view, heterosexuality functions as a regulatory norm in a regime of sexual control designed to stifle erotic creativity, diversity, and dissent. This sex-radical feminist critique of heterosexuality was put forward most forcefully by Gayle Rubin in her influential contribution to sex-radical feminist thought, "Thinking Sex: Notes for a Radical Theory of the Politics of Sexuality" (1984). In this essay, Rubin describes married, monogamous, "vanilla" heterosexuality as occupying the center of a "charmed circle" of "good, normal, natural, blessed sexuality," relegating all other manifestations of human sexual capacity to the "outer limits" of "bad, abnormal, unnatural, and damned sexuality" (281). A central goal of Rubin's sex-radical feminism was to decenter heterosexuality and subvert the "system of erotic stigma" that maintained its normative status (280, 282).

This shared critical orientation toward heterosexuality is not surprising when one considers the formative influence lesbian feminism exerted on both antipornography and sex-radical feminism. Formulated in the early 1970s as a reaction to the homophobia and heteronormativity of both the moderate and more radical liberationist wings of the women's movement, lesbian feminism figured lesbianism as the sine qua non of feminist politics (Radicalesbians [1970] 1971; Myron and Bunch 1975). As lesbian-feminist author and activist Ti-Grace Atkinson famously put it, "Feminism is the theory; lesbianism is the practice" (Koedt 1971). While lesbian feminism has been recognized as a crucial antecedent to antipornography feminism, it also made important contributions to the development of sex-radical feminism (Bronstein 2011).[26] For example, the original sex-radical feminists were lesbian sadomasochists who came together in the San Francisco Bay

Area to found the lesbian S&M support group Samois because they felt excluded from established lesbian feminist institutions. The influence of lesbian feminism is evident throughout some of Samois's earliest and most influential writings. The author's note at the beginning of Barbara Ruth's contribution to *What Color Is Your Handkerchief? A Lesbian S/M Sexuality Reader* is representative in this regard. "I believe," Ruth explains, "that sadomasochism as a liberating practice is only possible for women within a lesbian-feminist context. . . . S-M can equalize a power imbalance in a love relationship, but only between members of the same sexual caste. As a lesbian-feminist, I believe it would be extremely self-destructive for any woman to play either role in an S-M relationship with any man. . . . Such an action would be . . . counter-revolutionary" (Lipschutz 1979, 8). While not all sex-radical feminists looked on heterosexuality with such severe suspicion, the lesbian-feminist strain in sex-radical feminism is strong and should not be downplayed or dismissed.[27]

One final affinity between antipornography feminism and sex-radical feminism that the catfight narrative conceals almost entirely is their shared commitment to politicizing sex and sexuality in ways that ran counter to the hegemonic liberalism of their day. I will take the case of antipornography feminism first. Because antipornography feminists understood pornography to be an eminently political practice, the purpose of which was to bolster systems of male and white supremacy, they were willing to use a variety of tactics, including letter-writing campaigns, consumer boycotts, zoning regulations, and civil rights laws, to limit its visibility and accessibility. This willingness to bring political power, including but not limited to the power of the state and the law, to bear on sexually explicit expression set antipornography feminists in frequent and often bitter conflict with their liberal contemporaries, who saw pornography by and large as apolitical and harmless speech that should be exempt from governmental regulation in the name of individual liberty and privacy.

While sex-radical feminists did not share (and in fact vehemently criticized) antipornography feminists' desire to curtail the production and consumption of pornography, they did share with antipornography feminists a desire to politicize sex in ways that ran counter to liberal convention. While liberals had traditionally defended a narrow range of sexually explicit expression as private, apolitical, and harmless speech, sex-radical feminists insisted that all forms of sexual expression, as well as all consensual sexual acts, including the most stigmatized and marginalized, ought to be publicly affirmed, even celebrated, as indispensable to human freedom and identity.[28] This radical vindication of sexual freedom sat uneasily alongside the tepid politics of individual liberty, privacy, and free speech embraced by pornography's liberal defenders. It is thus no surprise that these groups often found themselves in bitter conflict with one another.

This third and final affinity between antipornography feminism and sex-radical feminism, their shared critical orientation to the sexual politics of liberalism, is central to the core project of *Why We Lost the Sex Wars*. As I have already stated, the aim of the present work is to debunk the catfight narrative and call into question the implicitly liberal sexual politics it has worked insidiously to normalize within contemporary feminist discourse. Foregrounding the battles that raged between civil libertarian opponents of obscenity regulation and their antipornography feminist and sex-radical feminist critics during the sex wars constitutes one of the most crucial aspects of this rethinking.

This discussion of conflicts between antipornography feminists, sex-radical feminists, and liberals leads me to one final term that I must clarify before proceeding to a fuller statement of the main arguments of *Why We Lost the Sex Wars*. "Liberalism" is a notoriously promiscuous term that can be used to signify everything from progressivism to its opposite.[29] In the present work, I use the term to denote a range of positions premised on "the belief that the freedom of the individual is the highest political value" and that "freedom of conscience, freedom of occupational choice, privacy and family rights all place limits on what governments may do" (Ryan 2012, 362, 366, 364, 377). At the heart of liberalism so conceived is a distinction between the public and the private where the public is figured as a sphere of justice in which law serves as a neutral guarantor of liberty among free and equal individuals, while the private is figured as a sphere "beyond justice" in which law and liberty are fundamentally at odds (Okin 1989, 25).[30] While liberals have traditionally presented the public/private distinction as a means of securing individual liberty against the encroachments of overweening governments, feminist political theorists have noted its utility for other purposes. As Carole Pateman incisively observes, given "the way in which women and men are differentially located within private life and the public world," liberalism's public/ private distinction "obscures the subjection of women to men within an apparently universal, egalitarian individualist order" (1989b, 120). It is liberalism in this sense that played such a crucial role during the sex wars.

I should note here that my use of the term "liberal" differs in significant respects from a usage more typical of histories of feminism's so-called second wave. This usage, which is ubiquitous in introductory women's and gender studies curricula and the like, is operative wherever the women's movement of the latter half of the twentieth century is parsed in terms of a liberal versus radical split with figures like Betty Friedan cast in the role of liberal and figures like Shulamith Firestone cast in the role of radical. In this usage, "liberal" means, roughly, a political actor who engages in conventional forms of political activism (e.g., forming a political lobby like the National Organization for Women) in the service of conventional political goals (e.g., equal treatment for women under the law), while "radical" means essentially the opposite: a political actor who engages in unconventional forms of political activism (e.g., forming a radical feminist consciousness-raising group like Redstockings and conducting Zap actions at hearings of the New York State Joint Legislative Committee on Public Health) in the service of unconventional political goals (e.g., abortion on demand and the liberation of women from male supremacy). In the present work, I eschew this rather vague usage of the term "liberal" in favor of the more rigorous and precise usage common among political theorists, political philosophers, intellectual historians, and historians of political thought.

My use of the term "liberal" in the present work also differs in significant respects from the usage of other scholars who have written specifically about the sex wars. For instance, in her discussion of the American women's movement of the 1960s and 1970s, historian Christine Stansell uses the term "liberal" to distinguish feminists who favored "incremental change and electoral politics" from "radicals," whom Stansell describes as practicing a "searing, melodramatic, and rambunctious . . . politics of confrontation, catharsis, and personal transformation" (2010, 222–23). In my view, applying the term "liberal" in this sense to the sex wars breeds much in the way of confusion and misunderstanding. Consider, for example, antipornography feminists like Susan Brownmiller, Andrea Dworkin, Dorchen Leidholdt, and Catharine MacKinnon. By crafting and advocating on behalf of a municipal ordinance that made pornography a legally actionable civil rights violation, these antipornography feminists engaged in the style of politics that Stansell calls liberal. However, as they engaged in this liberal politics, each of these antipornography feminists offered searing indictments of the liberals who opposed their legislation as well as the conceptualizations of harm, liberty, and privacy firmly rooted in the liberal political tradition that undergirded this liberal opposition. Additionally, many antipornography feminists who engaged in Stansell's liberal politics also engaged in a politics that Stansell would undoubtedly call radical. For instance, Andrea Dworkin, who both lobbied elected officials on behalf of the antipornography legislation she coauthored with Catharine MacKinnon and who also served as what Stansell aptly describes as the "obsessed melodramatic polemicist of the antipornography feminist movement," is a prime example of an antipornography feminist who confounds Stansell's liberal/radical dichotomy (2010, 346). I aim to avoid such confusion by using the term "liberal" in the more precise manner that I have just described.

One more prefatory remark regarding my use of the term "liberal" in the present work. Using "liberal" to signify political claims arising from normative commitments to individual liberty, limited government, and the public/private distinction is also warranted by the peculiarly American context of the sex wars with which *Why We Lost the Sex Wars* is primarily concerned. As scholars of American history have long observed, liberalism in the sense that I invoke here has exerted a tremendous influence on American politics from the founding era onward. Inspired in large part by the liberalism of John Locke, the American revolutionaries declared, fought for, and ultimately won their independence. A decade later, the country they formed adopted a constitution heavily influenced by Lockean liberalism. In the definitive work on the subject, *The Liberal Tradition in America: An Interpretation of American Political Thought since the Revolution*

(1955), Louis Hartz documents and describes the central role that liberalism, for better or for worse, has played in delimiting the boundaries of political possibility in the United States all the way up through the New Deal. More recently, scholars have amended and extended the Hartzian thesis, further establishing liberalism as among the core "multiple traditions" comprising American political life (Smith 1993). Just as liberalism in the sense I use it here has fundamentally shaped debates across American history over everything from the structure of the U.S. Constitution to the most arcane provisions of the Internal Revenue Code, so too it has shaped debates about pornography, commercial sex, S&M, and a whole host of other issues pertaining to sex and sexuality, including those that transpired during the feminist sex wars.

In the late 1950s, for example, it was liberalism that provided the ideological foundation for a campaign waged by a cadre of devout civil libertarians, including book and magazine publishers, film distributors, and attorneys like Barney Rossett, Hugh Hefner, Charles Rembar, Herald Price Fahringer, and Edward de Grazia, to roll back the Comstock-era regime of obscenity regulation and clear the way for the virtually unregulated private consumption of sexually explicit material in the United States. Beginning in the early 1970s, this campaign drew fire from both antipornography and sex-radical feminist quarters. Antipornography feminists assailed these liberal champions of the so-called freedom to read for utilizing conceptions of harm, liberty, and the public and the private too rigid and formalistic to accommodate even the most basic pleas for justice on behalf of women. Sex-radical feminists took a somewhat different tack, criticizing civil libertarians for defending pornography and sexuality more generally by relegating them to an apolitical private sphere where their political potential as instruments of community building, identity articulation, and erotic subversion would languish unrealized.

Thus, in the 1970s and early 1980s, the relationship between antipornography feminism, sex-radical feminism, and liberalism was profoundly strained. Antipornography and sex-radical feminists challenged conventional liberal notions of the public and the private by insisting on the eminently political character of sexuality, while liberals insisted on viewing sexual matters like pornography through the prism of expressive freedom, personal choice, and private morality. Then, beginning in the early 1980s, as antipornography feminists championed an ordinance that would have made pornography actionable as a violation of women's civil rights, the relationships between antipornography feminism, sex-radical feminism, and liberalism began to shift. Influential liberals began defending antipornography feminist arguments and legislative proposals. Meanwhile, sex-radical feminists began to strategically use the liberal rhetoric of civil liberties and free speech that they had once so roundly criticized in order to resist the passage of antipornography feminist legislation. In short, what began in the late 1970s as a triangular argument between tepid liberal defenders, impassioned antipornography feminist critics, and sex-radical feminist proponents of pornography expanded over the course of the 1980s and 1990s into an even more complicated array of positions, with liberalism inflecting virtually all sides.

Why We Lost the Sex Wars is the first account of the history of the sex wars to excavate these long-neglected relationships between antipornography feminism, sex-radical feminism, and liberalism in something close to their full nuance and complexity. However, as I mentioned earlier, Carolyn Bronstein's history of the American antipornography feminist movement does bring a small sliver of antipornography feminism's early and often contentious relationship with liberalism into view. Unfortunately, Bronstein's discussion of this relationship is limited to one confrontation between antipornography feminists and civil libertarians at a single academic colloquium in the winter of 1978 and is thus far from complete. Additionally, Bronstein's characterization of this confrontation as a clash between classical liberalism, represented by the civil libertarians, and a communitarian social position, represented by the antipornography feminists, is inaccurate and confused. Contrary to Bronstein's claim, antipornography feminists did not put forward a communitarian critique of liberalism at this colloquium or anywhere else. They did not argue, as Bronstein claims they did, that "sometimes the interests of the group [have] to be taken into account and given priority over those of the individual to achieve a common good" (Bronstein 2011, 182). Nor did they assail liberals for their aspirations to universality at the expense of particularity, their atomized vision of the self, or their tendency to denigrate the claims of tradition, culture, and community, three other common communitarian critiques of liberalism (Walzer 1990). In fact, antipornography feminists often expressed what can only be described as anticommunitarian views. For instance, at the very colloquium Bronstein discusses, Florence Rush blamed the sexual abuse of children on traditional notions of marriage and family, and Andrea Dworkin impugned appeals to the common good as ideological ploys used to dupe women into defending laws that afford them no protection and in which "they have absolutely no stake" (Law 1979, 225, 242). Thus, while Bronstein shows great insight in highlighting this colloquium, as well as the clash between antipornography feminists and liberals that transpired there, her account fails to apprehend the nature of the political and theoretical chasm that divided antipornography feminists and liberals during this phase of the sex wars.

Unlike antipornography feminism's relationship to liberalism, which chroniclers of the sex wars have largely neglected, the relationship between sex-radical feminism and liberalism has been a matter of frequent discussion among scholars for decades. However, almost invariably, scholars have grossly misapprehended the nature of this relationship, mischaracterizing sex-radical feminism as a species of liberalism rather than as a critical engagement with it. One of the earliest examples of such a mischaracterization appears in the edited volume *Against Sado-masochism: A Radical Feminist Analysis* (Linden et al. 1982). Philosopher Bat-Ami Bar On's contribution accuses sex-radical feminist defenders of sadomasochism of "taking liberal trends to their logical conclusion" and using "a liberal conception of sexual liberation in which sexual conduct is a matter of individual expression" devoid of any "relational context" (1982, 72). Two years later, in the *Feminist Review,* Marie France proffered a similar reading of sex-radical feminism, accusing sex-radical feminists of defending sadomasochism "by means of the liberal credo, a strategy based on a distinction between public and private morality where law only regulates public activity" (1984, 35). In that same year, Ann Ferguson's aforementioned *Signs* article appeared, in which she characterizes sex-radical feminists as "libertarians" (1984, 107). In 1990, this interpretative thesis reached its apogee with the publication of Dorchen Leidholdt's and Janice Raymond's *The Sexual Liberals and the Attack on Feminism.*

Throughout this collection, the politics of sex-radical feminists like Gayle Rubin are lumped together with those of civil libertarians like Hugh Hefner, and both are derided for their "sexual liberalism" (xi, 15, 133).

As I argue at length in chapter 3, such interpretations of sex-radical feminism's relationship to liberalism are mistaken.[31] Not only do they overlook the substantial political differences that existed between sex-radical feminists and liberals on issues like pornography, public sex, intergenerational sex, and gay rights in the late 1970s and early 1980s, but they also obscure many of sex-radical feminism's most distinctive features. As I demonstrate, sex-radical feminists condemned defenses of sexual behavior rooted in appeals to privacy, rejected individualistic conceptions of sexual identity and freedom, questioned portrayals of sexual desire as natural, innate, or prepolitical, and demanded a sexual freedom so expansive that it entailed the destruction of the complex of laws, norms, and social practices that Gayle Rubin influentially dubbed "the system of sexual oppression" and the cultivation of diverse sexual identities and counterpublics (1984, 293). Taken together, all of this indicates that sex-radical feminism was not a species of liberalism but rather a critical engagement with it. An important contribution of *Why We Lost the Sex Wars* is a thorough refutation of any interpretive thesis claiming otherwise.

To circle back, then, the primary objective of *Why We Lost the Sex Wars* is to press contemporary understandings of the sex wars beyond Barnard— that is, beyond the reductive categories of the catfight narrative—by re-thinking the sex wars in richer, more complex, and more dynamic terms. The central players in the alternative narrative *Why We Lost the Sex Wars* proposes are antipornography feminists, sex-radical feminists, and Black and third world feminists on the feminist side, and liberals who perceived feminist incursions into the domain of sexual politics as either a threat to or an extension of core liberal values on the liberal side. Rethinking the sex wars along these lines provides a more accurate account of what actually happened during this important historical episode; it also pro-vides a critical, unsettling, and potentially productive view on some of the most prominent and controversial aspects of feminist sexual politics today, including the transnational antirape protest movement known as

SlutWalk, calls for trigger warnings on college and university campuses, and the sweeping cultural reckoning occurring around issues of sexual harassment, abuse, and assault under the sign of #MeToo. *Why We Lost the Sex Wars* is thus a feminist history that is urgently interested in the feminist present. By recovering the sex wars in all, or at least some, of their repressed complexity, *Why We Lost the Sex Wars* aims to provide what Michel Foucault terms "a critical ontology of ourselves," "a critique of what we are" that "is at one and the same time the historical analysis of the limits that are imposed on us and an experiment with the possibility of going beyond them" (1984, 50). As political theorist Wendy Brown observes, "Theory's most important political offering is [the] opening of a breathing space between the world of common meanings and the world of alternative ones, a space of potential renewal for thought, desire, and action" (2009, 81). My intention in *Why We Lost the Sex Wars* is to do just that: to gain critical purchase on feminism's present by turning to feminism's past, where I hope to find not only "a critique of what we are saying, thinking, and doing," but also "the possibility of no longer being, doing or thinking what we are, do or think" (1984, 46).

PLAN OF THE BOOK

Why We Lost the Sex Wars begins with a chronicling of the complex and shifting relationship between antipornography feminism and liberalism from the early 1970s to the mid-1990s. In chapter 1, I show how antipornography feminism was born in the early 1970s out of white-hot hostility to a particular liberal project inaugurated in the 1950s that sought to upend the legal regulation of obscenity in the United States in the name of privacy and free speech. After delineating the political and theoretical contours of this postwar liberal anticensorship crusade, I lay out antipornography feminism's rich and colorful history of contesting it, including the occupation of Grove Press by early antipornography feminist leader Robin Morgan, and Andrea Dworkin's barnstorming tours of colleges and universities to debate some of pornography's most outspoken liberal defenders, like noted civil libertarian and criminal defense lawyer Alan Dershowitz. This chapter also underscores the trenchancy of antipornography feminism's critical engagement with liberalism by highlighting the significant inroads that antipornography feminist concepts, ideas, and arguments made in the discipline of political theory by way of the early feminist work of Carole Pateman.

In chapter 2, I recount what constitutes a distinct second phase in the relationship between antipornography feminism and liberalism: an improbable convergence that began in the mid-1980s and continued well into the 1990s. This convergence was largely one-sided. While antipornography feminists for the most part retained their original critical comportment toward liberalism, prominent liberal political philosophers, legal theorists, and jurists, including Cass Sunstein, Martha Nussbaum, and Elena Kagan, began to see antipornography feminism as something more than a censorious assault on privacy and individual liberty. However, the story of the convergence of antipornography feminism and liberalism during this widely overlooked second phase of their relationship is not one of liberals seeing the light and forswearing their deeply held liberal principles in favor of a critical antipornography feminist analysis. As I show in this chapter, the thinkers who pioneered what I call antipornography liberalism effected significant reconfigurations, modifications, and attenuations of antipornography feminism's core concepts, especially its broad and deeply political conception of pornography's harms, to make the convergence of antipornography feminism and liberalism possible. The end result of this process was a set of liberal arguments that portrayed pornography as a serious problem about which little could be done. While coercion, violence, and any other illegal activity engaged in in the course of producing pornography could and should be vigorously addressed by criminal law, these liberal antipornography feminists argued, individual liberty, privacy, and expressive freedom rendered pornography's other undesirable political consequences, namely the subordination of women, unreachable in any systematic or meaningfully political way.

Having devoted the first two chapters to charting the complex and shifting relationship between antipornography feminism and liberalism, chapter 3 turns to liberalism's equally intricate and dynamic relationship with sex-radical feminism. The chapter begins with an unearthing of sex-radical feminism's long-neglected but extensive history of critical engagement with the sexual politics of postwar liberalism. While sex-radical feminists did not engage in dramatic public debates and confrontations with liberals on the scale of those engaged in by antipornography feminists in the 1970s and early 1980s, they did register their opposition to liberalism's narrow and ambivalent politics of anticensorship and free speech. Most significantly, sex-radical feminists like Pat (now Patrick) Califia voiced audacious demands for a vibrant and diverse public sexual culture that stood in stark contrast to the restrained pleas of midcentury liberals for a somewhat wider berth for certain normative forms of sexual expression. In this sense, sex-radical feminism, much like its foil, antipornography feminism, must be seen, this chapter insists, as a critical response to the sexual politics of postwar liberalism.

After elucidating the sex-radical feminist critique of liberalism in the first half of the chapter, chapter 3 proceeds to chart the emergence of a strategic alliance between sex-radical feminists and civil libertarians to oppose the Dworkin–MacKinnon antipornography ordinance in the early 1980s. Unlike the convergence of antipornography feminism and liberalism during this same period, the alliance between sex-radical feminism and liberalism was driven primarily by sex-radical feminists looking to gain legal and political leverage over their antipornography feminist rivals. To this end, sex-radical feminists like Gayle Rubin and Amber Hollibaugh threw their lot in with civil libertarians like Nadine Strossen and David Richards to form the Feminist Anti-Censorship Taskforce (FACT). By combining sex-radical feminist arguments regarding the inherent social and political value of sexual expression with more restrained liberal arguments regarding the dangers of state censorship, FACT proved to be an effective force against the Dworkin–MacKinnon ordinance. However, this effectiveness came at a price. Aspects of sex-radical feminism that were not readily assimilable to a liberal politics of anticensorship and expressive freedom were obscured or abandoned, and by the mid-1990s, sex-radical feminism had been almost completely overtaken by a markedly narrower liberal project: anti-censorship/pro-sex feminism.

In chapter 4, the second dimension of the core project of *Why We Lost the Sex Wars* begins to unfold. While the first three chapters work to dismantle the two-dimensional structure of the catfight narrative by highlighting relationships between antipornography feminists, sex-radical feminists, and liberals during the sex wars, chapter 4 chips away at the reductive catfight narrative by bringing yet another overlooked dimension of the sex wars into view. During the sex wars, as antipornography and sex-radical feminists engaged in struggles on one front with each other and on another front with liberals of various stripes, Black and third world feminists opened up still more lines of conflict and contestation within the feminist sexuality debates. Some aligned themselves with the antipornography feminist movement; others threw in their lot with antipornography feminism's sex-radical feminist critics. But regardless of where they were positioned on the pleasure/danger continuum, this diverse assortment of Black and third world feminists waded into the fray of the sex wars with a common objective: to disrupt what I call, following sociologist Deborah King, the "monistic" sexual politics prevalent among both antipornography feminists and sex-radical feminists during the sex wars (1988, 52).[32] What Black and third world feminists brought to the sex wars debates on both the antipornography and sex-radical feminist sides was an attentiveness to the ways in which the domains of sex and sexuality are imbricated with inequalities of race, class, and gender, particularly in the lives of women of color. By foregrounding the interventions these Black and third world feminists made during the sex wars, chapter 4 makes a vital contribution to the core objective of *Why We Lost the Sex Wars*: complicating the binary categories of the catfight narrative and renarrating the sex wars according to something other than a simple pro-sex/anti-sex division. Chapter 4 also provides important insights into a possible causal mechanism driving the improbable liberal convergences described in the book's first three chapters. A monistic focus on the sexual needs, experiences, and desires of white women may have blunted the radicalism of antipornography and sex-radical feminism, leaving both of these feminist approaches to sexual politics susceptible to liberal co-optation and appropriation, their critical orientation toward the anemic sexual politics of liberalism aside.

Having thus fully fleshed out my alternative to the catfight narrative, in the conclusion, I take up several aspects of contemporary feminist sexual politics that the history excavated in the previous four chapters helps cast in a politically and theoretically productive new light. Taking antirape

SlutWalk protests, calls for trigger warnings on college and university campuses, and the #MeToo movement as case studies, I trace the origins of these seemingly disparate phenomena back to the liberal–feminist convergences that my sex wars counternarrative has unearthed, highlighting the limitations liberalism has placed on contemporary feminism's ability to engage in what is arguably feminism's most fundamental work: resistance to sexual oppression and injustice. In short, *Why We Lost the Sex Wars* concludes with a plea. I urge contemporary feminists who are serious about fighting against sexual oppression and for sexual freedom to return to the sex wars to reconsider antipornography feminism, sex-radical feminism, and the intersectional variants of these positions theorized by Black and third world feminists before their attenuation by liberalism. Pretensions of the catfight narrative aside, the sex wars were not a straightforward and decisive vindication of a tacitly liberal sex positivity. Rather, they were a remarkably fecund moment for feminist political thought when antipornography feminists, sex-radical feminists, and Black and third world feminists formulated visions of sexual freedom that burst existing liberal strictures asunder and opened up radical new vistas of sexual political possibility. That these visions seem scandalous and utopian even today gives me hope that they might once again fire feminist imaginations and fuel the vital political work of fighting for sexual freedom beyond the bounds of liberal convention in the present.

1

"Pornography Is the Theory. Rape Is the Practice."

THE ANTIPORNOGRAPHY FEMINIST CRITIQUE OF LIBERALISM

Before the advent of antipornography feminism in the mid-1970s, the most prominent critics of pornography were conservatives. Conservatives opposed the widespread availability of sexually explicit materials on the grounds that such materials are obscene, a term taken from the Latin for "filthy" and "inauspicious," and therefore corrosive of the moral foundation of a well-ordered society.[1] One prominent expositor of this conservative view in the United States was Anthony Comstock, a nineteenth-century antivice crusader and champion of the sweeping federal obscenity law that bears his name, the Comstock Act.[2] In *Traps for the Young,* an advice manual for concerned parents, Comstock likens a wide range of so-called obscene materials, including both pulp novels and classic works of literature like Boccaccio's *Decameron,* to contagious diseases imported from abroad threatening the future stewards of American society: boys and young men (1883, x). Nearly eighty years later, echoes of Comstock's views reverberate in Patrick Devlin's influential second Maccabaean Lecture delivered to the British Academy, "The Enforcement of Morals" (1959). Framed as a critique of the philosophical underpinnings of liberal arguments for the decriminalization of homosexuality, Devlin's lecture argues that every society has an essential right to preserve itself by "eradicat[ing]" threats to its "public morality," including pornography and other forms of sexual malfeasance (1965, 17).

The feminist critique of pornography that emerged in the 1970s bore little resemblance to these conservative critiques. Unlike conservatives, antipornography feminists did not object to sexually explicit materials tout court; nor did they consider such materials obscene. In fact, many antipornography feminists vigorously criticized the whole notion of obscenity, called for the outright repeal of all obscenity laws, and affirmed many materials and practices conservatives abhorred, including erotica, sex education literature, and lesbianism.[3] What antipornography feminists did object to was pornography. In their view, pornography was defined not by its prurience or its morally deleterious effects, but by its politics—that is, its contribution to the subordination of women. As Susan Brownmiller, an early leader in what would eventually become a full-fledged antipornography feminist movement, explains, "The feminist objection to pornography is based on our belief that pornography represents hatred of women, that pornography's intent is to humiliate, degrade, and dehumanize the female body for the purpose of erotic stimulation and pleasure" (1980, 254). "Pornography," Brownmiller declares elsewhere, "is the undiluted essence of anti-female propaganda" (1975, 394).

This newfangled feminist perspective on pornography differed not only from traditional conservative perspectives but also from well-established liberal perspectives. In the course of fending off conservative calls for censorship, liberals had long portrayed pornography as a private, apolitical, and essentially harmless vice deserving of moral opprobrium and some forms of government regulation, but not full-on censorship. John Stuart Mill's remarks in *On Liberty* concerning "offences against decency" reflect this quintessentially liberal view. "There are many acts," Mill writes, "which, being directly injurious only to the agents themselves, ought not to be legally interdicted, but which, if done publicly, are a violation of good manners, and coming thus within the category of offences against others, may rightfully be prohibited" ([1869] 1989, 98). "Of this kind," Mill continues, "are offences against decency; on which it is unnecessary to dwell, the rather as they are only connected indirectly with our subject, the objection to publicity being equally strong in the case of many actions not in themselves condemnable, nor supposed to be so" (98). Mill's equivocal defense of private indecency lived on well into the twentieth century, shaping the thinking of some of pornography's most prominent liberal defenders. For instance, liberal political philosopher Ronald Dworkin vindicates a "right to pornography," construed as a right to the voluntary consumption of "depressingly obscene photographs and films" in private while simultaneously defending prohibitions against the public display of such photographs and films (1981, 182). Joel Feinberg (1984), another liberal luminary, takes a similar tack, arguing that voluntary private consumption of pornography is harmless to others and therefore ought to be tolerated, but that the public display of pornography may be prohibited to protect others from moral offense. Thus, for more than a century, liberals have considered pornography to be at best an undignified diversion, and at worst a potential source of offense to others.[4]

This liberal take on pornography flew in the face of the antipornography feminist charge that pornography is tantamount to "blueprints for female enslavement and gynocide" (Barry 1979, 214). Given this fundamental disagreement, it is perhaps not surprising that the earliest encounters between antipornography feminists and liberals were marked by grave suspicion, and at times outright hostility. Antipornography feminists saw liberals as well-heeled shills for the pornography industry and the patriarchal power it served. One prominent antipornography feminist, for instance, went so far as to describe the American Civil Liberties Union as the center of "the pro-pimp lobby" (MacKinnon 1997, 11). Liberals for their part reciprocated this contempt by portraying antipornography feminists as little more than Victorian bluenoses in radical feminist drag. For instance, Ronald Dworkin accused antipornography feminists of being in league with religious conservatives. "Old wars over pornography and censorship have new armies in radical feminists and the Moral Majority," Dworkin warned, repeating an allegation that dogged the antipornography feminist movement for much of its existence (1985, 1).[5]

Thus, throughout the 1970s and early 1980s, the relationship between antipornography feminists and liberals was profoundly strained. Then, beginning in the early 1980s, as antipornography feminists championed a municipal ordinance that would define pornography as the "graphic sexually explicit subordination of women"[6] and give individuals who could prove they had been harmed by pornography the right to sue its producers and distributors for damages, this relationship began to change (Dworkin and MacKinnon 1988, 113). Influential liberal thinkers began to mount recognizably liberal defenses of antipornography feminist claims and legislative proposals, giving rise to a truly improbable political position: antipornography liberalism. In this chapter and the next, I tell the story of how the feminist critique of pornography, which emerged in the early 1970s as an emphatic critique of liberalism, was remade over the course of the 1980s and 1990s into a widely accepted tenet of liberalism itself.

"THE END OF OBSCENITY"

To appreciate the improbability of the emergence of antipornography liberalism in the latter half of the 1980s, one must first appreciate just how far removed the liberal position on pornography was from the anti-pornography feminist position in the 1970s and early 1980s. Before the mid-1980s, when a variety of recognizably liberal perspectives on the issue of pornography began to emerge, the conversation concerning the regulation of sexually explicit material in the United States was dominated by liberals of a distinctly civil libertarian bent. Since the days of Anthony Comstock's reign as postal inspector (1873–1915), liberals in the United States had been fighting conservative efforts to regulate sexual expression. Through organizations like the National Liberal League (1876), the National Defense Association (1878), and the Free Speech League (1902), liberals lobbied for the amendment or outright repeal of the federal Comstock Act and its state-level progeny.[7] Some of these liberals, like Free Speech League founder Theodore Schroeder, advocated what has since come to be known as an absolutist interpretation of the First Amendment, insisting that "all present State and Federal laws against 'obscenity'" are unconstitutional (1911, 11).[8] Others, like National Liberal League president Thaddeus Wakeman, took a more moderate line, arguing that government regulation of obscenity was permissible, but that the legal definition of obscenity should be a narrow one, applicable only to works that "excite the amative passions, [and] arouse lascivious and lewd thoughts" (Horowitz 2002, 428).[9] Despite the efforts of these liberal reformers, Comstock-era obscenity regulations remained in force in the United States well into the twentieth century.[10] However, when the United States Supreme Court revamped federal obscenity standards in *Roth v. United States* (1957), a cadre of civil libertarians, including book and magazine publishers, film distributors, and attorneys, saw an opportunity to succeed where their forebears had failed.[11]

At first glance, the *Roth* decision does not appear to hold out much hope for liberal opponents of obscenity regulations. *Roth* presented the high court with an opportunity to declare the Comstock Act and its ilk prima facie unconstitutional, but the majority demurred. In fact, the central holding in *Roth* is that the First Amendment "was not intended to protect every utterance" and that obscenity is "outside the protection intended for speech and press." Nevertheless, ingenious liberal auditors of the court's work discerned in *Roth* what one has described as "a subsidiary theme—a freedom-favoring tail that would, in time, powerfully wag the censorship dog" (de Grazia 1992, 320). This was the *Roth* majority's contention that obscenity is speech "utterly without redeeming social importance" that "deals with sex in a manner appealing to the prurient interest." To conservatives, these seemingly trivial pieces of dicta were mere statements of the obvious. To liberals, however, they were an opportunity. If the court meant what it said here, that a work is obscene if it "utterly" lacks "redeeming social importance" and appeals to a "prurient interest" in sex, then it follows, liberals reasoned, that a work with even a modicum of social importance that appeals to a healthy and normal interest in sex is not obscene and is therefore entitled to the protection of the First Amendment. No sooner had the *Roth* decision been handed down than civil libertarian attorneys like Charles Rembar, Edward de Grazia, Ephraim London, and Albert Bendich were successfully using this innovative interpretation to vindicate works whose publication had been unthinkable before *Roth*.

At the forefront of this postwar crusade against the regulation of obscenity was the alternative publishing house Grove Press, along with its maverick owner, Barney Rosset.[12] As Loren Glass emphasizes in his history of Grove, the press was no mere publishing house; it was the siege engine in what Rosset once described as "a carefully planned campaign, much like a military campaign" against the entire legal regime of literary censorship in the United States (2013, 101). The first victory in Rosset's campaign came in 1959 in *Grove v. Christenberry*, a case that ended a decades-long ban on the publication of D. H. Lawrence's 1928 novel *Lady Chatterley's Lover*. The next decade would bring many more victories for Rosset and Grove, including hard-fought exonerations of Henry Miller's *Tropic of Cancer* (1934) and William S. Burroughs's *Naked Lunch* (1959).[13]

After successfully championing what might best be described as the "literary obscene," Rosset turned Grove's energies and resources to the publication of more straightforwardly pornographic materials: erotic texts, mostly from the nineteenth and early twentieth centuries, that had previously been available only "under the counter" in the United States (Glass 2013, 131). Among these black-market staples were the wildly explicit works of the Marquis de Sade, a French aristocrat, revolutionary, and libertine from whose name the words "sadism" and "sadistic" are derived. In 1965, accompanied by comparatively little controversy, Grove issued the first volume in what would be a massive three-volume collection of Sade's work. In the following year, Grove published the first American edition of *My Secret Life* (ca. 1888), an eleven-volume anonymous autobiography documenting the sexual adventures of a Victorian gentleman known only as Walter. By the end of the 1960s, Grove had exhumed an entire catalog of Edwardian and Victorian pornography, issuing titles like *Man with a Maid* (1968), the erotic saga of the notorious Fanny Hill's only daughter, and *The Pearl* (1968), a nineteenth-century magazine of "voluptuous reading," under a series of new imprints such as Venus Library, Zebra Books, and Black Circle (Glass 2013, 140).

Buoyed by his success as a publisher of sexually explicit books, Rosset decided to try his hand at the distribution of sexually explicit motion pictures. To this end, in 1967, Grove licensed *I Am Curious (Yellow)*, an arty Swedish film that mixed leftist politics with explicit sex, for distribution in the United States. When customs officials confiscated the six 35mm reels containing the film at the U.S. border, Rosset and his legal team successfully sued the federal government for their release.[14] Later, in 1969, when the owners of a Boston movie theater screening *I Am Curious (Yellow)* were indicted for violating state obscenity laws, Grove Press and the defendants successfully fought the case all the way up to the Supreme

Court.[15] In the wake of these legal victories, Grove quickly became a major distributor and exhibitor of pornographic films (Glass 2013, 140). In the summer of 1969, Rosset's reputation as an unrepentant pornographer was cemented when *Life* magazine christened him "The Old Smut Peddler" (Glass 2013, 143).

"THE UNDILUTED ESSENCE OF ANTI-FEMALE PROPAGANDA"

Barney Rosset's all-out war against the regulation of obscenity in the United States set the stage for the first confrontation between the distinctive brand of liberalism animating his crusade and the emerging feminist critique of pornography. On April 13, 1970, a group of thirty women forcibly occupied Grove Press's executive offices in Greenwich Village.[16] The occupation was in part a response to the firing of several employees who had been working to unionize Grove, an action widely perceived (and eventually confirmed by the National Labor Relations Board) to be union busting. However, it was also a protest against Grove's involvement in the publication and distribution of materials the occupiers believed degraded women.[17] In a set of demands issued just before their arrest, the occupiers accused Grove and its subsidiaries of profiting from "the basic theme of humiliating, degrading, and dehumanizing women through sadomasochistic literature, pornographic films, and oppressive exploitive practices against its own female employees" (Lederer, 1980a, 269). "In self-defense," the occupiers declared, "we women are holding the Grove offices in trust [until] all publication of books and magazines, and all distribution of films that degrade women [are] stopped" (269). Looking back on these events, Robin Morgan, one of the occupation's organizers who would go on to coin the defining antipornography feminist slogan "Pornography is the theory. Rape is the practice." (Morgan 1977, 169), and who cofounded the Women's Anti-Defamation League, the predecessor organization to WAP,[18] described the takeover of the Grove Press offices as "the first time feminists openly declared pornography as an enemy" (268).[19] It was also the first time feminists openly called into question liberal efforts to cast pornography as private, harmless, and constitutionally protected speech.

Over the next five years, feminists built on the critique of pornography that had inspired the Grove Press occupation, and as they did so, the conflict between liberalism and what would eventually cohere into a full-fledged antipornography feminist ideology became increasingly explicit. For example, in her groundbreaking[20] feminist history of rape, *Against Our Will: Men, Women, and Rape*, Susan Brownmiller, who would go on to serve as the first president of WAP in 1979,[21] berates liberals for placing the rights of producers, purveyors, and purchasers of "ugly smut" above the rights of women (1975, 392). "The case against pornography and the case against prostitution are central to the fight against rape," Brownmiller writes, "and if it angers a large part of the liberal population to be so informed, then I would question in turn the political understanding of such liberals and their true concern for the rights of women" (390). In the course of mounting this blistering critique of the liberal position on pornography, Brownmiller draws parallels between the early opposition of the American Civil Liberties Union (ACLU) to feminist efforts to reform rape law and current efforts to make "obscenity the new frontier in defense of freedom of speech" (390). The same "defense lawyer mentality" that blinded civil libertarians to the injustice and sexism of the corroborative proof requirements written into the rape laws of many states[22] blinds them now, Brownmiller argues, to the fact that "'adult' or 'erotic' books and movies" are not "a valid extension of freedom of speech that must be preserved as a Constitutional right," but "the undiluted essence of anti-female propaganda" (390, 394–95).

In January 1977, just over a year after the publication of Brownmiller's *Against Our Will*, Andrea Dworkin brought her distinctive brand of anti-pornography feminism to the campus of the University of Massachusetts at Amherst. In response to a controversy surrounding student government funding for student organizations hosting screenings of sexually explicit films on campus,[23] Dworkin delivered a speech entitled "Pornography: The New Terrorism." The speech's grandiose prose, vivid analogies, and blistering indictment of civil libertarianism would elevate it above its narrow provenance and make it an instant antipornography feminist classic (Dworkin 1993a).[24]

As the title of Dworkin's speech proclaims, in her view, pornography is a form of terrorism aimed at frightening women into "silent acceptance of female degradation as a fact of life" (1993a, 201). As the "tiger cages" of Côn Sơn Island were to the South Vietnamese and the death camps of the Third Reich were to the Jews of Europe, so are pornographic words and images, in Dworkin's words, "death threats to a female population in rebellion" (201). This means that in Dworkin's view, civil libertarians like Barney Rosset, who purported to be fighting for the right of free speech, were in fact fighting to win constitutional protection for a reactionary campaign of terror against women. "The concept of 'civil liberties' in this country," Dworkin thunders, "has not ever, and does not now, embody principles and behaviors that respect the sexual rights of women," and those who "ritualistically claim to be the legal guardians of 'free speech'" are in fact "the legal guardians of male profit, male property and phallic power" (202).

One year later, at a colloquium at the New York University School of Law entitled "Obscenity: Degradation of Women versus Right of Free Speech" (1979), Dworkin delivered this influential speech once again, only this time her audience consisted of more than just sympathetic college students. Sponsored by the *New York University Review of Law and Social Change,* the colloquium brought leading civil libertarians, including Herald Price Fahringer, attorney for adult entertainment moguls Al Goldstein and Larry Flynt, together with leading antipornography feminists, including Dworkin and Brownmiller, to discuss the issue of pornography. The stated aim of the colloquium was to quell the rancor between antipornography feminists and liberals and to identify possible opportunities for collaboration between them. "We hoped," Lisa Lerman, the colloquium's coordinator, explains in her preface to a transcript of the event published in the *New York University Review of Law and Social Change,* "to get the civil libertarians 'unstuck' from addressing only the obsolete moralistic objections to pornography, and also to discuss what legal remedies may be available to women subjected to the dehumanization and the physical threats posed by violent pornography" (1979, 181). By practically all accounts, these aims went unfulfilled. As Lerman herself describes it, the colloquium was marked by "a general failure of communication." "The attorneys . . . interpreted the [feminist] outcry against violent pornography as a call for censorship and . . . focused on defending the first amendment" and the feminists "described the evils of violent pornography in subjective, emotional terms" and "were oblivious to the need for specificity, proof of injury, or 'hard evidence'" (182–84). In short, Lerman concludes, "the lawyers spoke legalese; the feminists spoke feminese" (184).[25] However, the colloquium was a success in at least one respect: by bringing antipornography feminists and liberals directly into conversation with one another for the first time, it clarified the nature and extent of the theoretical chasm that divided them.[26]

Nowhere was this theoretical chasm more evident than in a confrontation between Paul Chevigny, a law professor and former civil liberties lawyer, and Andrea Dworkin during a panel entitled "Effects of Violent Pornography." The first shots in this spirited exchange were fired by Chevigny. "There is *nothing* to be said, nothing *rational* to be said," Chevigny declares in his opening statement, "for any government censorship of any writings that relate to sex. It would be an inexcusable interference with the freedom of everyone . . . in this country" and a destructive intrusion into "the emotional relations between men and women" (1979, 232–33). Having painted his antipornography feminist interlocutors as irrational busybodies, Chevigny proceeds to criticize them for failing to address the panel's topic. While they may have shown that "women are an oppressed class" and that "pornography is a form of propaganda" that "creates an atmosphere which is degrading to women," they had not, Chevigny admonishes, offered any evidence that pornography "really hurts women" (233). "No one here has said any of the things I thought we were going to hear about effects of pornography," Chevigny exclaims, "I did not hear anything about any specific effects. *Not a syllable.* Nothing" (233). Chevigny expresses a similar frustration later in the panel—this time, the transcript indicates, while "banging on the table" (241).

Later, when it was her turn to speak, Andrea Dworkin fired back. Taking up Chevigny's charge that she and her fellow antipornography feminists had failed to speak directly to pornography's effects, Dworkin insists that "we have been here all day discussing the issue of pornography [and] articulating our social situation as women and the fact is that it didn't take, did it? No matter how often we explain rape to the rapist, we explain woman battering to the woman batterer, we explain pornography to the pornographers or the consumers of pornography, we explain that law is usually a weapon used against us to the lawyers, no matter how often we explain it reasonably in a realm of rational discourse, within which we are told to stay, it doesn't take" (Dworkin 1979, 238).[27] "Women," Dworkin continues, "are denied freedom of expression by rape, by battering, . . . by violence on every level, by sexual harassment . . . , by being unable to make the decent living that gives one the freedom to speak one's mind. . . . When I tell you that pornography silences me . . . and Phyllis Chesler has testified to it, and Leah Fritz has, and Florence Rush has,[28] and women all over the country have, and we are told we haven't said anything about the effects of pornography . . . , then we understand that we are operating in a moral vacuum" (239).

This exchange between Chevigny and Dworkin is a synecdoche for the conflict that defined the relationship between antipornography feminism and liberalism throughout the 1970s. Chevigny's insistence that antipornography feminists were right regarding pornography's role in women's subordination but wrong in their presumption that, in pointing to this role, they were saying anything at all about pornography's "effects" evinces his investment in a quintessentially liberal notion of the public and the private. For Chevigny, the "degrading atmosphere" that pornography begets is not properly considered an "effect of pornography" because, in his conventionally liberal view, this "degrading atmosphere" does not, as he puts it, "really hurt women." What Chevigny means by this is not that living in a culture that widely sanctions women's subordination is good for women, but that the subordination of women through pornography is a "private," as opposed to a "public," harm that admits of no legal remedy.[29] If a legal remedy for such a harm were adopted, so Chevigny's liberal reasoning goes, then the implications for individual liberty would be disastrous. Such a law would ride roughshod over the public/private distinction and subject fundamentally private matters such as "the emotional relations between men and women" to government regulation and control (Law 1979, 234).

In her response to Chevigny, Dworkin challenges this liberal analysis head on. By insisting that pornography "silences" women, Dworkin both contests liberal figurations of women's subordination through pornography as a merely "private" harm and radically calls into question the status of liberalism's public/private distinction as a safeguard for individual liberty. After all, if practices liberals cordon off from the reach of law and government in the name of individual liberty actually work to systematically undermine the liberty of women, then liberalism's public/private distinction begins to look less like a bulwark against tyranny and more like an instrument of patriarchal domination.

As this exchange between Chevigny and Dworkin attests, despite its organizers' best efforts, the colloquium seems to have left civil libertarians and antipornography feminists even more deeply divided over the issue of pornography. As the 1970s gave way to the 1980s, liberals and feminists remained at odds. By the summer of 1980, Aryeh Nair, then the national executive director of the ACLU, had dubbed pornography's feminist critics "the new censors" in an editorial in the *Nation* (Neier 1980, 737). In spring 1981, a debate between Andrea Dworkin and outspoken civil libertarian defense attorney Alan Dershowitz at the Schlesinger Library at the Radcliffe Institute for Advanced Study turned so rancorous that it made earlier clashes between antipornography feminists and liberals look almost congenial in comparison. According to an account published in the *Boston Phoenix,* the debate was "a classic confrontation between the radical and liberal" (Diamant 1981). Dworkin gave "a dramatic speech about male supremacy" and Dershowitz, who had just successfully defended Harry Reems, the male star of the 1972 film *Deep Throat,* in an obscenity trial in Memphis, Tennessee, followed with "a series of outraged gasps about dangers to the First Amendment" (Diamant 1981). According to Dershowitz, the predominately feminist audience tried to "censor" his speech with chants of "Down with the pornocrats!" (1982, 190). Dershowitz also claims that a leather-clad contingent of Dworkin's supporters carried chains into the auditorium and "threatened violence" (190). Tensions between Dershowitz and Dworkin reached a fever pitch when Dershowitz suggested that feminist opposition to pornography would culminate in the censorship of Dworkin's own writings. "You can't have it both ways," Dershowitz admonished the audience. "You want Dworkin,

you've got to take pornography" (Diamant 1981). Dworkin responded by
giving him the finger (Dershowitz 2002).[30]

Clearly, by the end of the 1970s, antipornography feminists and liberals had reached an impasse. Holding fast to the public/private distinction and the liberty they believed it safeguarded, liberals either rejected
antipornography feminist claims regarding pornography's harmfulness
altogether or insisted that these harms, though regrettable, could not
justify any serious efforts to curtail pornography's production, distribution, or consumption. Meanwhile, in the face of what they perceived as
liberals' calloused obstinacy, antipornography feminists condemned what
they perceived as liberals' fanatical adherence to conceptions of harm,
liberty, and the public and the private too narrow and formalistic to accommodate even the most basic pleas for justice on behalf of women. "I
think the inviolability of the First Amendment has replaced God, mother-
hood, and patriotism as a sacrosanct refuge for those who prefer to rely
on sacred cows rather than the working out of complex societal problems
in the public arena," Brownmiller told the audience at Women Against
Violence in Pornography and Media's (WAVPM) Feminist Perspectives
on Pornography conference in 1978, summing up what was at the time a
rapidly growing consensus among antipornography feminists concerning
the limits of liberalism (Bronstein 2011, 161). As the 1970s gave way to the
1980s, and antipornography feminists began to champion an ordinance
figuring pornography as legally actionable sex discrimination as opposed
to constitutionally protected speech, the already profound theoretical
differences separating antipornography feminists and liberals seemed
poised to deepen.

In the fall of 1983, at the request of the city of Minneapolis, Andrea
Dworkin and Catharine MacKinnon drafted the first version of their
pornography civil rights ordinance. Premised on the defining dogma of
antipornography feminism that pornography threatens women's physical,
political, and economic well-being, the ordinance consisted of a series
of amendments to Minneapolis's existing civil rights code. It singled
out pornography as a form of sex discrimination and defined specific
acts, including "trafficking in pornography," "coercion into pornographic

performances," "forcing pornography on a person," and "assault or physical attack due to pornography,"[31] as civil rights violations (Dworkin and MacKinnon 1985, 101). As Dworkin, MacKinnon, and their sympathizers frequently emphasized, the ordinance was a civil, as opposed to a criminal, law, and one that placed "enforcement in the hands of the victim," not police and prosecutors (MacKinnon 1987b, 203).[32] More specifically, the ordinance gave women, as well as any other persons who could prove to the satisfaction of a trier of fact that their civil rights had been violated through a particular piece of pornography, a cause of action to sue the producers and distributors of the material implicated in the civil rights violation for damages as well as a permanent injunction against the sale, exhibition, and distribution of that material (Dworkin and MacKinnon 1988, 101).

Perhaps the most controversial aspect of Dworkin and MacKinnon's Minneapolis ordinance was its definition of pornography. In order for materials to be deemed pornographic and therefore actionable under the ordinance, the ordinance stipulated that materials had to "graphically" depict, in either pictures or words, "the sexually explicit subordination of women" (Dworkin and MacKinnon 1985, 101). Actionable materials also had to include at least one of nine additional elements: women[33] presented "dehumanized as sexual objects, things, or commodities," "as sexual objects who enjoy pain or humiliation," "as sexual objects who experience sexual pleasure in being raped," "as sexual objects tied up or cut up or mutilated or bruised or physically hurt," "in postures of sexual submission, servility, or display," in such a way that they are "reduced to [their] body parts—including but not limited to vaginas, breasts, or buttocks," "as whores by nature," "as being penetrated by objects or animals," or "in scenarios of degradation, injury, abasement, torture, shown as filthy or inferior, bleeding, bruised, or hurt in a context that makes these conditions sexual" (Dworkin and MacKinnon 1988, 101). Materials found by a trier of fact to meet the ordinance's definitional requirement would be subject to civil action by any individual alleging that their civil rights had been violated through those materials.

The Minneapolis city council passed two versions of what eventually came to be known as the Dworkin–MacKinnon ordinance, the first in December 1983 and the second in July 1984. The city's mayor, Don Fraser, vetoed both of them, citing First Amendment concerns.[34] Over the next two years, versions of the ordinance were also considered in Indianapolis, Indiana; Madison, Wisconsin; Suffolk County, New York; Bellingham, Washington; Los Angeles County, California; and Cambridge, Massachusetts. The ordinance also sparked interest at the federal level, and between summer and winter 1985, MacKinnon, Dworkin, and two other prominent antipornography feminists, Dorchen Leidholt and Diana Russell, accepted invitations to testify about the ordinance before the Attorney General's Commission on Pornography, known as the Meese Commission for Edwin Meese, attorney general under President Ronald Reagan from 1985 to 1988. In its final report, issued in July 1986, the commission expressed its "substantial agreement with the motivations behind the ordinance and the goals it represents" and recommended that Congress "conduct hearings and consider legislation recognizing a civil remedy for harm attributable to pornography" (62, 186).

Despite these early successes, in the summer of 1986 the ordinance's momentum began to flag. This was in large part due to the Supreme Court's summary affirmance of the decision in *American Booksellers Ass'n, Inc. v. Hudnut.* In this decision, handed down in August 1985, the U.S. Court of Appeals for the Seventh Circuit struck down Indianapolis's version of the Dworkin–MacKinnon ordinance on First Amendment grounds, holding that the law amounted to a content-based restriction on speech that was not neutral in regard to viewpoint. Invoking the same quintessentially liberal notions of the public and the private that antipornography feminists had been assailing since the 1970s, Judge Frank Easterbrook, writing for the majority in *Hudnut,* likened the Dworkin–MacKinnon ordinance to "thought control" (328). Granting that "depictions of subordination tend to perpetuate subordination," Easterbrook nevertheless maintains that legal interventions aimed at curtailing subordinating depictions of women were illegitimate (325). According to Judge Easterbrook, "all of [pornography's] unhappy effects depend on mental intermediation," and to permit the mitigation of these effects through the regulation of pornography would be to invite the government into the "private" sphere of thoughts and intimate relations, to establish in law "an approved view of women [and] of how the sexes may relate to each other," and to leave "the government in control of all of the institutions of culture, the great censor and director of which thoughts are good for us" (328).

While the court's finding of unconstitutionality in *Hudnut* was based solely on the ordinance's ambition to establish what Judge Easterbrook calls an "'approved' view of women" and its consequent failure to remain neutral in regard to the content of the speech it sought to regulate, the *Hudnut* opinion echoes many other well-worn liberal ideas concerning the regulation of sexually explicit materials. For instance, the *Hudnut* majority is critical of the ordinance's definition of pornography because it fails to take into account "literary, artistic, political, or scientific value" (325). "Under the ordinance," Judge Easterbrook observes, "speech that . . . presents women as enjoying pain, humiliation, or rape, or even simply presents women in 'positions of servility or submission or display' is forbidden, no matter how great the literary or political value of the work taken as a whole" (328). The *Hudnut* decision also takes the Dworkin–MacKinnon ordinance to task for eschewing the established liberal framework for the regulation of "obscenity." "The Indianapolis ordinance does not refer to the prurient interest, to offensiveness, or to the standards of the community," Judge Easterbrook remarks, and "under the ordinance . . . speech that portrays women in positions of equality is lawful, no matter how graphic the sexual content" (324, 328). Finally, and most significantly, the *Hudnut* opinion affirms the long-standing liberal view that nonobscene sexually explicit materials, even those that by the *Hudnut* majority's own admission "lead to affront and lower pay at work, insult and injury at home, battery and rape on the streets," are, for all intents and purposes, harmless (329). All of these "unhappy effects depend on mental intermediation," Judge Easterbrook writes (329). The implication here is that, as liberals have long maintained, the alleged harms pornography inflicts are not truly harmful—or at least not harmful in a sense that would justify the sort of regulation represented by the Dworkin–MacKinnon ordinance (329). In summarily affirming the *Hudnut* ruling, the Supreme Court effectively ratified all of these long uncontested liberal views.

Without a doubt, the *Hudnut* ruling was a victory for civil libertarians. The ACLU and numerous other affiliated civil liberties organizations dealt a fatal blow to the Dworkin–MacKinnon ordinance and hastened the decline of the antipornography feminist movement that had been its champion.[35] However, the defeat of the Dworkin–MacKinnon ordinance and the subsequent decline of the antipornography feminist movement did not mark the end of antipornography feminism's influence and relevance. In fact, as the ordinance's momentum waned, and as the antipornography feminist movement disintegrated, antipornography feminist ideas underwent a renaissance of sorts at the hands of some unlikely allies. In the mid-1980s, prominent liberal jurists and political philosophers began translating the feminist critique of pornography into a liberal idiom, and in so doing, they dramatically reconfigured the relationship between antipornography feminism and liberalism.

THE SEX WARS COME TO POLITICAL THEORY

Before chronicling the surprising turns the relationship between antipornography feminism and liberalism took in the wake of the defeat of the Dworkin–MacKinnon ordinance, I want to explore one noteworthy mark that these conflicts between antipornography feminists and liberals made in the discipline of political theory. Several key concepts, ideas, and arguments developed by antipornography feminists in the course of their critical engagements with civil libertarian defenses of pornography exerted a significant influence on the work of Carole Pateman, a feminist political theorist who has been one of the discipline's most incisive critics of liberalism for the past four decades. Such a detour will, I hope, help readers who may be skeptical of antipornography feminism's strident, and at times fanatical and dogmatic, politics to give their critical engagement with liberalism a second look, and at the very least acknowledge it for the compelling contribution to feminist politics and thought that it was.

In 1980, in what is widely regarded as the flagship journal of the discipline of political theory, *Political Theory,* Carole Pateman published an article entitled "Women and Consent." This article, which forms a link between Pateman's earlier work in *The Problem of Political Obligation: A Critique of Liberal Theory* (1979) and her later and more expressly feminist work in *The Sexual Contract* (1988), draws explicitly on feminist analyses of the laws and "social beliefs and practices" surrounding rape in an effort to bring what Pateman describes as "the suppressed problems of consent theory" to the surface (1980, 156). In Pateman's estimation, consent theory is far from the radical antipatriarchal doctrine it purports to be. In fact, according to Pateman, it is merely a novel means of justifying the patriarchal relationships that voluntarist theories of society and politics threaten to undercut. That the concept of consent functions in this conservative manner is especially obvious, Pateman argues, in the laws, social beliefs, and practices surrounding rape where submission, including enforced submission, is routinely identified with consent and where gendered conventions of appropriate sexual behavior render notions such as "consent" and "non-consent" virtually meaningless (156, 161).[36]

Among the feminist works informing Pateman's (1980) analysis is Brownmiller's *Against Our Will*. Pateman explicitly references Brownmiller's 1975 book twice in her article. The first reference is in a footnote supporting her claim that rape is a widespread phenomenon affecting all women, even those who could not plausibly be said to have "precipitated" an assault, such as the very old, the very young, and the heavily pregnant. As Pateman puts it in this footnote, "No woman is immune" (1980, 166). Pateman's second reference to Brownmiller's book is in a footnote supporting her claim that rapes are intentional acts perpetrated by rational men rather than mistaken or accidental acts perpetrated by "stupid or careless" men. Taken together, these two claims comprise what might be described as the thesis of *Against Our Will*, summed up here in one of the book's most familiar passages: "Rape is nothing more or less than a conscious process of intimidation by which all men keep all women in a state of fear" (Brownmiller 1975, 15).

By the time "Women and Consent" was published, arguments Brownmiller makes in *Against Our Will* regarding the centrality of rape to women's oppression, the practical indistinguishability of rape and consensual sex, and the interrelationship of rape, pornography, and prostitution had become central tenets of antipornography feminist politics and ideology. Indeed, in the year leading up to the publication of Pateman's article, Brownmiller herself became a leading voice in the antipornography feminist movement, leveraging her notoriety as the author of *Against Our*

Will to found WAP, the first national antipornography feminist organization in the United States.

In "Women and Consent," Pateman (1980) does not directly reference Brownmiller's influential claims concerning the interrelation of rape, pornography, and prostitution.[37] She does, however, repeat and affirm other closely related claims, which, at the time of the article's publication, were widely and publicly embraced by the antipornography feminist movement.[38] For instance, Pateman challenges the conventional distinction between rape and consensual sex. Pateman resists the view that "rape is . . . a unique act that stands in complete opposition to the consensual relations that ordinarily obtain between the sexes," characterizing it instead as "the extreme expression or an extension of the accepted and 'natural' relation between men and women" (161). Brownmiller puts forward an almost identical argument in *Against Our Will.* "The real reason for the law's everlasting confusion as to what constitutes an act of rape and what constitutes an act of mutual intercourse," Brownmiller writes, "is the underlying cultural assumption that it is the natural masculine role to proceed aggressively toward [insertion of the penis], while the natural feminine role is to 'resist' or 'submit'" (1975, 383).

Thus, for both Pateman and Brownmiller, the naturalization and normalization of force in conventional heterosexual relations makes the line between mutual heterosexual sex and rape difficult, even impossible, to determine. In Brownmiller's influential antipornography feminist analysis, this claim plays a crucial role: it serves as the opening premise in a line of argument linking pornography (as well as prostitution) to rape. According to Brownmiller, both pornography and prostitution are among the most potent cultural forces at work naturalizing and normalizing force in putatively consensual heterosexual sex. In Brownmiller's words, pornography and prostitution "promote and propagandize [the ideology of rape]" and "offer men, and in particular, impressionable adolescent males . . . the ideology and psychologic encouragement to commit their acts of aggression without awareness, for the most part, that they have committed a punishable crime" (1975, 391). This argument is the sine qua non of antipornography feminism, and the fact that Pateman's "Women and Consent" recapitulates its foundational premise shows that by 1980, antipornography feminist ideas and arguments regarding the continuity between rape and "consensual" heterosexual sex had made inroads into Pateman's political theorizing.

Pateman's article bears other marks of antipornography feminist influence. For instance, in "Women and Consent," Pateman, much like her antipornography feminist contemporaries, privileges sexuality as a site in which women's more generalized subordinate status is rendered especially visible and obvious. In Pateman's view, modern liberal societies' laws as well as their less formalized beliefs and attitudes concerning rape and "consensual" heterosexual sex reveal something deeper about the status of women in these societies, namely that, "notwithstanding their formal civic status, women are regarded as men's 'natural' subordinates, and hence as incapable of consent" (1980, 154). Brownmiller draws a similar inference from the voluminous data on sexual assault she compiles in *Against Our Will.* According to Brownmiller, the failure of modern liberal societies to acknowledge and redress the sexual injuries sustained by women living within them evinces that the "male liberal tradition" is steeped in the "philosophy of rape" and consequently views women "as anonymous panting playthings, adult toys, dehumanized objects to be used, abused, broken, and discarded," not as free and equal rights-bearing individuals (1975, 391, 394). For both Pateman and antipornography feminists like Brownmiller, then, sex and sexuality have pride of place analytically because they are seen as giving the lie to claims that gender equality is an accomplished fact in modern liberal regimes.

Pateman's analysis privileges sex and sexuality in another way that is wholly consonant with antipornography feminism. Like Brownmiller in *Against Our Will,* in "Women and Consent," Pateman figures rape as a prime mover driving, exacerbating, and reinforcing women's social, political, and economic subordination. "Rape is central to the problem of women and consent in everyday life," Pateman writes (1980, 156), echoing the claims of antipornography feminists like Brownmiller that "the ideology of rape" permeates "every level of our society" and affects "all women" (Brownmiller 1975, 15, 389). Similarly, when Pateman argues that the morass of problems concerning women and consent in modern liberal societies presents "an entirely sufficient argument, not only for the democratic reconstruction of the liberal state, but for a simultaneous reconstruction of our sexual lives" (1980, 163), she echoes the claims of Brownmiller and antipornography feminists more generally that rape and the constellation of patriarchal myths and attitudes surrounding it may be "the central key" to understanding and unlocking women's oppression (Brownmiller 1975, 397).

While Pateman's "Women and Consent" bears many marks of antipornography feminist influence—namely its interrogation of the conventional distinction between "consensual" heterosexual sex and rape, its privileging of sex and sexuality as sites and sources of women's subordination, and its frustration with traditional liberal responses to the problem of the sexual oppression of women—it stops short of advocating a full-blown antipornography feminist agenda. In "Women and Consent," Pateman's primary aim is political theoretical. She is not out to criticize pornography, prostitution, or the ideology of male supremacy that they support, but to expose the inegalitarian implications of liberal consent theory as it has been applied in the context of rape law. Eight years later, Pateman would expand on this project and amplify her critique of the concept of consent in *The Sexual Contract* (1988). In this work, Pateman also advocates and pursues a recognizably antipornography feminist agenda, including figuring both pornography and prostitution as crucial sites, sources, and symptoms of women's subordination.

Pateman's principal argument in *The Sexual Contract* is this: far from signaling the end of patriarchal rule and ushering in a new epoch of egalitarian and consensual social relations, the social contract described by classic contract theorists like Hobbes and Locke is a "sexual contract" that supplants the rule of men as fathers (a political arrangement Pateman terms "classical" patriarchy) and establishes "a specifically modern form of patriarchy," "fraternal patriarchy," or the rule of "men as men" (1988, 1–3).[39] The excavation of the neglected sexual dimensions of the classic social contract stories, as well as an elucidation of their implications for contemporary politics and theory, comprise the bulk of *The Sexual Contract*.

In the preface to *The Sexual Contract*, Pateman signals that her book is meant to be more than just another work of "mainstream political theory"

(1988, x). In fact, she marks the book as an expressly feminist project and situates it in the broader context of "radical feminist" theory and activism. "Some of my arguments," Pateman writes, "have been prompted by writers customarily labeled radical feminists . . . [and] my deepest intellectual debt is to the arguments and activities of the feminist movement" (x–xi). Pateman later reveals that one of the radical feminist writers to whom she is most deeply indebted is Adrienne Rich. An acclaimed poet, essayist, and activist, Adrienne Rich was also a founding member of WAP and the author of an afterword to the antipornography feminist anthology *Take Back the Night: Women on Pornography,* in which she likens pornography to "witch burning, lynching, pogroms, fascism," and "slavery" (1980a, 314, 318). In "Compulsory Heterosexuality and Lesbian Existence," Rich portrays pornography as an integral part of "compulsory heterosexuality," a "political institution" comprised of a "pervasive cluster of forces" that "enforce women's total emotional, erotic loyalty and subservience to men" and "assure male right of physical, economic, and emotional access" to women (1980b, 637, 640, 647). By exerting a powerful "influence on consciousness," Rich believes pornography brainwashes both women and men into believing "that women are natural sexual prey to men and love it," effectively reifying what Rich calls "the law of male sex right to women" (641, 645).

In *The Sexual Contract,* Pateman references Rich's concept, "the law of male sex right," directly: "The original pact is a sexual as well as a social contract: it is sexual in the sense of patriarchal—that is, the contract establishes men's political right over women—and also sexual in the sense of establishing orderly access by men to women's bodies. The original contract creates what I shall call, following Adrienne Rich, 'the law of male sex-right'" (1988, 2). Here Pateman positions her book's central argument that the contract is the distinctively modern means of "establishing orderly access by men to women's bodies" and shoring up "the law of male sex-right" as a supplement to Rich's account of compulsory heterosexuality (2). Building on Rich's contention that men secure access to women by way of a multifaceted "political institution," Pateman suggests that in modern liberal societies, one aspect of this political institution is contract (2). Far from "exemplifying and securing individual freedom" Pateman argues that contracts, especially those to which women are practically by definition a party, such as the marriage contract, the prostitution contract, and the surrogacy contract, inevitably give rise to "relations of domination and subordination" in which a woman (whether as a wife, a prostitute, or a surrogate mother) places the "right of command" over her body (evasively termed "the property in her person" in the language of contract) in the hands of a man (8, 4–5).[40] This argument—the defining argument of Pateman's book—can be seen as a continuation and elaboration of Rich's account of compulsory heterosexuality. It is an attempt to use the canonical texts and analytical tools of political theory to come to terms with precisely how the political institution that ensures men's ready access to women and their unique capacities that Rich describes as compulsory heterosexuality functions and is legitimated in modern liberal societies.

This continuity between Pateman's *The Sexual Contract* and Rich's "Compulsory Heterosexuality and Lesbian Existence" signals a wider continuity between Pateman's book and antipornography feminist thought. Perhaps the most obvious feature common to both *The Sexual Contract* and virtually all antipornography feminist writing is the figuration of pornography as a key site, source, and symptom of women's subordination to men. While it would be misleading to suggest that pornography is among Pateman's central concerns in *The Sexual Contract,* it would be equally misleading to suggest that concern with pornography is completely absent from Pateman's text. For instance, Pateman observes that "men still eagerly press for the enforcement of the law of male sex-right and demand that women's bodies, in the flesh and in representation, should be publicly available to them" (1988, 14). Pateman later expands on this remark. "The general display of women's bodies and sexual parts, either in representation or as live bodies," Pateman writes, "is central to the sex industry and continually reminds men—and women—that men exercise the law of male sex-right, that they have patriarchal rights of access to women's bodies" (1988, 199).

Such portrayals of pornography as a means by which men both proclaim and exercise their "patriarchal rights of access to women's bodies" is typical of antipornography feminist writing, such as Rich's "Compulsory

Heterosexuality" (1980b). It is also prominently featured in the title of Andrea Dworkin's antipornography feminist manifesto, *Pornography: Men Possessing Women* ([1981] 1991). The following passage from Dworkin's text is exemplary in this regard. "In the male system," Dworkin writes, "women are . . . the whore who belongs to all male citizens. . . . Buying her is buying pornography. Having her is having pornography" (202). Thus, for both Pateman and antipornography feminists like Rich and Dworkin, pornography is one common, highly visible, and virtually unregulated way in which men possess, control, and dominate women in contemporary liberal societies. However, it must be borne in mind that neither Pateman nor antipornography feminists believed pornography to be the sole means by which this was accomplished. Rather, as the passages quoted above intimate, both Pateman and antipornography feminists believed pornography worked in concert with another key institution of "the law of male sex right": prostitution.[41]

Perhaps the most prominent antipornography feminist to draw a link between pornography, prostitution, and women's subordination to men is Susan Brownmiller. "The case against pornography and the case against toleration of prostitution are central to the fight against rape," Brownmiller notes (1975, 390). In Brownmiller's view, critiquing prostitution and pornography is crucial to antirape efforts because both pornography and prostitution "institutionalize the concept . . . that sex is a female service that should not be denied the civilized male"—just the sort of belief in masculine sexual entitlement that, Brownmiller argues, lurks behind acts of rape (391–92). "When young men learn that females may be bought for a price," Brownmiller reasons, "then how should they not also conclude that that which may be bought may also be taken without the civility of a monetary exchange?" (391).

Andrea Dworkin also posits a fundamental relation between prostitution, pornography, and women's subordination to men. In fact, in Dworkin's view, this relationship is so fundamental that it has left its mark on the word "pornography" itself. "Pornography," Dworkin explains, "derived from the ancient Greek *pornē* and *graphos*, means 'writing about whores'" or "the graphic depiction of women as vile whores" ([1981] 1991, 199, 200). After making this etymological point, Dworkin proceeds to argue that the connection between pornography and prostitution runs even deeper. According to Dworkin, pornography does not merely represent women as "vile whores"; it actually reduces them to this degraded status. "In the system of male sexual domination," Dworkin contends, "women are *porneia,* in our real live bodies the graphic depictions of whores, used as whores are used, valued as whores are valued" (223–24).

Kathleen Barry, another notable antipornography feminist,[42] posits a similar relationship between pornography, prostitution, and women's subordination to men. In *Female Sexual Slavery,*[43] a 1979 book primarily concerned with laying bare the most horrific aspects of the international sex trafficking industry, Barry devotes an entire chapter—the book's longest—to elucidating the role pornography plays in the perpetuation and legitimation of forced prostitution. According to Barry, pornography embodies and promotes "the ideology of cultural sadism"—an ideology that in her view helps maintain "female sexual slavery" by making the sexual use and abuse of women appear normal, natural, and inevitable (1979, 182). By making men into "the powerful, objectifying aggressor" and women into "the naturally masochistic sexual object existing only for male sexual use and satisfaction," pornography, Barry explains, "encourage[s] and support[s] sexual violence, defining it into normal behavior," thus enabling the forced prostitution of women and girls to flourish on a global scale with "safety, support, and impunity" (174, 184–85).

As these examples demonstrate, critiques of prostitution as an institution of men's sexual dominance are part and parcel of antipornography feminist thought. In the antipornography feminist view, prostitution, like pornography, embodies and perpetuates the belief that women are objects that exist solely for men's sexual use, a belief that then serves as the cornerstone of male supremacy. In *The Sexual Contract,* Pateman echoes this antipornography feminist critique of prostitution. In the chapter entitled "What's Wrong with Prostitution?," Pateman argues that, contrary to the sanguine views put forward by libertarians and even some feminists, prostitution is not "merely a job of work," but an institution of "sexual mastery" (1988, 190, 207). "When a man enters into the prostitution contract," Pateman explains, "he is not interested in sexually indifferent, disembodied services;" he contracts to "obtain unilateral right of direct sexual use of a woman's body" (207, 204). He contracts, in other words, to constitute himself as a "civil master for a time" (207). In this way, Pateman argues, through prostitution, "the law of male sex-right is publicly affirmed and men gain public acknowledgment as women's sexual masters" (208). This, Pateman forcefully concludes, "is what is wrong with prostitution" (208).

It is also, in Pateman's view, what is wrong with sadomasochism. According to Pateman, the fact that the sex industry caters to "a vigorous demand for 'bondage and discipline' or fantasy slave contracts" is further evidence that pornography and prostitution are primarily about the shoring up of "the law of male sex-right" (1988, 199). Responding directly to Pat (now Patrick) Califia's sex-radical feminist defense of S&M,[44] Pateman argues that sadomasochism is not "a rebellious or revolutionary fantasy" but rather "a dramatic exhibition of the logic of contract and of the full implications of the sexuality of the patriarchal masculine 'individual'" (186). Bearing in mind that Pateman's central argument in *The Sexual Contract* is that contract is a modern means of instituting patriarchal domination, the characterization of sadomasochism she offers here is tantamount to an accusation that defenders of S&M like Califia are patriarchal collaborators.

Such accusations are commonplace in antipornography feminist writing. For instance, in the introduction to *Against Sadomasochism* (1982), a volume that features contributions from several antipornography feminist leaders including Women Against Violence in Pornography and Media (WAVPM) cofounders Kathleen Barry, Susan Griffin, and Diana Russell, sadomasochism is described as "firmly rooted in patriarchal sexual ideology" (Linden et al. 1982, 4). In her contribution to this volume, Russell, who is also one of the volume's coeditors, offers a response to defenses of sadomasochism that emphasize its consensual nature. Russell's response closely resembles the position staked out by Pateman in *The Sexual Contract*. Rather than questioning whether or not S&M encounters are actually consensual, as their defenders maintain, Russell asserts that "wanting or consenting to domination and humiliation does not make it nonoppressive. It merely demonstrates how deep and profound the oppression is" (1982, 177). For Russell, as for Pateman, the presence of genuine consent does not indemnify S&M against the charge that it is a reflection and affirmation of women's subordinate status. In fact, that defenders of S&M so fervently and frequently invoke the language of consent and the "logic of contract" is further evidence of their complicity in modern modes of patriarchal domination.

Thus, it is not only in Pateman's scattered remarks concerning pornography but also in her much more developed critiques of prostitution and sadomasochism that we see the influence of antipornography feminist ideas and arguments on *The Sexual Contract*. Like many antipornography feminists, including those she directly references in her text like Brownmiller, Barry, and Rich, Pateman conceives of pornography, prostitution, and sadomasochism as institutions of male dominance. They are not harmless or potentially liberating avenues of sexual exploration and expression to which both women and men should be permitted unfettered access, as some particularly adventurous civil libertarians and all sex-radical feminists maintain. Rather, they are key means through which "the law of male sex-right" is proclaimed and enforced; further, as Pateman is at continual pains to emphasize, the liberal ideology that is so oftern used to legitimate these sexual practices offers women little in the way of genuine sexual freedom and autonomy.

Perhaps the most compelling evidence that a significant continuity inheres between the critiques of pornography, prostitution, and sadomasochism offered by Pateman in *The Sexual Contract* and those offered by antipornography feminists throughout the 1970s and 1980s is Pateman's own remarks on the matter. In 1990, a year after the publication of *The Sexual Contract*, Pateman published a review of Catharine MacKinnon's 1987 *Feminism Unmodified: Discourses on Life and Law*, a collection of speeches and writings composed by MacKinnon at the height of her involvement in the antipornography feminist movement. On the whole, Pateman's review of MacKinnon's book is sympathetic. She endorses MacKinnon's view that "the cornerstone of men's claim to jurisdiction over women is that they have right of sexual access to women's bodies" (1990, 402, 401). She describes "MacKinnon's insistence that women's subordination to men is different from the subjection of other groups or categories of people because it is sexual" as "the most important contribution of *Feminism Unmodified*" and draws parallels between it and her own argument regarding the establishment of "the law of male sex right" through "the (story of the) sexual contract" in *The Sexual Contract* (401).

Pateman also commends MacKinnon's unsparing critique of pornography. "In pornography," Pateman writes, adopting MacKinnon's own forceful rhetorical style, "what men can do when they have one of us has no limits. Women are represented as freely available for sexual use, whether or not they are willing, and violence, degradation, and humiliation are represented as sex; the meaning of womanhood is proclaimed to be sexual submission" (1990, 407).[45] Pateman even goes so far as to tentatively endorse the Dworkin–MacKinnon ordinance, which was, by the time Pateman's review appeared, all but a lost cause thanks to the Supreme Court's summary affirmance of the *Hudnut* ruling in 1986. "Use of law" to regulate pornography, Pateman writes, "brings its own problems, such as black markets, smuggling, and the well-known problems of defining 'pornography,' but perhaps," Pateman concludes, "the law is a necessary recourse for women given the scale of the [pornography] industry" (407).[46] That as late as 1990 Pateman was willing to give the Dworkin–MacKinnon ordinance the benefit of the doubt is powerful evidence of the influence antipornography feminist concerns, concepts, and arguments exerted on her political theorizing during this period.

Pateman's favorable review of MacKinnon's *Feminism Unmodified* and sympathetic deportment vis-à-vis the Dworkin–MacKinnon ordinance appear even more striking when they are considered alongside the chilly reception that one of Pateman's contemporaries, feminist political theorist Wendy Brown, offered MacKinnon's ideas and legislative proposals around this same time. In a review of MacKinnon's *Feminism Unmodified* published in summer 1989, just a few months before Pateman's review appeared, Brown offers a scathing critique of MacKinnon's book and the antipornography feminist politics it elaborates. Brown's review begins with an attack on MacKinnon's oratorical style. "Oratory," Brown writes, "is MacKinnon's necessary medium, for her critical claims are hardly meditative reflections upon one of the most complex and subtle dimensions of our political and epistemological universe—gender power. They are searing manifestos intended to stir the sleeping, spur the complacent, and scorn the apologetic" (1989, 489).[47] Brown is also highly critical of

MacKinnon's "infelicitous reliance" on Marxism (490). "I am quite sure," Brown writes, "that [Marxist] method," with "its affinity with scientific discourse, its penchant for unambiguous categories, and its drive toward theorizing a totality," "is anathema to intelligent analysis of gender or sexuality" (490). Moreover, Brown continues, MacKinnon's thesis that gender inequality is "created, operationalized, and expressed through *sexuality*" in a manner analogous to the way in which class inequality is created, operationalized, and expressed through work in Marx's theory is inconsistent with her claim that sexual difference and sexuality are socially constructed (489). In Brown's words, "MacKinnon ends up casting women, men, and sexuality as thoroughly socially constructed at the same time she speaks of men *expropriating* female sexuality—as if this sexuality had some existence prior to and innocent of its social construction" (490).

Perhaps the most serious fault Brown finds with MacKinnon's book is its failure to articulate what she calls "a political theory of sexuality" (1989, 491). Such a theory, Brown explains, "would have to explore rather than denounce the complex faces of power in sexuality. . . . It would also have to account for rather than consign to the pathos of false consciousness the fact of female sexual diversity as well as the paradox that women have been profoundly injured sexually and women are alive and kicking sexually" (491). In Brown's view, MacKinnon's "linear, systematic argument" concerning the way in which sexuality is forcibly constructed by and through male dominance is polemically powerful but in the final analysis irrelevant, even violent, "to the variegated character of sexual life and gender within and among diverse cultures, races, and epochs" (491).

In Brown's view, the shortcomings of MacKinnon's theory are nowhere more evident than in her analysis of pornography. "MacKinnon reads pornography," Brown writes, "like cops read street signs: unambiguous directives to action that are never contradictory, complex, subversive, or contestable in meaning" (1989, 491). According to Brown, MacKinnon's blanket assertions "that all pornography depicts the sexual subordination of women . . . and that all pornography is for men" are flat-out wrong (491). Regarding what is in her view MacKinnon's reductive and misleading characterization of pornography as a straightforward and all-powerful instrument of male dominance, Brown writes, "It is as if acknowledgment of cracks in the totality negate the possibility of feminism itself and as if complexity is incompatible with political struggle—sure symptoms, both, of political theory destined to colonize rather than illuminate or liberate its subject" (491).

The only kind words Brown has for *Feminism Unmodified* can be found in the final two paragraphs of her review. "MacKinnon's feminist critique of liberalism," Brown writes approvingly, "plunders every boundary operating within liberal discourse to obscure women's situation," "scathes every arm of the state and the law," and "makes *Feminism Unmodified* a book worth reading" (1989, 492). However, Brown is quick to note that MacKinnon's "incisive" and "graceful" critique of liberalism stands awkwardly alongside her turn to the liberal state and "the meager palliative of civil rights law" to redress women's subordination (492). Ultimately, in Brown's view, the single worthwhile aspect of MacKinnon's book— its searing indictment of liberalism—is undermined by MacKinnon's "relentless depiction" of women as powerless victims of sexually predatory men, for it is this depiction that drives MacKinnon's simplistic and problematically state-centered antipornography feminist politics (492).

Brown's and Pateman's assessments of MacKinnon's *Feminism Unmodified* and the antipornography feminist politics it outlines could not be more different. Whereas Brown sees MacKinnon's feminist political theory and the legislation it inspired as founded on faulty, sexist, and ultimately freedom-denying premises, Pateman praises MacKinnon's theory of women's sexual subordination and grants that the Dworkin–MacKinnon ordinance is perhaps a "necessary recourse" in women's struggle for freedom and equality (Brown 1989, 492; Pateman 1990, 407). While it would be misleading and inaccurate to collapse Pateman's position into MacKinnon's, or those of the other antipornography feminist theorists and activists Pateman cites and draws from, there are affinities between Pateman's early feminist work and the ideas and arguments of the original antipornography feminists that cannot be denied, and that Pateman herself acknowledged. These affinities are evidence not only of the powerful influence antipornography feminism exerted over feminist thinking during the late 1970s and early 1980s but also of the extent to which critical engagement with the core concepts of liberal theory was a central part of the antipornography feminist project at this time. Antipornography feminism was born of white-hot feminist hostility to the liberalism espoused by midcentury civil libertarian opponents of obscenity regulation, like Barney Rossett, Charles Rembar, and Alan Dershowitz. Attuning ourselves to the antipornography feminist resonances in the work of Carole Pateman, one of political theory's most respected and unsparing critics of liberalism, underscores this important fact and moves us toward a richer and more accurate view of the antipornography feminist project. Whether we find their analyses of sexual politics incisive and persuasive or crude and unsophisticated, we must at the very least follow Wendy Brown in acknowledging that, insofar as they "plunder[ed] every boundary operating within liberal discourse to obscure women's situation," antipornography feminists were engaged in serious and worthwhile feminist work.

2

Free Speech, Criminal Acts

LIBERAL APPROPRIATIONS OF
ANTIPORNOGRAPHY FEMINISM

As the clashes between pornography's feminist critics and liberal defenders throughout the 1970s and early 1980s demonstrate, a critical orientation toward liberalism was as fundamental to antipornography feminism in its earliest articulations as was a critical orientation toward pornography and other institutions of sexual oppression. Andrea Dworkin offers a quintessential expression of the regnant antipornography feminist appraisal of liberalism during this period in a brief and pugnacious essay, written in 1981, criticizing the ACLU (1993a, 212). In Dworkin's view, the "First Amendment absolutists" at the ACLU, who pride themselves on defending "pornographers, the Nazis, and the Klan," operate on an "unembodied," and therefore "dangerous," principle (212). "No matter what blood flows," Dworkin charges, "the principle comes first; consequences do not matter; physical acts are taken to be abstractions; genocidal ambitions and concrete organizing toward genocidal goals are trivialized by male lawyers who are a most protected and privileged group. Meanwhile, those who are targeted as victims are left defenseless" (212). In the eyes of early antipornography feminists like Dworkin, liberalism was an instrument of domination, an ideology that shored up brutal regimes of inequality by placing them beyond the reach of law and government in the name of individual liberty.

Just as a critical orientation toward liberalism was a defining feature of antipornography feminism in its first decade, a broad consensus regarding antipornography feminism prevailed among liberals during this period. In the liberal view, pornography was disgusting, offensive, and degrading, but not harmful or oppressive in the manner antipornography feminists alleged.[1] Therefore, liberals insisted, the problem of pornography could be satisfactorily addressed by private action—namely avoidance on the part of those who find it displeasing. Herald Price Fahringer, general counsel for the First Amendment Lawyer's Association and attorney for both Larry Flynt, publisher of *Hustler,* and Al Goldstein, publisher of *Screw,* gave voice to this widespread liberal view. "I find much of the sexually explicit material available today personally distasteful, and I recognize that some of it degrades women," Fahringer confessed to a mixed audience of feminists and civil libertarians at the New York University School of Law in 1978 (1979, 251). "However," he continues, "those who believe that this country's new breed of publishers and filmmakers should have their mouths washed out with soap for using four-letter words or publishing pictures of nude women in obstetric poses must remember that no one is compelled to either see or read what is repulsive to him or her" (251). "Those who are appalled by these materials can ignore them," Fahringer concludes. "And the few who gain some satisfaction from them should be allowed that small comfort" (251).

Thus, in the 1970s and early 1980s, antipornography feminists saw liberalism as the creed of the "pro-pimp lobby," while liberals saw antipornography feminism as a renascent "puritan moralism" (MacKinnon and Dworkin 1997, 11; Richards 1979, 237). However, in the mid-1980s, in the aftermath of the defeat of the Dworkin–MacKinnon ordinance, all of this began to change. At a time when antipornography feminism's prospects appeared most bleak and its relationship to liberalism most strained, influential liberals took up the antipornography feminist cause. Dissatisfied with both traditional antipornography feminist representations of the problem of pornography and pat liberal dismissals of antipornography feminist claims regarding pornography's harmfulness, in the mid-1980s, liberal political philosophers and legal theorists began articulating an improbable ideological amalgam: antipornography liberalism.

ANTECEDENTS TO ANTIPORNOGRAPHY LIBERALISM

While the emergence of a full-fledged liberal variant of antipornography feminism could not have been foreseen amid the rancor and hostility that defined the relationship between antipornography feminism and liberalism during the 1970s and early 1980s, in retrospect, antecedents are discernible as early as the late 1970s. For instance, in 1978, at the same New York University School of Law colloquium where Paul Chevigny pounded on the table as he chided feminists for failing to offer proof of pornography's harmful effects, two self-identified civil libertarian feminists and one anonymous audience member attempted to find a middle ground.

One colloquium participant who sought to reconcile civil libertarian concerns about the First Amendment and feminist concerns about pornography was Marjorie Smith, the deputy commissioner of the New York City Department of Consumer Affairs and former staff attorney for the Women's Rights Project of the ACLU. In the midst of a starkly polarized gathering, Smith attempted to thread the needle, arguing that the strategy and tactics of the Los Angeles based antipornography feminist organization Women Against Violence Against Women (WAVAW) were consistent with "civil liberties principles" (250). Founded in 1976, WAVAW's original mission had been to stop *Snuff*, a 1976 film purporting to document the actual sexual assault and murder of a woman, from being shown in Southern California theaters. Through a combination of protests, pickets, and appeals to local authorities to seize the film on the grounds that it violated state obscenity statutes, WAVAW succeeded in driving *Snuff* out of Southern California in less than a month. By December 1978, when Smith offered her defense of the organization at the New York University colloquium, WAVAW had moved on to coordinating a national boycott against the recording industry for using images that "trivialized, glorified, sensationalized, or romanticized" violence against women to promote their products (Bronstein 2011, 97).[2] Smith defended WAVAW's use of "consumer boycott techniques such as picketing and letter-writing campaigns" against the recording industry as in keeping with the values enshrined in the First Amendment (1979, 247).[3] Conceding that "it is possible . . . for reasonable people to disagree about whether the problem of media glorification of violence against women in pornography or elsewhere . . . has sufficiently serious consequences to warrant involvement in the activities of a group such as Women Against Violence Against Women, the decision to become involved," Smith insisted, "can be made by a civil libertarian feminist without abandoning civil liberties principles" (250).

Smith's defense of antipornography feminists' use of private action to combat pornography met with grudging approval from her civil libertarian peers. The predominant view among civil libertarians at the colloquium was that private action against pornography, though technically in accord with civil liberties principles as Smith had argued, was a frivolous misallocation of feminist energy and resources. Law professor David Richards's comments on this score are representative. "I want to say that pornography is, with respect to feminism, not a significant issue," Richards lectured the feminists in the audience, adding that "the significant issues seem to me to be family and occupational structure, sex roles, and the like" (1979, 237). "To persist in the argument of prohibiting pornography," Richards emphasized, "trivializes feminism" (237). Nevertheless, Richards continued, if feminists insist on drawing attention to pornography, then they should confine themselves to private action. "Inform men of how you feel about these fantasies that they find natural. . . . Make men feel guilty and ashamed," Richards advised (237).

While Smith was willing to defend only private action undertaken by feminists in their crusade against pornography, a second self-identified civil libertarian feminist at the colloquium was willing to grant antipornography feminists a much wider field. Brenda Feigen Fasteau, a former director of the ACLU's Women's Rights Project and a national vice president of the National Organization for Women, began her prepared remarks with the following declaration: "As a feminist and a lawyer I do not think it is possible to be a feminist without believing in the first amendment" (1979, 282). "If we don't recognize the first amendment," Fasteau warned her fellow feminists, "then *Ms. Magazine* will end up being banned" (284). With her liberal bona fides firmly established, Fasteau went on to recommend two legal avenues feminists might pursue to curtail the production and distribution of pornography. Her first recommendation involved a creative expansion of existing libel laws to invent "a new tort" that would allow "for a class action to be brought by a group of women injured both mentally and physically by a particular movie or magazine" (292). "I think it is possible to create that," Fasteau remarked, "without offending the first amendment if you can show damage" (300). Fasteau's second recommendation was to enact "a statute prohibiting incitement of violence against women" that "would prohibit publications that demonstrated how to rape a woman, how to mutilate a woman" (300). "I think that such a statute would not offend first amendment values," which, Fasteau reminded the audience, she considered "practically sacrosanct" (300).

As Carolyn Bronstein (2011) has noted, the legal reforms Fasteau recommended at the New York University colloquium foreshadowed the antipornography ordinance Catharine MacKinnon and Andrea Dworkin would put forward in Minneapolis just a few years later. As this affinity might lead one to expect, Fasteau's proposals met with substantial resistance from her fellow civil libertarians at the colloquium. For instance, Ephraim London, a noted civil liberties attorney who handled a string of landmark obscenity cases in the 1950s and 1960s, rejected Fasteau's recommendations, arguing that even a film documenting the rape of a woman ought to be accorded constitutional protection. "It has been suggested that it should be unlawful to show a film of a woman being raped. But," London reasoned, "that is not an act of rape then taking place. It is a statement of what is said to have occurred previously" (Redlich 1979, 285). "Even if the film is intended to titillate," London added, "the exhibition of the film should not, in my view, be prevented" (285). London further rejected Fasteau's suggestion that "a new tort" might be created that would allow women who "can show damage" to sue pornographers without offending the First Amendment. "I am willing to assume for the purpose of discussion," London granted, "that pornography dealing with the torture of women, the rape of women, the degradation of women is harmful" (284). Nevertheless, London continued, "one solution we cannot resort to is government intervention. . . . The minute you give the government power to regulate what is to be read or seen or heard, you violate our constitutional freedom of expression" (284). "One cannot take the position that the first amendment prohibits government censorship of any kind except that which relates to the degradation of women," London concluded (284). In 1978, Fasteau was clearly a woman apart among her liberal peers.

Aside from Smith's and Fasteau's remarks, there was one other instance at the New York University colloquium that in retrospect can be seen as anticipating the surprising shift that liberal thinking regarding the feminist critique of pornography would undergo in the late 1980s. This instance came at the end of a panel discussion on the regulation of pornography, when an audience member whom the transcript does not identify spoke eloquently of the serious challenge the feminist critique of pornography posed for civil libertarians. "As lawyers and civil libertarians," the audience member began, "we want a society that provides for the free and robust exchange of ideas" (Redlich 1979, 297). "Some of us," the audience member continued, "have only recently come to the realization that we also want a society free from the kind of statistics [dealing with the kind and degree of violence being perpetrated on women by men] that have been quoted today" (297). "Once we accept these values as perhaps of equal interest," the audience member explained, "then the problem becomes one of reconciling these values to create a society that reflects both interests as best it can . . . , a society where the free exchange of ideas creates a climate in which women will grow up and live free from violence" (298). "Some restrictions on speech may be supportable as a means of reaching that kind of society," the audience member concluded, adding, "the first amendment has to be reconciled with . . . the welfare of women" (298).

According to the colloquium's official transcript, this unknown audience member's suggestion that the liberal commitment to a society that provides for the "free and robust exchange of ideas" may have to be balanced against "the welfare of women" was not addressed by any of the colloquium's participants. As the transcript has it, after the unknown audience member finished speaking, another audience member asked a question, and the discussion among the panelists quickly turned to "building codes" and "local health laws" (Redlich 1979, 298). The colloquium's transcript also indicates that just a few moments before the unknown audience member spoke, Susan Brownmiller said to Ephraim London,[4] "Each of [the women's movement's] issues seems to cause the liberal establishment to have to do a lot of rethinking of its positions" (292). On that particular day in 1978, the "liberal establishment" appeared decidedly unwilling to rethink its position on pornography. However, some six years later, leading liberal theorists would undertake such a rethinking in earnest, making Brownmiller's comment to London seem less ironic and more prescient.

"WITHOUT POSING SIGNIFICANT THREATS TO A WELL-FUNCTIONING SYSTEM OF FREE EXPRESSION"

One of the earliest examples of antipornography liberalism can be found in the work of American legal scholar Cass Sunstein. In a string of articles and essays published between 1986 and 1993 in the wake of the defeat of the Dworkin–MacKinnon ordinance in *American Booksellers Ass'n, Inc. v. Hudnut,* Sunstein (1986, 1988, 1992, 1993) endeavors to breathe new life into feminist efforts to curtail the production and distribution of pornography. Distancing himself from the characteristic liberal tendency "to dismiss the case against pornography as the product of prudishness or inhibition," Sunstein unequivocally asserts that pornography is a cause of "serious harm, mostly to women" that could be legally regulated "without posing significant threats to a well-functioning system of free expression" (1986, 594, 591, 601, 626).[5] Sunstein also distances himself from the "speech is speech position," according to which "all speech stands on the same ground and . . . government has no business censoring speech merely because some people or some officials are puritanical or offended by it" (1993, 267, 262). Instead of these traditional liberal views, Sunstein explicitly advocates for the regulation of pornography. According to Sunstein, "Sexually explicit speech should be regulated not when it is sexually explicit (the problem of obscenity) but instead when it merges sex with violence (the problem of pornography). The problem of pornography does not stem from offense, from free access to sexually explicit materials, from an unregulated erotic life, or from the violation of community standards. Instead it is a result of tangible real-world harms, produced by the portrayal of women and children as objects for the control and use of others, most prominently through sexual violence" (1993, 263–64).

Judged solely on the basis of these broad claims, Sunstein's position appears largely consonant with the positions of earlier antipornography feminists like Susan Brownmiller, Andrea Dworkin, and Catharine Mac-Kinnon, all of whom Sunstein cites directly in the works considered here. However, when we look beyond these generalities and examine Sunstein's arguments in more detail, differences between what I call Sunstein's anti-pornography liberalism and the antipornography feminism that preceded it begin to emerge—and what might easily have been mistaken for a revival begins to look much more like a revision.[6]

The most obvious difference between Sunstein and the antipornography feminists who preceded him is that Sunstein is a committed liberal formulating an approach to pornography regulation that conforms to, as opposed to defies or confounds, conventional liberal notions of harm, liberty, and the public and the private. Sunstein's allegiance to liberalism is most readily evident in the range of materials he singles out for critique and regulation. From the women's liberationists who occupied the offices of Grove Press in 1970 to the WAVAW activists who coordinated a three-year nationwide boycott of Warner Bros. Records from 1976 to 1979, the original antipornography feminists were out to criticize a startlingly wide range of materials. For the Grove Press occupiers, the target was the publisher's ever-expanding catalog of books, magazines, and films that, in their view, "degrade[d] women" (Lederer 1980, 269). For the activists at WAVAW, the target was "images of physical and sexual violence against women in mass media," including those used to promote best-selling albums like *Love Gun* by Kiss (1977) and *Black and Blue* by the Rolling Stones (1976).[7] Eventually, and despite the reservations of some movement leaders, antipornography feminists began to use the term "pornography" as a kind of shorthand for a broad swath of materials that they believed sanctioned the sexual abuse and degradation of women.[8] As Laura Lederer and Diana E. H. Russell explain in the November 1977 issue of the WAVPM newsletter, the materials WAVPM opposed were "films . . . [,] books and magazines . . . [,] record album photos, fashion and men's magazine layouts, department-store window displays, and billboards in which women are shown bound, gagged, beaten, whipped, and chained" (Lederer 1980, 24). All of these materials, Lederer and Russell contend, share "the message . . . that beating and raping women, urinating and defecating on women, is erotic and pleasurable for men, and that women desire this kind of treatment, or at least expect it" (Lederer 1980, 24). In her contribution to the antipornography feminist anthology *Take Back the Night* (1980), feminist philosopher Helen E. Longino argues that this message was the sine qua non of pornography. "Pornography," Longino writes, "is material that explicitly represents or describes degrading and abusive sexual behavior so as to endorse and/or recommend the behavior as described" (1980, 44). Underscoring the expansiveness of this definition, Longino adds that "the pornographic view of women [is] no longer confined within plain brown wrappers" but is instead "thoroughly entrenched in a booming portion of the publishing, film, and recording industries" (1980, 44, 46).

When Andrea Dworkin and Catharine MacKinnon put forward their antipornography civil rights ordinance in the early 1980s, their intention was to target a narrower range of materials than these earlier antipornography feminists had.[9] This is not to say that Dworkin and MacKinnon did not believe messages condoning the sexual abuse and degradation of women permeated the culture. They did.[10] However, as Dworkin and MacKinnon explain in a self-published defense of their civil rights approach to pornography regulation, *Pornography and Civil Rights: A New Day for Women's Equality* (1988), their ordinance was designed to reach a highly specific set of materials. While "it is true," Dworkin and MacKinnon grant, "that pornography exists on a larger social continuum with other materials that objectify and demean women" and "that many materials (such as some religious works and sociobiology texts) express the same message as pornography," the ordinance takes the view that pornography is a distinct product manufactured, marketed, and sold by a distinct "industry" (1988, 36). "No pornographer has any trouble knowing what to make. No distributor has any trouble knowing what to carry. No retailer has any trouble knowing what to order. No consumer has any trouble knowing what to buy," Dworkin and MacKinnon observe (36). Because pornography is so distinct and the pornography industry so clearly defined, in Dworkin's and MacKinnon's view, defining pornography is a rather straightforward task: one must simply "look at the existing universe of the pornography industry and . . . describe what is there" (37).

Dworkin and MacKinnon's ordinance vividly describes "what is there" in the pornography industry. Their ordinance defines pornography as "the graphic sexually explicit subordination of women through pictures and/or words that also includes one or more of the following": women presented "dehumanized as sexual objects, things, or commodities," "as sexual objects who enjoy pain or humiliation," "as sexual objects who experience sexual pleasure in being raped," "as sexual objects tied up or cut up or mutilated or bruised or physically hurt," "in postures of sexual submission, servility, or display," in such a way that they are "reduced to [their] body parts—including but not limited to vaginas, breasts, or buttocks," "as whores by nature," "as being penetrated by objects or animals," "in scenarios of degradation, injury, abasement, torture, shown as filthy or inferior, bleeding, bruised, or hurt in a context that makes these conditions sexual" (1988, 101). The ordinance also provides that "the use of men, children, or transsexuals in the place of women" in materials bearing these features would be actionable (101). In *Only Words* (1993), a defense of the ordinance published nearly a decade after it was first proposed, MacKinnon gives a concrete sense of the range of materials this definition was meant to cover. "[The ordinance's] definition is coterminous with the [pornography] industry," MacKinnon explains, "from *Playboy,* in which women are objectified and presented dehumanized as sexual objects or things for use; through the torture of women and the sexualization of racism and the fetishization of women's body parts; to snuff films, in which actual murder is the ultimate sexual act, the reduction to the thing form of a human being and the silence of women literal and complete" (MacKinnon 1993, 22–23). As MacKinnon emphasizes here, the Dworkin–MacKinnon ordinance was designed to reach the entire range of wares peddled by the pornography "industry," from "hardcore" materials in which women "are bound, battered, tortured, humiliated and killed" to "softcore" materials in which women are "merely taken and used," no more and no less (1987, 198).

The reason Dworkin and MacKinnon opted to eschew a broader definition of pornography and tailor their ordinance more specifically was their belief that pornography, as the ordinance defines it, does something that other media purveying "the same message of sexualized misogyny" does not: actively subordinates women (Dworkin and MacKinnon 1988, 37). On the basis of their own research as well as testimony presented at public hearings conducted for the ordinance in Minneapolis, Indianapolis, Los Angeles, and Boston, Dworkin and MacKinnon argue that pornography is "a major force for institutionalizing a subhuman, victimized, and second-class status for women" (MacKinnon 1987, 200–201). [11] It does this, they believe, in a variety of ways. First, pornography subordinates women through its production. Unlike "mainstream media," where "violence is done through special effects," "in pornography women shown being beaten and tortured report being beaten and tortured" (MacKinnon 1993, 27). As MacKinnon once succinctly put it, "Pornography has to be done to women to be made" (1993, 39). Additionally, Dworkin and MacKinnon argue, many women who appear in pornography "are poor and without options and formerly abused if not overtly coerced or tricked into being there" (1988, 40). Such conditions are, in their view, "what it takes to make women do what is in even the pornography that shows no overt violence" (MacKinnon 1993, 20), and in this way, pornography creates a powerful incentive to maintain women in positions of relative inequality and powerlessness.

Dworkin and MacKinnon also believe pornography subordinates women through its use. As survivor after survivor at the public hearings held on behalf of the ordinance testified, and as Dworkin and MacKinnon are at continual pains to emphasize, pornography, including "nonviolent materials," is sometimes used by rapists to plan their crimes or to silence and humiliate their victims (1988, 40). It is also used, as Dworkin and MacKinnon note, to intimidate and harass women in the workplace (MacKinnon 1987, 198–99). Most significantly, the use of pornography "change[s] attitudes and impel[s] behaviors in ways that are unique in their extent and devastating in their consequences" (MacKinnon 1993, 37). It "increase[es] the acceptability of forced sex," "diminish[es] men's vision of the desirability and possibility of sex equality," "[reduces women] to subhuman dimension to the point where they cannot be perceived as fully human," and "makes orgasm a response to bigotry" (Dworkin and MacKinnon 1988, 40, 38; MacKinnon 1987b, 200). "Pornography," in MacKinnon's words, "makes the world a pornographic place" and creates a "hostile, unequal living environment" for women (MacKinnon 1993, 25, 36). It "is an eight-billion-dollar-a-year industry of rape and battery and sexual harassment, an industry that both performs these abuses for the production of pornography and targets women for them society wide" (MacKinnon 1987b, 198).

While Dworkin and MacKinnon were convinced that their ordinance offered a "closed, concrete, and descriptive" definition of pornography that would reach only those materials that subordinated women through their production and use, their critics were not. As Alan Dershowitz quipped, "the novels of Henry Miller and D. H. Lawrence are as dangerous and pornographic to MacKinnon as the video *Sex Kittens*" (2002, 165). The amici who opposed the ordinance in *American Booksellers Ass'n, Inc. v. Hudnut* shared Dershowitz's view. Their briefs alleged that the ordinance would lead to the suppression of "works from James Joyce's *Ulysses* to Homer's *Iliad*" (325). The diversity of the plaintiffs in *Hudnut,* who, taken together, made, sold, or read everything "from hard-core films to W. B. Yeats' poem 'Leda and the Swan'" also indicates that concerns regarding the breadth of the ordinance's definition of pornography were widespread among its opponents (327).[12]

Surprisingly, these concerns appear to have been shared by Sunstein as well. While Sunstein was in broad agreement with Dworkin and MacKinnon that pornography was harmful and that its legal regulation could be justified, he also agreed with Dworkin and MacKinnon's critics that parts of their ordinance, as he put it, "might be faulted for overbreadth" (1988, 844). Thus, Sunstein proposed an alternative approach to the regulation of pornography that targeted a much narrower range of materials than Dworkin and MacKinnon had hoped to reach.

As Sunstein explains, "properly regulable pornography (a) [is] sexually explicit, (b) depict[s] women as enjoying or deserving some form of physical abuse, and (c) ha[s] the purpose and effect of producing sexual arousal" (1986, 592). The most readily apparent difference between the definition of pornography Sunstein offers here and the definition Dworkin and MacKinnon offer in their ordinance is that Sunstein's definition describes pornography in terms of "physical abuse" whereas Dworkin and MacKinnon's describes it in terms of "subordination." Unlike Dworkin and MacKinnon, who target graphic, sexually explicit materials that subordinate women through a variety of means, including "objectification" and "express violence" (1985, 39), Sunstein argues for the regulation of only what he calls "violent pornography" (1992, 21). Sunstein is forthcoming about his departure from Dworkin and MacKinnon in this regard. "The approach proposed here," he concedes, is "tightly targeted to . . . portrayals of sexual violence" and "excludes sexually explicit materials that do not sexualize violence against women" (1986, 616, 592). This exclusion, Sunstein acknowledges, makes his approach "somewhat narrower than the one suggested by the Indianapolis ordinance, which created liability for graphic sexually explicit subordination of women as 'sexual objects'" (592).

Just how much narrower Sunstein's approach is becomes clear when one considers the examples Sunstein furnishes of the sorts of materials his regulation was designed to cover. Whereas Dworkin and MacKinnon had their sights set on the entire range of materials produced by the so-called pornography industry, Sunstein emphasizes that his proposed legislation would cover only a fraction of those materials. On the basis of a study published in the *American Journal of Psychiatry,* Sunstein estimates that 17.2 percent of "pornographic magazines" sold in New York City would fit his definition of pornography because that was the percentage of magazines surveyed in the study whose covers "were explicitly devoted to violent themes such as bondage and domination" (1986, 593). The title of this study, "Pornographic Imagery and the Prevalence of Paraphilia," sheds additional light on precisely what type of material Sunstein intended for his definition to cover: "Paraphilia," fringe material, magazines with titles like "*Black Tit and Body Torture, Tit Torture Photos,* and *Chair Bondage,*" was Sunstein's quarry, not mainstream materials like *Deep Throat* and *Playboy* (1986, 593). Sunstein justifies the narrower focus of his proposed legislation by referring to scientific research into the effects of sexually explicit material on individual attitudes and behavior. In Sunstein's view, "There is empirical support for drawing a distinction between violent and nonviolent sexually explicit materials" because "it appears that 'the aggressive content of pornography . . . is the main contributor to violence against women'" (592).

That Dworkin and MacKinnon thought Sunstein's narrower definition of pornography deeply misguided is undeniable. In a passage that could have been addressed specifically to Sunstein, Dworkin and MacKinnon insisted that "limit[ing] the definition of pornography to violent materials" ignores the fact that "nonviolent materials are also known to be harmful . . .—for instance, in their use by rapists and child molesters, in increasing the acceptability of forced sex, and in diminishing men's vision of the desirability and possibility of sex equality" (Dworkin and MacKinnon 1988, 40). MacKinnon had made a similar point several years earlier in her 1984 Francis Biddle Memorial Lecture at Harvard Law School. "As to that pornography covered by [Andrea Dworkin's and my] definition in which normal research subjects seldom perceive violence, long-term exposure," MacKinnon maintained, "still makes them see women as more worthless, trivial, non-human, and objectlike, that is, the way those who are discriminated against are seen by those who discriminate against them" (1985, 54). "You may think snuff is one thing, *Playboy* another," MacKinnon told the audience at the National Conference on Women and the Law in spring 1985, but "our law says something very simple: a woman is not a thing to be used, any more than to be abused" ([1985] 1987, 200). Sunstein's narrow definition of pornography, which left what MacKinnon once described as "so-called sex only materials" untouched, clearly set his approach apart from the approach embodied in the Dworkin–MacKinnon ordinance (MacKinnon 1987a, 187).

Sunstein's definition of pornography was also narrower than Dworkin and MacKinnon's in other ways. For instance, unlike the Dworkin–MacKinnon ordinance, which defined pornography as "the sexually explicit subordination of women through pictures or words," Sunstein believed that "antipornography legislation should be addressed only to movies and pictures" (1992, 24). Such a limitation is justified, Sunstein explains, because "abuse of participants will occur only in movies and pictures" (24). "Moreover," Sunstein adds, "the evidence on pornography as a stimulus to violence deals mostly with movies and pictures, and the immediacy and vividness of these media suggest a possible distinction

from written texts" (24). In short, in Sunstein's view, crafting antipornography legislation in such a way as to "exempt the written word" meant
that the legislation would be more precisely tailored "to the cause of the
harm: the production and dissemination of portrayals of sexual violence"
(1992, 24; 1986, 616).

Sunstein was also amenable to the idea of grafting customary exemptions to obscenity laws onto his proposed antipornography legislation.
For instance, Sunstein suggests, "it might be desirable to limit antipornography legislation so that it applies to work 'taken as a whole' or at
the very least protects 'isolated passages' in longer works" and exempts
"material having significant social value" (1986, 624; 1988, 844).[13] Sunstein
was willing to accept these exemptions because in his view, "materials
that have pornographic components," such as "a motion picture [that]
contains pornographic scenes as part of a more general enterprise[,] . . .
are . . . less likely to produce sexual violence" and "may on the whole
generate little of the relevant harm" (1986, 624). Dworkin and MacKinnon, of course, were reluctant to incorporate such exemptions into their
ordinance.[14] As Dworkin and MacKinnon saw it, "taking the work 'as a
whole' ignores that which the victims of pornography have long known:
legitimate settings diminish the perception of injury done to those whose
trivialization and objectification they contextualize" (MacKinnon 1985,
21). Regarding exemptions for material that possesses "significant social
value," MacKinnon protested, "If a woman is subjected, why should it
matter that the work has other value?" (21).[15]

The relatively narrow range of materials Sunstein aimed to reach with
his proposed antipornography legislation points to another significant difference between Sunstein and the antipornography feminists that preceded
him: his comparatively narrow view of pornography's harms. As Sunstein
explains, in his view, pornography contributes to "three categories of
concrete, gender-related harms: harms to those who participate in the
production of pornography, harms to the victims of sex crimes that would
not have been committed in the absence of pornography, and harms to
society through social conditioning that fosters discrimination and other
unlawful activities" (1986, 595). Some six years later, Sunstein offered a
similar description of pornography's harms: "The harms [of pornography]

fall in three categories. First, the existence of the pornography market produces a number of harms to models and actresses. . . . Second, there is a causal connection between pornography and violence against women . . . Third, and more generally, pornography reflects and promotes attitudes toward women that are degrading and dehumanizing and that contribute to a variety of forms of illegal conduct, prominently including sexual harassment" (1992, 23–25). On the basis of these descriptions, it is clear that Sunstein, like virtually all antipornography feminists who came before him, believes that pornography contributes to widespread violence and illegal acts of discrimination and harassment against women. However, notably absent from Sunstein's catalog of pornography's harms is a harm that had been of central concern to earlier antipornography feminists: objectification.

As far back as the occupation of Grove Press in 1970, antipornography feminists had called attention to objectification as a principal way in which women were oppressed, and therefore harmed, by pornography.[16] "No more using of women's bodies as filth-objects," the Grove Press occupiers demanded. "No more peddling . . . movies . . . that force women to act out their bestialized oppression while the whole world is watching! . . . No more male radicals who can ignore the oppression of women . . . as sex objects" (Lederer 1980, 271). Several years later, in *Against Our Will,* Susan Brownmiller presented "objectification" as a harm endemic not only to pornography but also to rape. "Pornography, like rape," Brownmiller contends, "is a male invention, designed to dehumanize women, to reduce the female to an object of sexual access" (394). In the November 1977 issue of WAVPM's newsletter, *NewsPage,* Diana Russell and Laura Lederer repeated Brownmiller's claims regarding the harm of objectification. When asked if they object to "pornography in which there is no violence," Russell and Lederer said yes. "Not all pornography is violent," Russell and Lederer explain, "but even the most banal pornography objectifies women's bodies," and "an essential ingredient in much rape and other forms of violence to women is the 'objectification' of the woman" (Lederer 1980, 24). As these quotations illustrate, the earliest antipornography feminists believed that pornography did more than merely prime its consumers to physically harm or illegally discriminate against women. In their view, pornography objectified women, and objectification constituted a harm in and of itself.

This understanding of objectification as one of pornography's principal harms is reflected in the Dworkin–MacKinnon antipornography ordinance. The ordinance defines pornography as "the graphic sexually explicit subordination of women through pictures and/or words" that also includes at least one additional element. The ordinance's list of additional elements includes depictions of things generally recognized as harmful, like torture and mutilation, but it also includes depictions of things not generally recognized as such, like "women . . . dehumanized as sexual objects, things or commodities" and "women . . . in postures or positions of sexual submission, servility, or display" (Dworkin and MacKinnon 1988, 36). As Dworkin and MacKinnon make clear in their self-published defense of the ordinance, this was by design. "Some of the enumerated subparts [of the ordinance's definition of pornography]," they explain, "specify presentations of women that show express violence; some focus on acts of submission, degradation, humiliation, and objectification that have been more difficult to see as violation because these acts are most distinctively done to women and called sex" (39). Among the central aims of the Dworkin–MacKinnon ordinance is to make the harmfulness of these seemingly harmless acts legible, to make "the harm of being seen and treated as a sexual thing rather than as a human being" visible—and, most importantly, legally actionable (45). As MacKinnon emphasizes, even the public hearings organized on behalf of the ordinance were guided by this aim. "These hearings," MacKinnon writes in the introduction to *In Harm's Way: The Pornography Civil Rights Hearings,* "were the moment when . . . , against a backdrop of claims that [they] do not exist . . . , the harms of pornography stood exposed and took shape as potential legal injuries" (MacKinnon and Dworkin 1997, 4).

As Sunstein readily acknowledges, his proposals for regulating pornography differ from Dworkin and MacKinnon's in this regard. Whereas his legislative recommendations "deal with pornography as a subject of regulation only to the extent that it is associated with violence against women (an important ingredient in sexual inequality)," Dworkin and MacKinnon's, Sunstein explains, "deal far more broadly with the role of pornography in creating inequality, in part through its place in the sexual subordination and objectification of women" (1993, 393; 1992, 21).[17] In a review of MacKinnon's *Feminism Unmodified: Discourses on Life and Law*, Sunstein expresses serious reservations about this aspect of Dworkin and MacKinnon's project. "Some of MacKinnon's rhetoric [with respect to pornography's harmful effects] is overstated," Sunstein writes, adding that MacKinnon's claim that "the sexual objectification of women, and sexuality in general, [is] a central cause of sexual subordination" is the "aspect of MacKinnon's critique that has made her views so controversial" and stirred so much "resistance to the antipornography movement" (1988, 843, 835, 846). While Sunstein is willing to concede (once in a footnote) that "it is more than plausible to think that objectification is a serious social harm," he is not willing to support Dworkin and MacKinnon's efforts to secure for it legal recognition and redress (1992, 21). Sunstein may have been prepared to use the law to regulate materials that contributed to violence against women and other illegal conduct, but when it came to materials implicated in the not-yet-legally-recognized harm of objectification, he demurred.

It is impossible to discuss the reasons behind Sunstein's demurral without delving into one of the most fundamental differences between Sunstein and the antipornography feminists who preceded him. Unlike his antipornography feminist predecessors, who considered the silencing and objectification of women in and through so-called sex-only pornography to be full-fledged public harms, Sunstein is a committed liberal offering a critique of pornography that is rooted in a conventionally liberal conception of harm. Sunstein so scrupulously sets his sights on "violent pornography" because, he argues, only materials that combine sexual explicitness with violence contribute to what he tellingly describes as pornography's "principal" and "concrete, gender-related harms," like "violence against women," "sexual harassment," and other "illegal conduct" (MacKinnon 1987a, 187; Sunstein 1992, 21, 25; Sunstein 1986, 592, 595). As Sunstein acknowledges, "not all of those who focus on [the problem of pornography] treat pornography as a problem of sex discrimination only because it is associated with violence"; however, Sunstein believes that crafting antipornography legislation with a "broader understanding of the harms of pornography, including the very large category of objectification" in mind is a mistake (1992, 21). Sounding very much like one of antipornography feminism's liberal critics, Sunstein maintains that "one cannot find [pornography's silencing effects] to be a reason for regulation without making excessive inroads on a system of free expression" and raising "severe First Amendment difficulties" (25, 21). "The notion of objectification," Sunstein cautions, "is one with which it is extremely difficult for a legal system to work" (25). Far better, Sunstein advises, to adopt an approach to pornography regulation that "does not go so deep" and that "deals with pornography as a subject of regulation only to the extent that it is associated with violence against women" or other criminal acts (1988, 846; 1992, 21).

Of course, Sunstein's antipornography feminist forebears agreed that antipornography legislation designed to address pornography's harms, including the harm of objectification, bucked liberal convention and raised "severe First Amendment difficulties." This is precisely why many of them adopted such critical postures vis-à-vis conventional First Amendment doctrine and the liberal assumptions undergirding it.[18] "Liberal legalism," MacKinnon once declared, "is . . . a medium for making male dominance both invisible and legitimate by adopting the male point of view in law at the same time as it enforces that view on society. . . . In the liberal state, the rule of law—neutral, abstract, elevated, pervasive—both institutionalizes the power of men over women and institutionalizes power in its male form" (1989, 237–38). Similarly, Dworkin and MacKinnon describe the First Amendment as a means of shoring up "power disguised as rights protected by law that fosters inequality" (1988, 22). In an address delivered at the 1978 New York University colloquium "Obscenity: Degradation of Women versus Freedom of Speech," Susan Brownmiller put forward a similar view. "The first amendment of late has been stretched out of shape," she laments, and used by "a powerful group, a sick group, a mentally unstable group, an evil group" to secure "a protected right to promote sexual violence against an oppressed group for commercial exploitation and gain" (1979, 255).[19]

As these remarks indicate, antipornography feminists tended to view the First Amendment as the cornerstone of a dysfunctional system in which "the free speech of men [was permitted to silence] the free speech of women" (MacKinnon 1985, 65). To repair this dysfunction and bring about a system of free expression deserving of the name, Dworkin and MacKinnon proposed a "new model for freedom of expression" (MacKinnon 1993, 109). Under this "new model," as MacKinnon described it, "the free speech position" would "no longer support social dominance" because "the state [would] have as great a role in providing relief from injury to equality through speech and in giving equal access to speech as it has now in disciplining its power to intervene in that speech that manages to get expressed" (109). Under this new model, in other words, pornography, with its singular capacity to "deauthorize and reduce and devalidate and silence," would no longer be protected in the name of freedom of expression, but restricted (MacKinnon 1985, 63).[20]

While antipornography feminists like Dworkin and MacKinnon were out to break with convention and revolutionize the constitutional meaning of freedom of expression, Sunstein was out to accomplish something quite different. His goal was not to shift the parameters of existing constitutional law to accommodate the feminist critique of pornography but to fashion a feminist critique of pornography that conformed to the parameters of existing constitutional law. While Sunstein admits that "antipornography legislation tests constitutional doctrine in unexpected ways," he insists that "it is possible to defend such legislation within the confines of conventional doctrine" (1986, 626). In fact, in the conclusion of his earliest published antipornography effort, Sunstein explicitly states that his "purpose has been to show that pornography can be regulated without doing violence to the first amendment" (624).[21] Sunstein makes this same point even more forcefully some two years later in his review of MacKinnon's *Feminism Unmodified* for the *Harvard Law Review*. In what reads like a thinly veiled repudiation of Dworkin and MacKinnon's "new model for freedom of expression" (Lederer and Delgado 1995, 258), Sunstein contends that "first amendment doctrine furnishes the building blocks for a quite conventional argument for regulation of pornography" (1988, 844).

The "quite conventional argument for regulation of pornography" that Sunstein cobbled together out of "the building blocks" furnished him by the First Amendment goes something like this. Contrary to the claims of First Amendment absolutists, the First Amendment does not in fact accord equal protection to all speech. For example, commercial speech, labor speech, and other speech that is "far afield from the central concern of the First Amendment, which, broadly speaking is effective popular control of public affairs," has been found to fall within the category of "low-value" speech, and low-value speech may be regulated "on the basis of a far less powerful demonstration of harm" than is necessary in the case of high-value speech (Sunstein 1986, 602–3). Pornography, defined as sexually explicit depictions of women enjoying physical abuse designed to produce sexual arousal, is "more akin to a sexual aid than a communicative expression" and is therefore properly considered low-value speech (606). Pornography so defined is also linked to a number of harms, including violence against women and other illegal acts of sex discrimination. While the evidence of pornography's harmfulness is not dispositive, because pornography is low-value speech, the evidence is strong enough to permit regulation—provided, of course, that such regulation is sufficiently narrowly tailored to pornography's harms.

As Sunstein emphasized, his argument for the regulation of pornography "is hardly an endorsement of the broader position that the First Amendment should essentially be irrelevant to the debate, because it protects those who 'have' speech against those who 'have not' the power of speech" (1986, 624). Sunstein was not out to champion a radically new model of freedom of expression. In fact, Sunstein agreed with eminent liberal political philosopher Ronald Dworkin (one of MacKinnon's most outspoken critics) that the fact "that pornography sometimes plays a part in 'silencing women'—not by criminalizing their speech, but by discrediting it" is no reason to abandon a conventional and wholly negative understanding of the freedom of expression.[22] As Sunstein puts it, pornography's "silencing effect is an important part of the political argument against pornography; but it probably should not be part of the First Amendment debate" (1992, 25–26). What this shows is that although Sunstein was generally sympathetic to the feminist critique of pornography, he was also wary of those aspects of it that he believed raised "severe first amendment difficulties," made "excessive inroads on a system of free expression," "threaten[ed] areas thought to be personal and private," and "pointedly part[ed] company with certain aspects of mainstream liberalism" (1992, 21, 26; 1988, 835, 846). This wariness drove him "to generate a defense of antipornography legislation that," by his own admission, "does not go so deep," that uses a highly restrictive definition of pornography, and that addresses itself to a much narrower range of harms (1988, 846).

Of course, it should not be overlooked that Sunstein was also wary of many aspects of what had been, at least since the 1950s, the unquestioned liberal orthodoxy on pornography. Sunstein did not think that sexually explicit speech was for the most part harmless and deserving of constitutional protection, and he believed much liberal skepticism toward antipornography legislation was misplaced. Nowhere is this more evident than in his incisive critique of the Seventh Circuit Court's decision in *American Booksellers Ass'n, Inc. v. Hudnut*. In this decision, the court struck down the version of the Dworkin–MacKinnon ordinance adopted by the city of Indianapolis on the grounds that it amounted to a content-based regulation of speech that was not neutral in regard to viewpoint. In Sunstein's view, the distinction between "viewpoint-neutral" and "viewpoint-based" regulation that the court relied on in this ruling is unsustainable. "Regulation based on viewpoint is common in the law," Sunstein observed, citing examples such as bribery laws, which make it a crime to "offer $100 to tempt a person to commit murder," but permit "a $100 offer to build a fence" (1986, 613–14). Obscenity laws, Sunstein added, are also viewpoint based insofar as they prohibit only those sexually explicit materials that "portray sexual conduct in a patently offensive way, measured by 'contemporary community standards,'" and therefore necessarily draw a line "between messages on the basis of social attitudes toward sexual mores" (1986, 613–14, 595). The reason such laws are typically not construed as viewpoint based and struck down is because "one does not 'see' a viewpoint-based restriction when the harms invoked in defense of a regulation are obvious and so widely supported by social consensus that they allay any concern about impermissible government motivation" (615). Because the *Hudnut* court subscribed to the classical liberal notion that serious threats come "exclusively from the public sphere," a notion that, Sunstein emphasized elsewhere, represents "a quite narrow aspect of the liberal tradition," it "[undervalued] the harm pornography produces," "[misapplied] conventional doctrines requiring viewpoint neutrality" and "[overvalued] the dangers posed by generating a somewhat different category of regulated speech bound to have some definitional vagueness" (1988, 835; 1986, 626). In short, Sunstein faulted the *Hudnut* majority, and many of his liberal peers, for their failure to see that the purpose of "legislation aimed at pornography . . . [is] to prevent sexual violence and discrimination, not to suppress expression of a point of view" (1986, 612).

By breaking in all these ways with both his antipornography feminist and liberal peers, Sunstein, whether he intended to or not, pioneered a highly improbable argumentative position. Before Sunstein, liberals had for the most part been unwilling to take virtually any aspect of the feminist critique of pornography seriously. By limiting antipornography feminism's broad definition of pornography to violent pornography, and by narrowing its expansive conception of harm to violence and other illegal conduct, Sunstein changed this. He devised an antipornography approach that sought to mitigate "sexual inequality," without, in his words, "threaten[ing] areas thought to be personal and private" or offending "traditional First Amendment doctrine" (1992, 21; 1988, 835; 1986, 608).[23] He devised, in short, antipornography liberalism, a variant of antipornography feminism that relies on, as opposed to resists, fundamental liberal principles.

In the wake of Sunstein's pioneering efforts, scholars across a variety of disciplines began adapting the feminist critique of pornography to the strictures of liberalism and established constitutional law. For instance, in a series of articles published throughout the 1990s, philosopher Rae Langton ingeniously uses the theory of equality and rights laid out by Ronald Dworkin in *Taking Rights Seriously* (1978) to formulate a refutation of Dworkin's own defense of pornography in "Do We Have a Right to Pornography?" (1981; see Langton 1990, 1993, 1999). Langton's argument goes something like this. The cornerstone of Dworkinian liberalism is the principle of equal concern and respect. A "permissive policy" regarding "violent and degrading pornography" violates this principle because the policy is rooted in preferences that depend on the view that women are not deserving of equal concern and respect (1990, 353). In Dworkin's theory, such preferences are called "external preferences," and the policies they favor (racial segregation is the example Dworkin furnishes) can be overridden by the rights of anyone whom those policies disadvantage. As antipornography feminists have persuasively argued, a permissive policy regarding violent and degrading pornography disadvantages women, and therefore, "women as a group . . . have rights that are trumps" against it (346). In short, Langton concluded, "A prohibitive policy . . . is not only consistent with, but apparently demanded by, liberal theory" (354).

While Langton mined Dworkinian liberalism for antipornography feminist resources, others sought them in what had historically been the citadel of liberal opposition to pornography regulation: the liberal theory of John Stuart Mill. For instance, David Dyzenhaus has argued that pornography violates Mill's "harm principle" and therefore merits regulation. On Dyzenhaus's readings of both *On Liberty* and the "curiously neglected" *The Subjection of Women,* Mill is not solely, or even primarily, concerned with harms brought about through "state action" (1992, 537, 545). Rather, according to Dyzenhaus, "Mill clearly sees, that the practices of a moralistic majority," including a patriarchal one, "can be as coercive and as harmful to [the interest individuals have in autonomy] as any state action" (545). Because pornography makes "inequality . . . between men and women appear legitimate as well as sexy," Dyzenhaus argues, it contributes to "a regime of inequality" that "prevents women from articulating and living out conceptions of the good life which would be theirs to explore were they in a position of substantive equality" (536, 550). Pornography, in other words, harms the interest women have in autonomy. This, Dyzenhaus concludes, is why liberals laying claim to the Millian tradition "must be open to the legitimacy of coercive action to eradicate pornography" (536, 550).[24]

CRIMINALIZING PORNOGRAPHY

While Langton's and Dyzenhaus's contributions to antipornography liberalism in the early 1990s were significant, they pale in comparison to what came next. On March 5–7, 1993, some seven hundred lawyers, scholars, students, and activists convened at the University of Chicago

School of Law for a conference entitled "Speech, Equality, and Harm: Feminist Legal Perspectives on Pornography and Hate Propaganda." Conferees included veteran antipornography feminist leaders like Catharine MacKinnon, Andrea Dworkin, Dorchen Leidholdt, Laura Lederer, and Kathleen Barry as well as prominent liberal legal scholars like Cass Sunstein, Frank Michelman, Elena Kagan, John Powell, and Frederick Schauer and leading critical race theorists like Kimberlé Williams Crenshaw and Richard Delgado. Their goal in coming together was to address "the role of pornography and hate propaganda on the safety and status of women, people of color, gay men and lesbians"[25] by developing legal solutions to the problems of pornography and other forms of "harmful speech," defined by two of the conference's lead organizers, as "speech that harms the individual who is [its] target . . . and . . . perpetuates negative stereotypes, promotes discrimination, and maintains whole groups of people as second-class citizens, hampering their participation in our democracy" (Lederer and Delgado 1995, 5). While a handful of proposals presented at this conference bucked liberal conventions and concepts,[26] many were carefully tailored to accord with central liberal tenets, signaling a growing common ground between pornography's liberal and feminist critics.

Before this conference, the last time antipornography feminists and liberals had formally convened to discuss legal perspectives on pornography was in 1978 at the New York University School of Law colloquium, "Obscenity: Degradation of Women versus Right of Free Speech." As you will recall from chapter 1, the discussions at this colloquium were not particularly productive. In fact, according to the colloquium's organizer, the event was marked by "a general failure of communication," with liberals "interpret[ing] the [feminist] outcry against violent pornography as a call for censorship" and an attack on the First Amendment, and feminists "describ[ing] the evils of violent pornography in subjective, emotional terms," "oblivious to the need for specificity, proof of injury, or 'hard evidence'" (Lerman 1979, 182–84). By 1993, however, the dynamic between liberals and antipornography feminists had changed dramatically.

For instance, the University of Chicago conference featured presentations from a variety of experts purporting to offer "hard evidence" of pornography's harms. Evelina Giobbe, founder and executive director of

WHISPER, a nonprofit organization of ex-prostitutes, and Kathleen Barry, a sociologist specializing in the study of international sex trafficking, spoke to an alleged link between pornography and forced prostitution. Barbara Trees, a carpenter and labor organizer, and Olivia Young, a registered nurse, spoke to the role pornography played in their personal experiences of sexual harassment in the workplace. Additionally, the edited volume that grew out of the conference, *The Price We Pay: The Case against Racist Speech, Hate Propaganda, and Pornography* (1995), includes contributions from a number of psychologists presenting empirical evidence of pornography's harmful effects on adolescent male consumers as well as its contributions to sexist and racist discrimination and harassment in schools and workplaces. This same volume also includes contributions from several distinguished law professors, including Kimberlé Williams Crenshaw and Michelle J. Anderson, proposing new conceptual frameworks to facilitate the legal recognition of the harm of racist speech, hate propaganda, and pornography. Clearly, antipornography feminists were no longer "oblivious to the need for specificity, proof of injury, or 'hard evidence.'"

Liberals at this conference were also no longer inclined to perceive feminist concerns about pornography as attacks on fundamental liberal values. In fact, to a person, the liberal legal theorists who participated in the conference welcomed feminist insights into the role of pornography and other forms of "hate propaganda" in the reproduction of social inequality. Unlike their counterparts at the 1978 New York University colloquium, liberals at the 1993 University of Chicago conference saw these insights as vital contributions to the project of deepening and expanding freedom of expression. Frank Michelman's comments on this score are representative. According to Michelman, "conscientious civil libertarians," "committed" to the defense of "the values of expressive freedom in human life, and therefore of a legally established *system* of freedom of expression for *all*," are wrong to turn "a deaf ear to [feminist] claims of [pornography's] silencing [effects]" (1995, 273). Some speech, Michelman insisted, "degrade[s] the speech of others by summoning castelike perceptions of the others as unworthy to be heard . . . and in the process reinforces caste" (275). "How in all consistency," Michelman asked, "can [a society that values freedom of expression] read its Constitution to forbid absolutely restrictions of speech when those restrictions appear aptly and sincerely to be aimed against the evils of caste and subordination, as those evils are reasonably perceived to invade and inhabit and corrupt the system of freedom of expression itself?" (276). As Michelman's remarks demonstrate, by 1993, many liberals had gone from seeing the feminist critique of pornography as an assault on First Amendment values to an invaluable contribution to a more complete realization of those values.

Others adopted a slightly different view. Consider, for example, the proposals for pornography and hate speech regulation offered up at the conference by Elena Kagan, then a junior law professor at the University of Chicago law school. While Kagan expressed a great deal of sympathy for the view that "we live in a society [in which] certain forms of speech perpetuate and promote [racial and gender] inequality," she also insisted that "any attempt to regulate pornography and hate speech must take into account certain facts . . . of First Amendment doctrine" (Kagan 1995, 202). Kagan was particularly concerned that legal efforts aimed at curbing harmful speech give "the long-standing . . . principle of viewpoint neutrality" its due. According to this principle, which had been invoked by the majority in *American Booksellers Ass'n, Inc. v. Hudnut* to invalidate the Dworkin–MacKinnon ordinance, laws regulating speech must not do so on the basis of the viewpoint the regulated speech expresses. Undergirding this principle is a characteristically liberal anxiety regarding government interference in the "private" sphere of thoughts, values, judgments, and beliefs. To permit the government to regulate speech on the basis of viewpoint, so the liberal reasoning goes, is to permit the government to wield authority over fundamentally private matters, effectively deposing the individual as the ultimate arbiter of what is good, true, and worthy of consideration and what is not. It seems that Kagan embraced something very much like this conventionally liberal view, as each of the regulations she proposed was carefully designed to respect the principle of viewpoint neutrality and the public/private distinction it safeguards by refraining from regulating speech altogether.

According to Kagan, the most "realistic, principled, and perhaps surprisingly effective" legal measures that might be marshaled against "speech [that] perpetuate[s] and promote[s] inequality" would not regulate speech at all—or at least not in the first instance (Kagan 1995, 203). One such measure Kagan recommended was "hate crimes laws" or laws providing enhanced penalties for crimes committed because of the target's race, gender, sexual orientation, or other stipulated status (203). Another remedy proposed by Kagan was a law modeled after federal child pornography laws that "punish[ed] the distribution of materials whose manufacture involved coercion of, or violence against, participants" (205). Another was a law "prohibiting carefully defined kinds of harassment, threats, or intimidation, including but not limited to those based on race and sex" (204). What made each of these measures not only "feasible" but "proper" means of "eradicating the worst of hate speech and pornography," in Kagan's view, was that their ultimate aim was not to curb speech or extirpate undesirable beliefs or opinions from the minds of citizens, but to prevent illegal "conduct" like "racially based form[s] of disadvantage," "the violence and coercion that often occur in the making of pornography," and "harassment and intimidation" (203, 205).

Kagan's proposals to regulate inequality-engendering speech only where such speech intersects with illegal conduct reveals the extent to which liberal conceptions of harm, liberty, and the public and the private had merged with antipornography feminist thinking by the mid-1990s. While Kagan was convinced that pornography and hate speech "perpetuate and promote inequality," the upshot of her reform proposals, which were widely embraced by other feminist and antiracist opponents of pornography and hate speech at the time,[27] was that this alone does not amount to the sort of "public" harm that might justify the imposition of a legal remedy. By insisting that pornography and hate speech are "proper[ly]" regulated only indirectly through measures "aimed not at speech, but *acts,*" Kagan's antipornography liberal position reaffirmed traditional liberal figurations of pornography as "private" and harmless, and left liberalism's public/private distinction intact and unchallenged. Once irreconcilable opponents, by the mid-1990s, antipornography feminism and liberalism had become allies and complements.

Kagan was not the only opponent of pornography at the University of Chicago conference whose vision for reform was colored by liberal investments. In fact, even veteran antipornography feminist Dorchen Leidholdt,[28] no friend of liberalism in principle,[29] advocated an approach to pornography regulation at this conference that ceded much to liberal convention. Leidholdt's approach centered on figuring pornography as an illegal employment practice under Title VII of the Civil Rights Act. Drawing on precedents established over nearly two decades of sexual harassment litigation, Leidholdt argued that "the sexual harassment of women workers through pornography" can cause "psychological damage," "emotional distress," and "psychic trauma" severe enough "to undermine a woman worker's peace of mind, . . . disable her job performance," and "push her out of her job entirely" (217, 218). For these reasons, Leidholdt maintained, "pornography in the workplace" constitutes "a barrier to equal employment opportunities for women" and is actionable as sex-based employment discrimination (1995, 218, 231–32).

Leidholdt's proposal to use Title VII as a "legal wedge" to combat pornography in the workplace can be seen as a sort of pragmatic capitulation to liberal dictates (Lederer and Delgado 1995, 232). By figuring pornography as a discriminatory employment practice, Leidholdt ensured that pornography regulation would not extend beyond the workplace into other, more traditionally "private" settings.[30] Also, by casting pornography's harms in terms of well-established legal injuries like "trauma" and "emotional distress," both terms of art imported from tort law, Leidholdt moved away from the sweeping and highly politicized representations of harm characteristic of early antipornography feminism (e.g., "objectification," "subordination, "silencing," and the like) and toward the narrower and more conventional representations (e.g., "violence," "criminal acts," and "illegal conduct") preferred by antipornography liberals.

Even before the University of Chicago conference, antipornography liberalism was well enough established as a legible and credible argumentative position that, in a review of MacKinnon's *Toward a Feminist Theory of the State,* Drucilla Cornell was able to criticize MacKinnon for "fail[ing] to see that there are liberal arguments for some of the legal reforms she seeks to make" (1990, 2261). However, in the wake of the University of Chicago conference, antipornography liberalisms proliferated (Pollard 1990; Rorty 1990; Scoccia 1996; Schaeffer 2001; Adams 2002; Laden

2003; Brake 2004; Watson 2007; McGlynn and Ward 2009). In fact, by
the mid-1990s, antipornography liberalism had risen to such prominence
that Nadine Strossen, president of the ACLU from 1991 to 2008 and
adamant critic of the Dworkin–MacKinnon ordinance, was in a position to lament that "the Dworkin–MacKinnon approach to pornography
enjoys an enormous intuitive appeal to many feminists and liberals"
(1995, 83).

The enormity of antipornography liberalism's appeal in the mid-1990s
is evident in liberal political philosopher Martha Nussbaum's embrace of
many aspects of Dworkin and MacKinnon's critique of pornography in
Sex and Social Justice (1999). In Nussbaum's view, despite her self-styled
radicalism, her frequent and impassioned fulminations against liberalism,
and her unalloyed contempt for liberal feminism, Catharine MacKinnon
is, at bottom, "a Kantian liberal, inspired by a deep vision of personhood
and autonomy" (1999, 79).[31] "In my view," Nussbaum writes, "the radical
feminism of MacKinnon makes . . . a demand for equal respect, asking that
laws and institutions truly acknowledge women's equal worth in ways they
have not previously done" (20). "In so arguing," Nussbaum continues,
"MacKinnon . . . is making the Kantian demand that women be treated
as ends in themselves, centers of agency and freedom rather than merely
as adjuncts to the plans of men" (20). As if making a Kantian liberal out
of MacKinnon was not enough, Nussbaum goes a step further, arguing
that MacKinnon's keen insights into the ways in which the sexualities of
both men and women have "been shaped by long habits of domination and
subordination" were "anticipated" by none other than John Stuart Mill, a
thinker who, Nussbaum claims, "understood . . . that a moral critique of
deformed desire and preference is not antithetical to liberal democracy;
it is actually essential to its success" (12).

Having firmly established MacKinnon's liberal pedigree, Nussbaum
moves to demonstrate how MacKinnon's critique of the objectification of
women in pornography is rooted in her putatively liberal vision of personhood and autonomy. Accomplishing this is extraordinarily uncomplicated
for Nussbaum because, she argues, Kant's criticism of "sexual desire . . .
for leading people to treat one another as objects" is the "direct ancestor
of the arguments of MacKinnon," and thus a Kantian "notion of human-

ity . . . is implicit in most critiques of objectification in the MacKinnon/ Dworkin tradition" (1999, 152, 218). "The core idea of MacKinnon's and Dworkin's analysis [of objectification and pornography] is Kantian," Nussbaum explains (224). "Like Kant, [MacKinnon and Dworkin] start from the notion that all human beings are owed respect, and that this respect is incompatible with treating them as instruments, and also with denials of autonomy and subjectivity" (224). In Nussbaum's view, certain types of pornography—Nussbaum offers two examples: a "novel" (the scare quotes are Nussbaum's) entitled *Isabelle and Veronique: Four Months, Four Cities* and *Playboy* magazine—send the unambiguous message that the "[male reader] is the one with the subjectivity and autonomy" and that women "are things that look very sexy and are displayed out there for his consumption, like delicious pieces of fruit, existing only or primarily to satisfy his desire" (217, 234). This message, Nussbaum insists, following her stylized versions of MacKinnon and Dworkin, constitutes a "profound betrayal . . . of the Kantian ideal of human regard" (217, 234).

Given Nussbaum's interpretation of MacKinnon's critique of pornography as rooted in what are arguably some of liberalism's most fundamental values, it is not at all surprising that she is highly critical of liberals who have rather cursorily dismissed MacKinnon's and Dworkin's legal proposals to regulate pornography on the grounds that they "are in favor of the First Amendment" (1999, 247). "People who attack [MacKinnon's and Dworkin's] proposal on [these] grounds," Nussbaum writes in an uncharacteristically harsh passage, "are not saying anything intellectually respectable" (247). "The First Amendment," Nussbaum notes, "has never covered all speech" (247). Therefore, Nussbaum continues, "the argument must be made that [pornography] is the type of speech that ought to be protected by the First Amendment," not that "pornography is speech, so it must be protected" (247). Significantly, Nussbaum refrains from making the former argument. In fact, she praises MacKinnon's and Dworkin's proposed antipornography legislation for having "identified the right moral target" "in the sense that material depicting abuse and violence against women as sexy is morally problematic in a way that the traditional category of the 'obscene' does not seem to be" (23, 248). However, despite her wholehearted agreement with Dworkin and MacKinnon's moral critique of pornography, Nussbaum does not ultimately endorse their proposed legislation because she believes that "it is likely to be badly implemented in practice and . . . may exert a stifling effect on some valuable speech, including the feminist critique of pornography" (23).

While Nussbaum ultimately disagrees with Dworkin and MacKinnon's proposed legal remedy, she enthusiastically endorses their critique of pornography, describing pornography "as an urgent problem that needs to be treated with moral seriousness" (1999, 250). In making this endorsement, Nussbaum emblazons Dworkin and MacKinnon's critique of pornography with the imprimatur of canonical liberals such as Kant, J. S. Mill, and herself, and effectively casts those who "have simply refused to acknowledge that there is any moral problem in the representation of women as meant for abuse and humiliation" not only as antifeminist, but illiberal to boot (249).

Denise Schaeffer explicitly follows Nussbaum in arguing that "certain fundamental aspects of MacKinnon's work must be understood in a liberal framework" (2001, 699). Schaeffer's MacKinnon is both "a harsh critic" of as well as a "fervent adherent" to liberalism who invokes "liberal humanist ideals" such as "freedom, equality, and choice" at the same time that she castigates "liberal idealism" for failing to apprehend the distinctive ways in which women are excluded from these ideals (704, 706). "Paradoxically," Schaeffer writes, "MacKinnon wants liberals to see differently and to see more of what already tends to register as contrary to liberal principles" (705). Specifically, MacKinnon wants liberals to acknowledge "sexual use and abuse of women" as a phenomenon that institutes barriers to women's "individual choice and self-determination," and therefore constitutes "harm to another" of the sort that "justifies limitation to one's freedom" according to liberal doctrine (706). "If we could reach an agreement about how best to delineate the harm to women caused by the eroticization of dominance and submission," Schaeffer insists, "there is no inherent reason it could not be rectified from within a liberal perspective" (706). This shows, Schaeffer concludes, that "MacKinnon's work should be understood as part of a conversation within liberalism, not as a separate and fundamentally antagonistic enterprise" (700).

MacKinnon (2001), responding directly to Schaeffer (2001), insists that her theory, "while not liberalism in denial or disguise, is engaged in dialogue with liberalism" (709). In spite of what appears to be this small concession to Schaeffer and others who would assimilate her position to liberalism, MacKinnon is clear that she believes "we are long past the point where it makes sense to argue that liberal theory will produce sex equality on its own," and she is skeptical as to "whether liberalism would recognize its own concepts if they meant in reality what they are supposed to mean in theory . . . since they would no longer support power as currently organized" (709). "Any attempt to reinvent me as a born-again liberal," MacKinnon insists, "must contend with the fact that I criticize the liberal tradition for its methodological idealism . . . ; for its individualism . . . ; and for its relative blindness to organized power in diverse social forms" (709). "Certainly," MacKinnon concedes, "some contemporary liberal scholars, notably Martha Nussbaum (1999) . . . and Cass Sunstein (1993), contend productively with feminist concerns on liberal terrain"; but, she continues, "liberalism's ideology of consent and choice has made it impossible effectively to stop the pornography industry, even as some individual liberals . . . have opposed it" and "the existing liberal concept of harm has so far been incapable of seeing women as harmed when they are sexually objectified" (2001, 710). That MacKinnon felt the need to step forward in 2001 and publicly defend her record as a critic of liberalism and remind readers of the objections that antipornography feminists had been raising against liberalism since the early 1970s is evidence of just how firmly established antipornography liberalism had become by this time. By 2001, the long history of enmity between antipornography feminism and liberalism had been almost completely elided, and it was all but taken for granted that liberals and feminists were allies in an effort to curb pornography's harmful effects.

This elision of the prodigious scholarly efforts described in this chapter to reconcile antipornography feminism and liberalism has yielded several unfortunate consequences. First, it has caused antipornography feminism as it was originally conceived in the 1970s—a trenchant critique of the narrow and deeply masculinist sexual politics of postwar liberalism—

to be largely forgotten and the much more conventional position born of the conjunction of antipornography feminism and liberalism in the 1980s and 1990s, antipornography liberalism, to take its place. Second, antipornography liberalism's success in obscuring the historically contentious relationship between liberalism and antipornography feminism has made liberal arguments in favor of using state power, up to and including criminal law (e.g., antipornography regulations modeled after federal child pornography laws, expanded hate-crime laws), to regulate pornography for the sake of gender equality appear unremarkable, if not even natural and inevitable. It has, in other words, obscured the fact that concern for the equality of women to men in the so-called private sphere of sexual relations is far from indigenous to liberalism and that the significant shifts in liberal thinking that culminated in antipornography liberalism in the 1980s and 1990s were occasioned by at least a decade of concerted feminist struggle against liberalism's native impulses. It has also hidden from view the fact that the original antipornography feminists, unlike the antipornography liberals who came after them, refused to look to the law enforcement arm of what they viewed as an irretrievably masculinist and oppressive state for a remedy to pornography's harms. Susan Brownmiller's remarks on this score are representative: "A police department, like a prison or an army, is by nature and structure a traditionally male, authoritarian institution. . . . Operating through sanctioned force, the local police precinct has always been a bastion of male attitudes and responses that are inimical to women" (1975, 270). Even Catharine MacKinnon, who saw tremendous feminist potential in federal and state civil rights laws, was highly critical of attempts to address pornography's harms through criminal law generally and obscenity law specifically.[32] In short, the original antipornography feminists eschewed criminal legal remedies for pornography's harms, while the antipornography liberals who eventually eclipsed them invented novel ways to use criminal law to regulate pornography and curb its discriminatory effects.

Finally and perhaps most significantly, antipornography liberalism's success in concealing the history of liberalism's complex and contentious relationship with antipornography feminism has led many treatments of antipornography feminism's receptions and legacies to overemphasize various conservative co-optations of antipornography feminism (e.g., Phyllis Schlafly's 1987 volume *Pornography's Victims,* which reproduces sections of the 1986 *Final Report of the Attorney General's Commission on Pornography,* the so-called Meese Report, personally edited and annotated by Schlafly herself) while overlooking the influential liberal co-optations described in this chapter.[33] As I will argue in the conclusion, such partial and incomplete accounts of antipornography feminism's legacies have led to a failure on the part of contemporary scholars to theorize the significant role that liberalism has played in the rise of so-called carceral feminism, a political formation that mobilizes the emancipatory energies of feminism in the service of the expansion of the carceral state. Carceral feminism is not only the product of feminist and conservative convergences. The influence liberalism has exerted on feminist sexual politics since the mid-1980s has also worked to propel feminism in carceral directions.

In these first two chapters of *Why We Lost the Sex Wars,* I have explored antipornography feminism's complex and largely overlooked relationship to liberalism. I have shown how antipornography feminism emerged in the early 1970s as a critical response to a concerted campaign undertaken in the mid-twentieth century by liberals of a distinctly civil libertarian bent to roll back obscenity regulations in the United States. I have demonstrated how, for over a decade, liberals uniformly reacted to antipornography feminist critiques of this campaign with great suspicion and hostility, perceiving feminist analyses of pornography's role in normalizing sexual violence and perpetuating gender inequality as threats to expressive freedom and personal privacy. Then, beginning in the mid-1980s, as the antipornography feminist movement was on the wane and under attack even from within the feminist movement itself, I have shown how influential liberal legal theorists took up the antipornography feminist cause, fundamentally altering both liberalism and antipornography feminism in the process.

While the vicissitudinous relationship of antipornography feminism to liberalism has been my focus up to this point, in the next chapter, I turn to consider the similarly complex and shifting relationship between liberalism and antipornography feminism's primary feminist opponent during the sex wars, sex-radical feminism. Despite the many profound differences that divided antipornography feminists and sex-radical feminists during the sex wars, these warring feminist factions shared at least one significant commonality: a critical orientation to the narrow sexual politics of postwar liberalism that eventually gave way to an improbable feminist–liberal convergence, the influence of which is still palpable in feminist sexual politics today.

3

Ambivalent Liberals, Sex-Radical Feminists

On April 24, 1982, some eight hundred scholars, students, writers, artists, and activists convened at Barnard College for a conference entitled "The Scholar and the Feminist 9: Towards a Politics of Sexuality." As described in the introduction, this conference would prove the occasion for a historic clash between antipornography feminists, who mounted a dramatic protest against the conference just outside the gates of Barnard Hall, and sex-radical feminists, who had convened the conference in the hopes of formalizing and promoting a feminist alternative to the sexual politics of antipornography feminism. As the introduction also discussed, the clash between antipornography feminists and sex-radical feminists at Barnard that day would go on to become the foundation of what I have called the catfight narrative, an influential, albeit misleading and incomplete, account of the sex wars that presents the feminist sexuality debates of the 1970s, 1980s, and 1990s as a straightforward, two-sided, and wholly internecine feminist quarrel. According to the catfight narrative, sex-radical feminism burst forth fully formed onto the pages of feminist history at the Barnard conference as a direct response to the scurrilous attacks of those antipornography feminist picketers. My primary aim in this chapter is to push contemporary understandings of sex-radical feminism—its impetuses, aspirations, and legacies—beyond this specious portrait offered by the catfight narrative. While the Barnard conference was a significant moment in the development of sex-radical feminist politics and theory, sex-radical feminism predated the Barnard conference by nearly a decade and cannot be understood solely in relation to its conflict with antipornography feminism. In fact, as this chapter will demonstrate, sex-radical feminists articulated their trenchant critiques of heterosexuality, their scandalously expansive visions of sexual freedom, and their passionate defenses of some of the most stigmatized denizens of the sexual fringe in the course of a series of critical engagements with the very same postwar liberal anticensorship project that first spurred antipornography feminists into action in the 1970s. Then, in the mid-1980s, as Dworkin's and MacKinnon's antipornography civil rights ordinance gained momentum across the United States, sex-radical feminists made a crucial tactical decision. They aligned themselves with their longtime foes, anticensorship liberals, to defeat the Dworkin–MacKinnon ordinance. While sex-radical feminists' strategic deployment of liberal anticensorship rhetoric during this period proved effective insofar as it contributed to the defeat of the Dworkin–MacKinnon ordinance, this effectiveness came at a price. Aspects of sex-radical feminism not readily assimilable to a liberal idiom were obscured or abandoned, and by the mid-1990s, sex-radical feminism was completely overtaken by a markedly more liberal project: anti-censorship/pro-sex feminism.

"SEDUCTIO AD ABSURDUM": THE SEX-RADICAL FEMINIST CRITIQUE OF LIBERALISM

As described in chapter 2, in the late 1950s a cadre of civil libertarian attorneys, publishers, authors, and film producers launched a concerted campaign against the Comstock-era regime of obscenity regulation in the United States. This campaign, as I demonstrated, provided a crucial impetus for the emergence of antipornography feminism, which openly called into question its guiding premise: that sex is fundamentally private, apolitical, and harmless. Although sex-radical feminists did not engage in dramatic public debates and confrontations with liberals comparable to those engaged in by antipornography feminists in the 1970s and early 1980s, their audacious demands for a vibrant and diverse public sexual culture stood in stark contrast to the measured pleas of midcentury civil libertarians for a somewhat wider field for sexual expression.

As historian Whitney Strub has observed, throughout the mid-twentieth century, American liberals fought against censorship in ways that reinforced "a normative sexual regime" (2011, 44). Not even the stalwart civil libertarians who challenged the Comstock-era regime of obscenity regulation head on were willing to defend sexual expression qua sexual expression or sexual expression tout court. Consider, for example, the argument made by celebrated civil liberties attorney Charles Rembar in *Grove Press, Inc. v. Christenberry* (1959), the landmark case that exonerated the first unexpurgated American edition of D. H. Lawrence's *Lady Chatterley's Lover* (1928) from charges of obscenity and that pioneered the legal strategy that would lead to the exoneration of dozens of other sexually explicit works throughout the 1960s and 1970s. As Rembar explains in his firsthand account of the trial, in this case, he did not argue "that the Comstock Act as a whole was invalid, but that the First Amendment forbade its application to the book [he] was defending" (1968, 119). Rembar offers two reasons why *Lady Chatterley's Lover* ought to be exempt from regulation under the Comstock Act. First, despite its patent "lustfulness," the novel is not "utterly worthless," and Rembar produces a coterie of scholars, critics, and other literary "experts" to testify to the novel's status as a "modern classic" (119).[1] Because the Supreme Court, in *Roth v. United States,* had described obscenity "as utterly without redeeming social importance," a work with "literary merit" such as *Lady Chatterley's Lover* could not, Rembar argues, be adjudged obscene (119). Second, although the novel, in Rembar's words, "might arouse lust . . . , it was not the nasty kind of thing that could be called prurient" (124). And because the Supreme Court, also in *Roth v. United States,* had described obscenity as appealing to a "prurient," meaning "dirty, nasty, morbid, [and] unwholesome," interest in sex, a work that appealed to a "healthy" and "normal" interest in sex such as *Lady Chatterley's Lover* could not, Rembar reasons, be adjudged obscene (124).[2]

As these arguments indicate, in this pioneering liberal challenge to obscenity regulation, neither the legal category of obscenity nor its association with prurience is called into question. Indeed, Rembar's defense of *Lady Chatterley's Lover* invokes the very logic used to justify the work's suppression: productions that are merely "lustful" are of dubious value, and "prurience" is beyond the pale.[3] It is tempting, of course, to view this equivocal defense as born of necessity rather than principle. Rembar was, after all, an attorney out to win a lawsuit, not a philosopher accountable only to his own utopian imaginings. Surely, one might think, a more robust vision of sexual freedom must have been at work behind the scenes, animating these narrow legal arguments. However, there is much evidence to the contrary. For instance, within a decade of the resolution of *Grove Press, Inc. v. Christenberry,* Rembar could be heard publicly denouncing the more permissive sexual culture his groundbreaking legal victory helped bring about. "There is an acne on our culture," Rembar laments in the conclusion of his memoir chronicling his work representing defendants accused of obscenity, pointing to a glut of books, magazines, advertisements, and films that "play upon concupiscence" and "peddle sex with an idiot slyness" (1968, 491). "The current uses of the new freedom are not all to the good," Rembar observes. "We approach a *seductio ad absurdum*" (491).[4] Fortunately, Rembar continues, "the present distorted, impoverished, masturbatory concentration on representations of sex will diminish as the restraints on expression recede" (492). "As the courts move along their present path," Rembar predicts, "they hustle pornography off the scene, a billy in its back" (492).

Rembar's reflections on "the end of obscenity" reveal a profound ambivalence about sex at the heart of the postwar liberal campaign against obscenity regulation (1968). Undeniably, this campaign sought to broaden the legal boundaries for sexual expression in the United States. However, in doing so, it simultaneously sought to narrow the range of sexual expression on offer and to shore up conventional boundaries between healthy and pathological sex. Nowhere are these ambivalent sexual politics more vividly on display than in "The Playboy Philosophy," a series of editorial essays written by *Playboy* magazine's creator and editor, Hugh Hefner, and published in *Playboy* between December 1962 and May 1965. In this ungainly manifesto, Hefner excoriates the law of obscenity for its inability "to discern between the erotic wheat and the salacious chaff" (1963, 87). "Few censors comprehend the labyrinthian twistings and turnings that suppressed or perverted sexuality may take in the human animal," Hefner explains, and, as a consequence, "far more energy is expended ... in attempts to suppress appeals to the normally heterosexual than to the somewhat more subtle offerings to sadism, masochism, the homosexual and fetishism" (31). By "remov[ing] the primary heterosexual sources of stimulation from society," Hefner believes that censorship compels men "to affix [their] responses to something else—other men, perhaps, or perhaps a shoe or a bit of lace underwear" (90). "This is the kind of sickness," Hefner thunders, "that the unknowing censor can bring to society," and its only cure is the curtailment of the censor's power to suppress healthy and normal sexual expression (90). If this prescription is followed, Hefner promises, "perversion, neurosis, psychosis, unsuccessful marriage, divorce and suicide" will diminish and "happy and healthy" sex will flourish (82–83, 89).

This liberal faith in the capacity of sexual freedom to root out sexual perversion lived on well into the 1970s. For instance, Herald Price Fahringer, attorney for both Larry Flynt, publisher of *Hustler,* and Al Goldstein, publisher of *Screw,* confessed that he was "distress[ed]" by the "enormous demand for pornography" and the ubiquity of depictions of "gross sex" (1979, 289). "I find something very unhealthy," Fahringer explains, "about this preoccupation with . . . sex which is not tastefully portrayed," "which is not erotic," and which "is unlike that which is exciting, that which we saw eight years ago in *Playboy,* for example, a beautiful woman . . . portrayed very attractively" (290). The antidote to this distressing proliferation of "pornography" and "gross sex," Fahringer insists, is not censoring sexual expression but rather freeing it. "Obscenity," Fahringer explains, "breeds and multiplies in the dark crevices of a frightened society preoccupied with a sense of self-censorship" (253). "Once pornography is exposed to the strong sunlight of a completely free and uninhibited people," Fahringer prophesies, "its appeal will surely diminish" (253). Like John Stuart Mill, who famously argued that censorship "robs the human race . . . of the opportunity of exchanging error for truth" ([1869] 1989, 20), liberal opponents of obscenity regulation at this time believed that the censorship of sexually explicit materials robs the human race of the opportunity of exchanging obscenity's tawdry thrill for more dignified and authentic pleasures.

During the sex wars, sex-radical feminists assailed this ambivalent liberal sexual politics head on. Conceived in the late 1970s in the interstices of the women's liberation and gay liberation movements, sex-radical feminism sought to dethrone "vanilla" heterosexuality as the regnant norm governing sexual life and to expand the horizon of sexual possibility by engaging in controversial practices of identity articulation and community building for marginalized groups on the sexual fringe. While sex-radical feminism is often portrayed as a reaction against antipornography feminism's single-minded focus on sexual violence at the expense of sexual pleasure, and against its complicity in the marginalization of stigmatized sexual minorities like commercial sex workers and practitioners of S&M, antipornography feminism was not the only discourse on sex that sex-radical feminism challenged. Indeed, in its earliest articulations, sex-radical feminism offered a potent rebuke to the stiflingly narrow sexual politics of postwar liberalism.

For example, in response to the efforts of midcentury civil libertarians like Rembar, Hefner, and Fahringer to carve out a somewhat wider niche for sexual expression while simultaneously shoring up the boundaries between the obscene and the nonobscene, the prurient and the wholesome, and the perverse and the normal, sex-radical feminists set out to explode all of these boundaries for the sake of a sexual freedom that was not reducible to mere expressive freedom. This subversive aim is evident throughout sex-radical feminist writings, including the first expressly sex-radical feminist publication, *What Color Is Your Handkerchief? A Lesbian S/M Sexuality Reader*.[5] Published in June 1979 by the San Francisco–based lesbian feminist S&M group Samois, *What Color Is Your Handkerchief?* is a forty-five-page pamphlet on the practice and politics of lesbian sadomasochism. It opens with Samois's mission statement, in which the group's members identify themselves as "feminist lesbians who share a positive interest in sadomasochism" and "believe that . . . S/M can exist as part of a healthy and positive lifestyle" (1979, 2). With this simple act of identification, Samois's members directly challenge the notion, propagated by midcentury civil libertarians, that the only "healthy" and "positive" sex is vanilla (i.e., nonkinky) and heterosexual.

Samois's mission statement also challenged another boundary between the perverse and the normal, this one defended by many of their lesbian feminist peers. According to so-called political lesbians like Ti-Grace Atkinson and Rita Mae Brown, sex involving "power, dominance, role play, and oppression" runs counter to feminist values (Brown [1972] 1975).[6] This means that sadomasochism, which Samois defines as "an eroticized exchange of power negotiated between two or more sexual partners," was suspect, even counterrevolutionary, in the eyes of an influential swath of lesbian feminists (1979, 2). Samois's members flatly reject this proposition, arguing that it amounts to a feminist redescription of conventional notions of sexual propriety. "As radical perverts," Samois's members declare, "we oppose all social hierarchies based on sexual preference" (2). This includes hierarchies defended by nonfeminist liberals and radical lesbian feminists alike.

The most far-reaching interrogation of boundaries dividing the perverse from the normal included in *What Color Is Your Handkerchief?* is Gayle Rubin's essay "Sexual Politics, the New Right, and the Sexual Fringe." Here, Rubin, a founding member of Samois and a leading sex-radical feminist theorist, calls on the women's and gay liberation movements to work in solidarity with "sadomasochists," "prostitutes," "hustlers," "pedophiles," "pederasts," "lovers of young people," and "men cruising for sex in public places" to secure "legitimacy, rights, and recognition" for all "second class sexual citizens" (1979, 28–30). "At a time when feminists are called lesbians, when homosexuals are portrayed as child molesters, and when child 'molesters' are presented as the four horsemen of the apocalypse," it is "imperative," Rubin contends, "that the women's and gay movements develop more sensitivity to the problems, the humanity, and the legitimate claims of stigmatized sexual minorities" (1979, 29–30). Rubin's plea for understanding, "tolerance," and "simple justice" for groups whose sexual desires and practices are almost universally reviled underscores the extent to which sex-radical feminists were committed to the destabilization of sexual hierarchies and the subversion of virtually all norms regulating erotic life (Samois 1979, 29, 33).

The defenses of stigmatized and even criminalized sexualities offered up in *What Color Is Your Handkerchief?* point to another significant challenge sex-radical feminism posed to the sexual politics of postwar liberalism. Unlike midcentury civil libertarians, who sought little more than the easing of extant obscenity regulations, sex-radical feminists were out to upend what they viewed as a massive sociolegal regulatory apparatus aimed at the enforcement of erotic conformity. One of the most outspoken sex-radical feminists on this score was writer, sex educator, and Samois cofounder, Pat (now Patrick) Califia. While Califia is best known for his unsparing portraits of antipornography feminists as censorious prudes,[7] he was much more than a critic of antipornography feminism and an opponent of censorship.[8] In fact, in a pair of controversial articles published in the *Advocate* in the fall of 1980, Califia spoke out passionately in defense of "boy-lovers," gay men who have sex with male minors, and against laws criminalizing noncoercive, consensual intergenerational sex, including statutory rape and child pornography laws (Califia [1980] 1994a, [1980] 1994b). Just two years later, in another article for the *Advocate,* Califia came to the defense of "tearoom cruisers," men who have sex with other men in public restrooms, and forcefully condemns laws criminalizing public sex (Califia [1980] 1994c). In Califia's view, such laws are not sensible measures designed to protect children or the public but thinly veiled mechanisms for the punishment of erotic dissidence and the forcible maintenance of "the nuclear family and everything it stands for—middle-class values, homophobia, uniformity, and puritanism" (Califia [1980] 1994a, 50).

In her seminal contribution to sex-radical feminist theory, "Thinking Sex: Notes for a Radical Theory of the Politics of Sexuality," Gayle Rubin offers a similar critique of the sexual regulatory regime in the United States, even going so far as to compare certain aspects of it to "legalized racism" (1984, 291). In Rubin's view, laws prohibiting "same sex contact, anal penetration, and oral sex make homosexuals a criminal group denied the privileges of full citizenship" (291). Rubin also decries laws denying minors "access to 'adult' sexuality," such as age-of-consent laws, custody laws that "permit the state to steal the children of anyone whose erotic activities appear questionable," and certification laws that "require teachers arrested for sex offenses to lose their jobs and credentials" (290). In Rubin's view, such laws do not protect children so much as cut them off from unorthodox sexual possibilities, thereby ensuring "the transmission of conservative sexual values" from one generation to the next (290). "I don't think that any consensual sexual behavior should be illegal," Rubin states categorically, calling for the "repeal of all sex laws except those few that deal with actual, not statutory, coercion" and "the abolition of vice squads, whose job it is to enforce legislated morality" (294).[9]

In addition to calling for the restructuring of sex law to emphasize consent and punish coercion, sex-radical feminists also criticized many extralegal modes of sexual regulation. As Rubin observes, "although the legal apparatus of sex is staggering, most everyday social control is extra-legal," taking the form of "less formal, but very effective social sanctions" such as family violence; discrimination in employment, housing, and health care provision; psychiatric diagnoses; religious condemnation; zoning ordinances relegating sex-related businesses to marginal "sexual underworlds"; discriminatory enforcement of alcoholic beverage codes to shut down businesses catering to sexual minorities; and street harassment (1984, 292, 289, 295). Taken together with more formal legal regulations, sex-radical feminists like Rubin believed that these sanctions amounted to a "system of sexual oppression," a "Kafkaesque nightmare in which unlucky victims become herds of human cattle whose identification, surveillance, apprehension, treatment, incarceration, and punishment produce jobs and self-satisfaction for thousands of vice police, prison of-ficials, psychiatrists, and social workers" (293). Their ultimate goal was to dismantle this oppressive system and destroy what another sex-radical feminist evocatively described as "the sexual hell in which we all grew up" (Lipschutz 1979, 11; 1984, 293).

Sex-radical feminists' demands for liberation from the Kafkaesque nightmare of sexual oppression far outstripped anything civil libertarian opponents of obscenity regulation ever imagined.[10] As I have already described, postwar liberal defenders of the freedom of sexual expression did not seek to challenge sexual norms but to bolster them by swaddling sexually explicit materials appealing to what they deemed a healthy, normal, and natural (hetero)sexual desire in the protection of the First Amendment. Even *Screw* publisher Al Goldstein, who prided himself on his willingness to transgress boundaries of sexual propriety other pornographers dared not, was unwilling to question taboos concerning intergenerational sex, and he publicly supported stiff criminal penalties for child pornography as a delegate to the Libertarian Party national convention in 1991 (Buckley 1991).

The failure of midcentury liberals to confront the system of sexual oppression in all its facets and to offer a clear, consistent, and unqualified defense of sexual freedom beyond expressive freedom was a frequent target of sex-radical feminist criticism. For instance, in an article reflecting on the passage of the Protection of Children against Sexual Exploitation Act of 1977, Pat (now Patrick) Califia criticized attorney Heather Grant Florence, who represented the ACLU at the congressional hearings for the act, for neglecting to speak out on behalf of those targeted by the legislation. According to Califia, Florence's only objection to the bill, which made it a felony to photograph or film a child (defined as anyone under sixteen years of age) in the nude, engaged in sexual activity with another person, or masturbating, was the threat it posed to the First Amendment. She did not object to the committee's position that sex is bad for children and she even suggested that it would be appropriate for the committee "to increase the legal penalties for adults who have sex with minors" ([1980] 1994, 45). In Califia's view, Florence's testimony missed the point. What was at stake in the proposed law was not only or even primarily expressive freedom, but the sexual freedom of young people, their adult friends and lovers, and gay people generally, who were likely to bear the brunt of a law enforcement crack down on any kind of sex crime.

Califia made a similar point regarding the testimony civil libertarians offered before the Attorney General's Commission on Pornography, more commonly known as the Meese Commission. "A lot of the people who turned up to testify before the commission on behalf of the First Amendment," Califia notes, "did not focus their testimony on the issue of pornography" and "chose instead to speak about the dangerous impact that censorship could have on the arts, theater, and literature" (1994, 36). As Califia saw it, the failure of these liberals to "stand up at the Meese Commission and say, 'I want to be able to see somebody get spanked, tied up, and soundly fucked in a full-color film with a gorgeous soundtrack'" left an opening for the Justice Department to implement many of the Meese Commission's most draconian recommendations, including cracking down on the production, distribution, and display of gay and S&M pornography as well as comparatively uncontroversial "vanilla porn" (Califia 1994d, 36).

Sex-radical feminists were also critical of liberal responses to California's Proposition 6, more commonly known as the Briggs Initiative, a statewide ballot initiative put forward in 1978 that sought to ban gays, lesbians, and their supporters from working in California's public schools. For instance, Amber Hollibaugh, a sex-radical feminist writer and activist who played a critical role in the campaign to defeat the Briggs Initiative, spoke out against her anti-Briggs allies advocating a "human rights approach" (2000, 53). In Hollibaugh's view, "emphasizing the ways in which the Initiative violated civil rights and human rights" was a misguided strategy; it "swept [sexuality] under the covers" and left the sexual fears and anxieties animating support for the Initiative unaddressed (50, 52–53, 55). Hollibaugh's preferred approach, by contrast, was one that "directly confronted homophobia in all its cultural and political manifestations," "defended sexual freedom," and "talked about sexuality in an explicitly political way" (50). As Hollibaugh saw it, the Briggs Initiative was "an antigay issue" and framing it as an infringement of "civil rights" or "human rights" obscured this in an insidious and counterproductive way (52–53). "If you can't be gay when you're attacked as a gay person, but everybody knows you're gay," Hollibaugh explains, "you don't have anywhere to go, you can't do anything. . . . It forces people right back into the closet, it makes you dead, it makes you crazy" (53). Like other sex-radical feminists, Hollibaugh believed that the abstract liberal language of "civil rights" failed to grasp what Gayle Rubin once called "the political dimensions of erotic life" and hindered the cause of sexual liberation (1984, 310).

One final challenge sex-radical feminism posed to the sexual politics of postwar liberalism can be seen in the variety of political activities in which sex-radical feminists engaged. While the political activities of midcentury civil libertarians were almost exclusively juridical and focused on narrowing the parameters of the constitutional category of obscenity, the political activities of sex-radical feminists were primarily cultural and focused on a variety of objectives including identity articulation and community building among groups marginalized on account of their nonnormative sexualities. Nowhere were these multifaceted cultural politics more apparent than in the lesbian feminist S&M organization Samois. According to its mission statement, the purpose of Samois was to "build community, lessen isolation, and sharpen consciousness" among

S&M lesbian feminists (Samois 1979, 3). To this end, they engaged in a variety of activities aimed at developing a distinct lesbian feminist S&M identity and community.[11] They organized sex parties and educational workshops that catered to lesbians with feminist sensibilities and S&M sexualities. They published a guide to S&M businesses in San Francisco, an annotated bibliography of literature on lesbian S&M, and a glossary of lesbian feminist S&M terminology. Most significantly, they instituted the "handkerchief code," a system designed to provide S&M lesbians a way to publicly proclaim their sexual identities and preferences, identify one another on the street or in the bar, and cruise for prospective sexual partners. The code was simple enough to be practicable, yet complex enough to express an impressive degree of erotic variety. For instance, by sporting a red handkerchief in her left pocket, a woman could indicate that she was a "fist-fucker" (Samois 1979, 36). By moving that handkerchief from her left pocket to her right, she could identify as a "fist-fuckee" (36). If she switched her red handkerchief out for a black one, she could become either a "top" (left pocket) or a "bottom" (right pocket) into "heavy S/M and whipping" (36). All in all, thirty-six different sexual identities and preferences—including "breast fondler/breast fondlee" and "likes menstruating women/is menstruating"—could be expressed using Samois's handkerchief code. Lest neophytes have trouble keeping track of all of these permutations, Samois offered wallet-sized "hanky code cards" for sale by mail order.

In addition to working to build a S&M lesbian feminist community of their own, Samois also fought on behalf of S&M lesbian feminists for acceptance within existing gay, lesbian, S&M, and feminist communities. These battles often took the form of struggles for access to communal space. For instance, in 1979, Samois overcame the objections of the organizing committee and secured a permit to march in San Francisco's Gay Freedom Day Parade. Later that same year, Samois and its allies pressured the Oakland-based feminist bookstore A Woman's Place into stocking Samois's pamphlet on lesbian feminist S&M, *What Color Is Your Handkerchief?* In 1981, after much wrangling with wary staff members, Samois even managed to host an event for S&M lesbians in San Francisco's Women's Building. Throughout the four years it existed, Samois also fought many smaller battles to gain access to bars, bathhouses, and sex clubs traditionally reserved for gay men, "vanilla" lesbians, or straight S&M people.[12]

As Samois's variegated political activities indicate, the politics of sex-radical feminism exceeded a simplistic liberal politics of anticensorship and legal reform. While sex-radical feminists certainly sought to change laws, including those regulating the production and distribution of materials considered obscene, they also sought to carve out broad swaths of public space for sexuality in general and to make alternative sexualities more vibrant, visible, and accessible. Ending the censorship of sexual expression by the state was one part of this, but such anticensorship reforms were not the be-all and end-all of sex-radical feminist politics. Califia makes this point in the introduction to *Public Sex* (1994), a collection of his most influential sex-radical feminist writings. "Battles over freedom of expression," Califia writes, "have implications far beyond the mere ability of print to circulate without being hampered by agents of the state" (19). Also at stake in these battles, Califia observes, is the power of marginalized sexual minorities "to say what [their] sex means" (19). According to Califia, "The line between word and deed is a thin one" and "a desire that cannot be named or described is a desire that cannot be valued, acted upon, or used as the basis for an identity" (19). As this passage makes clear, sex-radical feminists like Califia valued expressive freedom not as an end in itself, but as the adjunct of a larger and more fundamental sexual freedom. This freedom was not the freedom Califia once described as the freedom "to visit sex as if it were a brothel or a shooting gallery, get [a fix], and then go home without getting busted and publicly labeled as" a pervert or a sex fiend (36). The freedom sex-radical feminists sought was the freedom to cultivate, craft, express, and live out their sexual desires, identities, and pleasures in public and in the context of erotically nurturing communities. It was the freedom Amber Hollibaugh thought gays and lesbians in San Francisco had finally achieved in the aftermath of the White Night riots. After the riots, Hollibaugh told the London-based journal *Gay Left*, "We have a different sense of how we're gay in this town. Not only gayer in the Castro, but gayer everywhere" (2000, 117). It was also the freedom Califia described when he brazenly declared, "I want the freedom to be as queer, as perverted, on the street and on the job as I am in my dungeon" (Samois 1981, 251). This freedom vastly exceeded the freedom sought by midcentury civil libertarians to peruse representations of so-called normal and healthy sex that possessed some modicum of redeeming social value in private.

Ellen Willis, an influential sex-radical feminist writer and activist who is perhaps best known for her work in founding the radical feminist consciousness-raising group Redstockings in New York City in 1969, calls attention to this distinction between the negative sexual freedom sought by liberals and the more expansive positive sexual freedom sought by her and her fellow sex-radical feminists. As Willis explains, "The philosophy of the 'sexual revolution' as we know it is an extension of liberalism: it defines sexual freedom as the simple absence of external restrictions—laws and overt social taboos—on sexual information and activity.... This is a superficial view.... From a radical standpoint ... , sexual liberation involves not only the abolition of restrictions but the positive presence of social and psychological conditions that foster satisfying sexual relations" (2014, 184–85). At bottom, sex-radical feminism was a political project devoted to cultivating these "social and psychological conditions that foster satisfying sexual relations." The sexual liberation sex-radical feminists sought was much grander in scope than some civil libertarian effort to curb the excesses of existing regimes of state censorship.

The foregoing argument—that sex-radical feminism posed a number of fundamental challenges to the sexual politics of postwar liberalism—cuts against a long-standing interpretation of sex-radical feminism as essentially classical liberalism applied to sex. I surveyed several influential instances of this interpretation from Bat-Ami Bar On (1982), Marie France (1984), Ann Ferguson (1984), and Dorchen Leidholdt and Janice Raymond (1990) in the introduction. In my view, such interpretations are gravely mistaken. Not only do they overlook the substantial political differences that existed between sex-radical feminists and liberals on issues like pornography, public sex, intergenerational sex, and gay rights in the late 1970s and early 1980s, but they also obscure many of sex-radical feminism's most distinctive features. Sex-radical feminists condemned defenses of sexual behavior rooted in appeals to privacy, rejected individualistic conceptions of sexual identity and freedom, questioned portrayals of (hetero)sexual desire as natural or innate, channeled significant effort into cultivating diverse sexual identities and erotic communities, and demanded a sexual freedom that entailed the destruction of what they theorized as a system of sexual oppression, a complex of laws, norms, customs, and social practices that privileged some sexual desires and behaviors while punishing others. Taken together, all of this indicates that sex-radical feminism was not a species of liberalism but rather a critical engagement with it.

THE FACT BRIEF AND THE RISE OF
ANTI-CENSORSHIP/PRO-SEX FEMINISM

In the late 1970s and early 1980s, sex-radical feminism stood as a defiant alternative not only to antipornography feminism but also to the much more prominent and influential sexual politics of postwar liberalism. During this period, sex-radical feminists like Gayle Rubin, Pat (now Patrick) Califia, Amber Hollibaugh, and Ellen Willis challenged the erotic hierarchies that liberals reified, demanding not merely the reform or repeal of extant obscenity laws but also an end to sexual oppression in all its guises. However, in the mid-1980s, as sex-radical feminists mobilized to combat Dworkin's and MacKinnon's antipornography civil rights ordinance, the lines between sex-radical feminism and civil libertarianism began to blur. In an effort to counter the lurid, and increasingly persuasive and legislatively successful, rhetoric of the antipornography feminist movement, sex-radical feminists made a strategic decision to use the potent civil libertarian rhetoric of anticensorship to position themselves as defenders of expressive freedom pitted against a prudish and paternalistic antipornography feminist movement seeking to impose its own personal code of sexual morality on the public. This strategic deployment of civil liberties rhetoric yielded ambiguous results for sex-radical feminism. While the Dworkin–MacKinnon ordinance was defeated and a space for a more robust defense of sexual expression than liberals had traditionally offered was opened up within the conceptual confines of liberalism, sex-radical feminism's most distinctive aspects—its expansive vision of sexual freedom, its concern with modes of sexual oppression beyond the censorship of sexual expression by the state, and its commitment to cultural projects of identity articulation and community building on the sexual fringe—were muted and ultimately displaced as sex-radical feminism was subsumed under the banner of anti-censorship/pro-sex feminism.

The displacement of sex-radical feminism by anti-censorship/pro-sex feminism began in the early 1980s as the Dworkin–MacKinnon ordinance gained momentum and sex-radical feminists began to organize in opposition to it. Although the ordinance was defeated twice by a mayoral veto in the city of Minneapolis, where it was originally proposed, it fared better in Indianapolis, where it passed into law in spring 1984.[13] Over the next two years, versions of the Dworkin–MacKinnon ordinance were also considered in Suffolk County, New York; Madison, Wisconsin; Bellingham, Washington; Los Angeles County, California; and Cambridge, Massachusetts. In most of these cities, coordinated opposition to the ordinance came primarily from antipornography feminism's longtime foes, civil libertarian opponents of obscenity regulation. However, in several instances, traditional liberal coalitions of booksellers, publishing trade associations, and state civil liberties unions were joined by sex-radical feminists acting under the aegis of a new organization, the Feminist Anti-Censorship Taskforce (FACT).

According to Carole Vance (1993a), an influential sex-radical feminist[14] and FACT cofounder, FACT was formed in the fall of 1984 in response to the introduction of a Dworkin–MacKinnon–style antipornography ordinance in Suffolk County, New York.[15] Within a year, FACT chapters had sprung up in Madison, Wisconsin; Los Angeles, California; and Cambridge, Massachusetts, "to oppose the enactment of Indianapolis-style antipornography laws" (Duggan and Hunter 2006, 242). To this end, FACT engaged in a variety of activities, including offering formal testimony at public hearings concerning the ordinance, organizing a street-theater action in protest of the 1986 Attorney General's Commission on Pornography, and publishing *Caught Looking* (Ellis and Hunter 1986), a tabloid-style book that paired essays criticizing antipornography feminism with sexually explicit photographs and illustrations.[16] However, FACT's most influential intervention was an amicus brief it submitted on behalf of the plaintiffs in a legal challenge to the version of the Dworkin–MacKinnon ordinance enacted by the city of Indianapolis, *American Booksellers Ass'n, Inc. v. Hudnut* (1986).

Written by feminist legal scholars Nan Hunter and Sylvia Law, and signed by what the radical feminist periodical *off our backs* described as "an extraordinarily wide range of feminists," including veteran sex radicals like Amber Hollibaugh and Gayle Rubin, and civil libertarian attorneys like Nadine Strossen and David Richards, the FACT brief sought to persuade the Court of Appeals for the Seventh Circuit that the Indianapolis ordinance was unconstitutional (Wallsgrove 1985, 12). To this end, the brief marshals two primary arguments. First, the brief maintains, the ordinance's definition of pornography is "unconstitutionally vague," and, when paired with the ordinance's trafficking provision, it amounts to a license to "censor" a "virtually limitless" number of materials in violation of the First Amendment's free speech guarantee (Hunter and Law 1987, 108, 89, 101). Second, the brief contends, by defining pornography in "gender specific terms as 'the graphic sexually explicit subordination of women,'" the ordinance "resonates with the traditional concept that sex itself degrades women" (132, 105). In FACT's view, "sexually explicit speech is not *per se* sexist or harmful to women," and a law designed to protect women from such a dubious harm "perpetuates central sexist stereotypes" and violates the Fourteenth Amendment's equal protection guarantee (89, 130).

Judged solely on the basis of these arguments, the FACT brief appears to be a conventional liberal effort. It figures sexually explicit expression as harmless, and it denounces attempts to regulate it as censorious encroachments on the freedom of speech. Even the FACT brief's novel deployment of the equal protection clause is largely in keeping with the traditional liberal claim that obscenity regulation is patronizing and paternalistic. However, despite these affinities, the FACT brief is no straightforward rehearsal of the liberal creed.[17] In fact, it flouts liberal convention in many ways. For instance, its bold vindication of "sexual speech" as "political" and "highly relevant to our decision-making as citizens on a wide range of social and ethical issues" is a far cry from liberals' traditionally ambivalent defenses of sexual expression as private and permissible only in a few discreet settings. Similarly, the FACT brief's argument that the Indianapolis ordinance would exacerbate the "massive discrimination" endured by "sexual minorities" by making their already marginalized "erotica" even more susceptible to suppression was not an argument that traditionally emanated from liberal quarters (Hunter and Law 1987, 109). In fact, liberals had traditionally argued just the opposite: that censorship laws unjustly targeted nonprurient, wholesome, healthy, and normal (read: conventionally heterosexual) materials for suppression, and did little to stanch the flow of prurience, filth, and smut. Finally, the FACT brief's dominant theme (apart from the threat the Indianapolis ordinance poses to expressive freedom in general, of course) is fear that, if enacted, the Indianapolis ordinance would furnish conservatives with "an effective tool" for the curtailment of women's "freedom to appropriate for themselves" the "traditionally male language" of sexuality (Hunter and Law 1987, 121–22). Such concern for women's, or anyone's, ability to express "unladylike, unfeminine, aggressive, power-charged, pushy, vulgar, urgent, confident, and intense" ideas about sex was a definite departure from liberal orthodoxy (Hunter and Law 1987, 122).

That the FACT brief defies even as it reproduces the conventional liberal line on free speech points to what is in my view the most significant aspect of FACT's intervention in the debate over the Dworkin–MacKinnon ordinance. Although many of FACT's founders and supporters were sex-radical feminists committed to an expansive vision of sexual liberation that exceeded liberal strictures,[18] the organization was guided by a strategic vision that held that "effective political action consists in appropriating, transforming and deploying the friendliest discourses, in order to counter the most hostile ones" (Duggan and Hunter 2006, 2).[19] In keeping with this strategy, FACT cofounder Lisa Duggan explains, FACT "appropriated the rhetoric of 'anticensorship'" along with the accompanying "framework of civil liberties" to construct a "bridge discourse" connecting the "reform politics of liberal and progressive groups" to the more radical politics of sex-radical feminism (2). By speaking in a liberal idiom, FACT was able to hitch sex-radical feminism's ambitious agenda, which included resisting sexual oppression in all its forms and creating a vibrant and diverse public sexual culture, to a familiar (and much less threatening) liberal politics of "free speech" and "civil liberties" (7). This enabled FACT to not only make an effective case against the

Indianapolis ordinance but also a lasting contribution to liberal thought: FACT's strategic deployment of liberal rhetoric led directly to the creation of a new liberal discourse on pornography and sexual freedom that provided a stark alternative to the ambivalent one liberals had traditionally used: anti-censorship/pro-sex feminism.[20]

A key figure in the articulation and popularization of this new liberal discourse was Nadine Strossen.[21] As president of the ACLU, founder of Feminists for Free Expression, and a member of the National Coalition Against Censorship's Working Group on Women, Censorship, and "Pornography," Strossen worked tirelessly to dispel the "widespread misperception," "encouraged," in her view, by "oversimplified, extremist, divisive, pronouncements by feminist pro-censorship leaders," that feminists and civil libertarians were fundamentally at odds over pornography (1993b, 1107; 1995, 32). According to Strossen, "feminism and civil liberties are inextricable," and the anticensorship position customarily grounded in free speech and First Amendment principles also finds sustenance in "feminist principles and concerns" (1987, 202; 1993, 1103). To support this claim, Strossen draws on the arguments and ideas of sex-radical feminists. "Censoring pornography," Strossen insists, would not only "violate . . . cherished First Amendment freedoms;" it would hinder "women's efforts to develop their own sexuality," exacerbate the oppression of lesbians and other sexual minorities, "harm women who voluntarily work in the sex industry," and undermine "essential aspects of human freedom," including "sexual freedom" (1995, 14; 1993, 1111–12). Such contentions, originally put forward by sex-radical feminists as critiques of the limited defenses of sexual freedom espoused by anticensorship liberals, became in Strossen's hands evidence of "the falseness of the purported dichotomy between feminist and civil libertarian principles" (1987, 201). Once a critical alternative to liberalism, sex-radical feminism was being remade by activists like Strossen into its ally and its complement.

This improbable union of sex-radical feminism and liberalism proved a potent one, not only contributing to the defeat of the Dworkin–MacKinnon ordinance, which, by the summer of 1986, was, legally speaking, a dead letter,[22] but also bringing about some noteworthy shifts in liberal discourse concerning expressive freedom. With the advent of anti-censorship/pro-sex feminism, liberals who had traditionally demurred from explicit and robust defenses of sexual freedom began to link their traditional concerns like censorship and free speech to a much broader set of concerns, including the freedom of sexual expression and the civil liberties of sexual minorities. A prime example of this new and expanded liberal discourse is *Polluting the Censorship Debate,* a report issued by the ACLU in July 1986 to criticize the findings of the Meese Commission. Throughout this report, the ACLU stakes out a series of positions that bear the unmistakable mark of sex-radical feminist influence and diverge significantly from the more sexually ambivalent species of civil libertarianism that animated the anticensorship campaigns of the 1960s and 1970s.

The most obvious difference between the 1986 ACLU report and the anticensorship arguments of civil libertarians of previous generations is that the ACLU report features a bold and unequivocal defense of sexual expression qua sexual expression. As the report states, the "presumption that there is a difference between sexually-oriented speech and all other kinds of speech is completely unwarranted," and "the First Amendment should protect all sexually explicit speech" without regard to notions such as prurience, offensiveness, or social value or utility (27–29). The report roots this sweeping defense of the freedom of sexual expression in the claim that sexually explicit speech, including pornography, "transmits ideas," "presents views of aesthetics and ethics about which public debate is certain and desirable," and "may . . . have as its purpose or effect the promotion of a political or ideological viewpoint" (30). Among the aesthetic, ethical, and political ideas expressed in pornography according to the ACLU report is the notion that "the kind of sexual activity depicted," no matter how widely stigmatized or seemingly "unpleasant," "is worth doing, or at least worth watching" (30). In other words, the ACLU report argues, pornography has an important role to play in "legitimating specific sexual practices" (30). To bolster this claim, the ACLU report quotes directly from an essay by sex-radical feminist theorist and activist Ann Snitow,[23] noting that pornography may also promote "the joys of passivity, of helpless abandon, of response without responsibility," ideas that deserve, the ACLU report insists, to be on the agenda for "public debate . . . in a society valuing free expression" (30).

The 1986 ACLU report also parts company with the arguments of the previous generation of civil libertarian opponents of censorship by emphasizing pornography's role in what the report describes as "'the achievement of self-realization,' . . . or 'self-fulfillment'" (31–32). By legitimating the viewers' "deepest emotions, reactions, or most peculiar rational ideas by showing that others share them," the ACLU report argues that pornography can play an important role in an individuals' search for sexual meaning, fulfillment, identity, and community (32). "In the area of sexuality," the report explains, "where social pressure and taboos frequently prevent the public airing of one's thoughts, it is difficult even in an otherwise open and tolerant society to find others who feel similarly. There is obvious political significance attached to the knowledge that there are others who think as you do. The social message of certain sexually explicit material may be viewed by some people, particularly those in sexual minorities, as beneficial to their self-identity and self-understanding" (32–33). This insistence on pornography's value as a medium of self-realization and self-fulfillment, particularly for sexual minorities, marks a definite shift from earlier civil libertarian defenses of sexually explicit expression, many of which were expressly homophobic and hostile to nonnormative sexualities, and shares an undeniable affinity with sex-radical feminist ideas and arguments.

The 1986 ACLU report also signals concern for the dignity and civil liberties of sexual minorities in other respects. For instance, in its discussion of the Meese Commission's recommendation that "Congress should amend the Mann Act to make its provisions gender neutral," the ACLU voices concern that such an amendment would simply "give prosecutors a new weapon against gay lifestyles" (122–23). The report also condemns the commission's recommendations that "state and local public health authorities" should crack down on violations by "'adults only' businesses" for similar reasons, decrying these recommendations as "transparent efforts to find new ways to criminalize or regulate consensual (albeit dangerous in some cases) behavior, largely of gay or bisexual men" (134–35). The ACLU report even takes steps toward condemning the stigmatization of practitioners of S&M and defending the pornography of this nearly universally reviled sexual subculture. "Although the [Meese] Report routinely includes the assertion that 'sado-masochistic themes'

are 'sexually violent,'" the ACLU report refers to "a whole body of literature . . . that suggests that much 's/m' activity is both wholly consensual
and non-violent" and insists that "portrayals of . . . sado-masochism . . .
are not inherently dangerous, harmful or unfair" (69, 120).

In all these respects, the ACLU's 1986 report departs from liberal
conventions of the 1960s and 1970s. However, the extent to which the
advent of anti-censorship/pro-sex feminism broadened liberal discourse
on sexual freedom should not be overstated. For instance, the ACLU
report does not call for the decriminalization of sex work but defends
"constitutionally protected expression" like pornography by insisting on
its distinctiveness from criminal conduct such as "pandering" (i.e., pimping) and "prostitution" (131). As the ACLU report argues, "If producing
film or pictures, not sexual gratification for money, is the primary purpose
of the actors' work, then that work can in no way be called prostitution,
and paying the actors' salaries can in no way be called pandering" (132).

The ultimately limited nature of the influence sex-radical feminism
was able to exert on liberal sexual politics is most visible in those aspects
of the 1986 ACLU report that touch on the sexuality of young people.
For instance, in response to the Meese Report's claim that "the most
frequent exposure to pornography is reported among adolescents between
12 and 17," the 1986 ACLU report does not offer a robust defense of the
sexual autonomy of young people. Rather, it insists that this statistic is
"unsubstantiated by the data in this report" and that "there is not a shred
of evidence to suggest that teenagers consume large amounts of pornography" (76–77). Such a reply, of course, begs the question of whether the
ACLU's position on pornography regulation might have been different had
the Meese Report offered credible evidence that young people consumed
large amounts of pornography.

The ACLU's critique of the Meese Commission's recommendation
that "Congress should enact legislation prohibiting producers of certain
sexually explicit visual depictions from using performers under the age of
twenty-one" is similarly limited (138). In the ACLU's view, "this proposal
constitutes a serious abridgment of the civil liberties of persons who are
fully adult in virtually all legal senses. Eighteen-year-olds vote, drive,
marry, make contracts, give legal consent to medical treatment, and die

on the battlefield. . . . Yet this change in the law would forbid them from freely choosing to pose for sexually explicit pictures" (138). Of course, concern for the civil and sexual liberty of those who are not yet legally adults is wholly absent from this response, which implicitly endorses the notion that it is permissible to forbid people under the age of eighteen from freely choosing to pose for sexually explicit pictures.

Also, the ACLU report's stance on laws regulating child pornography and intergenerational sex is vastly different from the position on these matters staked out by sex-radical feminists like Gayle Rubin and Pat (now Patrick) Califia. While Rubin and Califia opposed age-of-consent and child pornography laws as oppressive denials of the sexual autonomy of young people and unjust threats to the civil liberties and sexual freedom of their adult lovers, the ACLU report shows little concern for either of these matters. In fact, the 1986 ACLU report clearly states that although the ACLU believes that child pornography laws pose a threat to constitu-tionally protected speech, the organization also "agrees with [the Meese Commission] that the vast bulk of child pornography does represent the non-consensual violation of a child's rights" and that "the criminal law should proceed . . . with increased vigor against those who commit the underlying conduct which results in the sexually explicit photographs of children" (103, 105). "There is much to be done," the ACLU report continues, "to reach those who finance these photographic productions; those who procure the children (with various degrees of coercion) into making the photographs; those who engage in sexual activities with chil-dren, as well as other knowing and willful participants who aid and abet in molestation" (105).[24] The possibility that pictures of young people engaged in sexual conduct with adults depict benign and consensual sexual acts is neither mentioned nor entertained in the ACLU report. The ACLU's sole concern is for expressive freedom, not the sexual freedom of the young or oppressed sexual minorities.

In the course of its discussion of child pornography laws, the ACLU report also reproduces, rather than questions or challenges, characteriza-tions of pedophilia as dangerous and pathological. "The [Meese] Report speculates that stringent enforcement [of criminal bans on the production and distribution of child pornography] could decrease the market for such materials," the ACLU report explains, "but . . . given the deep pathologies of many pedophiles . . . such a result is quite unlikely. At its root, there is no basis to conclude that underlying sexual abuse would be stemmed by more child pornography laws" (106). What the ACLU has done here is invoke the specter of the incurably degenerate pedophile to argue against the criminalization of child pornography. Sex-radical feminists, who were as concerned with mitigating the social stigma endured by sexual non-conformists as they were with reforming sex law, would have stridently opposed such a strategy.

As this brief discussion of the 1986 ACLU report demonstrates, the amalgamation of civil liberties and sex-radical feminist rhetoric in anti-censorship/pro-sex feminism yielded ambiguous results. While the Dworkin–MacKinnon ordinance was defeated and a space for a more robust defense of sexual expression than liberals had traditionally offered was opened up within the conceptual confines of liberalism, these achievements came at a price. Many of sex-radical feminism's most distinctive aspects did not survive liberal translation, and a feminist political project that began the sex wars as a radical alternative to liberalism ended the sex wars as essentially a species of liberalism itself.

FEMINISM ECLIPSED

In this chapter, I have attempted to do for sex-radical feminism what I did for antipornography feminism in chapters 1 and 2: bring to light the history of its complex and shifting relationship with liberalism and, in doing so, move contemporary understandings of the sex wars beyond the catfight narrative. While sex-radical feminists did not engage in dramatic public confrontations with liberals on the scale of those engaged in by antipornography feminists in the 1970s and early 1980s, as this chapter has shown, they did register their opposition to the narrow and ambivalent sexual politics of postwar liberalism as they pursued an expansive program of sexual liberation. In this chapter, I have also described the emergence in the early 1980s of a strategic alliance between sex-radical feminists and civil libertarian liberals to oppose the Dworkin–MacKinnon antipornography ordinance. Unlike the convergence of antipornography feminism and liberalism during this same period described in chapter 2, the alliance between sex-radical feminists and anticensorship liberals was driven primarily by sex-radical feminists' desire to gain legal and political leverage over their antipornography feminist opponents. By combining what were at the time scandalous and unconventional sex-radical feminist arguments regarding the intrinsic social and political value of sexually explicit expression with more traditional liberal arguments regarding the threat posed by state censorship to expressive freedom, sex-radical feminists were able to mount an effective opposition to the Dworkin–MacKinnon ordinance. However, this effectiveness came at a price. Aspects of sex-radical feminism that were not reducible to a liberal politics of anticensorship and expressive freedom were obscured or abandoned, and by the mid-1990s, sex-radical feminism had been almost completely overtaken by a markedly narrower liberal project: anti-censorship/pro-sex feminism.

Thus, at this stage in my narrative of the history of the sex wars, we find ourselves in a curious position. Two monumentally significant contributions to twentieth-century feminist sexual politics and thought that were forged in white-hot hostility to the tepid and narrow sexual politics of postwar liberalism appear to have ended the sex wars in a much more ambiguous relation to liberalism than they began them. In the case of antipornography feminism, the feminist critique of pornography, which had emphasized the political character of pornography's harms and pursued remedies that deliberately flouted the bounds of traditional First Amendment jurisprudence, was supplanted by a much narrower liberal critique that represented pornography's harms in more conventional terms like "violence" and "crime," and pursued remedies that could be obtained within the bounds of long-standing liberal constitutional interpretation. In the case of sex-radical feminism, a project that began as an audacious demand for sexual freedom that far outstripped anything even the most daring anticensorship liberals had ever envisaged culminated in a moderately expanded liberal politics of expressive freedom that was willing, on occasion, to defend sexually explicit expression as socially and politically valuable rather than denigrating it is as deplorable but nevertheless legally permissible.

The surprising and counterintuitive liberal trajectories of both anti-pornography and sex-radical feminism that I have described in these last three chapters beg the following questions: How were these improbable liberal appropriations and transformations possible? How was liberalism, with its reluctance to mount even the meekest of challenges to heteronormativity, its squeamishness about defending a robust conception of sexual freedom that is not reducible to expressive freedom, and its principled refusal to bring sex, including many forms of sexual injustice, oppression, and harm, out of the so-called private sphere and into the public realm of the political, able to so thoroughly overtake and eclipse both of its radical feminist opponents during this period? In the next chapter, which considers the contributions of Black and third world feminists to the sex wars—contributions that, it is worth emphasizing, are even more neglected and misunderstood than the various antipornography and sex-radical feminist engagements with liberalism that I have discussed so far—a possible answer to these questions emerges. The failures of both white antipornography and white sex-radical feminists to take seriously the challenges offered by their Black and third world feminist allies during the sex wars prepared the way for the liberal appropriations and attenuations of antipornography and sex-radical feminism that I have just described.

4

Third World Feminism and the Sex Wars

In spring 2009, at a conference commemorating the twenty-fifth anniversary of the publication of her landmark essay "Thinking Sex: Notes for a Radical Theory of the Politics of Sexuality," Gayle Rubin responded to a question from an audience member about the relationship between two currents that dominated feminist politics and theory in the 1980s: Black feminism and the sex wars. Sharon P. Holland recounts the exchange:

> AUDIENCE MEMBER: I am wondering if you can talk a bit about the relationship of the emergence of black feminism at the time to the feminist sex wars, because that's always been fuzzy to me. As all of this stuff at Barnard was going on, what was the relationship of Audre Lorde and Barbara Smith . . . were those movements in conversation with each other at all, or were they happening separately?
>
> GAYLE RUBIN: I don't think it's a consistent relationship. There are other people who probably know more about that than I. But certainly, black feminism was emerging long before any of this happened, and the Combahee Collective document was printed in 1975 at least, maybe earlier, and the sex wars didn't really happen 'til later. And some black feminists were supporting the antiporn position and some were not. It's not a consistent relationship as far as I know. Certainly, people argued that pornography . . . one of their criticisms was they argued pornography was inherently racist and particularly racist in various ways. That was a controversial claim, although there was certainly racism—there was plenty of racism in pornography, but whether it was more racist than say, the rest of society, was an arguable point. (2011, 90–91)

In the course of this uncharacteristically fumbling response, Rubin mis-identifies the year in which the Combahee River Collective's pivotal work, "A Black Feminist Statement," was published (it was 1977, not 1975 or earlier) and reduces Black feminist engagement in the sex wars to either supporting or not supporting the presumptively white "antiporn position."

This tendency to drastically oversimplify or elide altogether the contributions of feminists of color to the sex wars is by no means confined to Rubin. In fact, some of the most prominent scholarship on the sex wars glosses over these contributions. For example, in her otherwise meticulous history of the antipornography feminist movement, Carolyn Bronstein downplays the contributions of Black feminists to antipornography feminist politics and theory. "Women of color," Bronstein writes, "were actively engaged in sex-related issues that affected the everyday health of women in their communities, including sterilization abuse, and access to reproductive care as well as abortion, but not antipornography" (2011, 271).[1] In her study of Black women in pornography, Mireille Miller-Young inverts Bronstein's mistake. Whereas Bronstein makes it seem as though virtually all women of color were skeptical or outright critical of antipornography feminism, Miller-Young makes it seem as though all Black feminists were antipornography feminists. Following a somewhat perfunctory rendition of the catfight narrative, Miller-Young writes, "Black feminists have often followed the antiporn feminist critique described above, arguing that pornography as an industry perpetuates harmful stereotypes about Black women's sexuality" (2014, 19–20). Jane Gerhard captures the range of views on pornography and sexuality expressed by feminists of color during the sex wars more accurately, acknowledging not only Black antipornography feminists like Audre Lorde and Alice Walker, but also the contributions of Black feminist scholars like Hortense Spillers to the critique of antipornography feminism articulated at the Barnard conference (2001, 189–90). Unfortunately, Gerhard's claim that the Barnard conference "embodied the accomplishment of minority feminists" because its participants "embraced and elaborated" their differences of class and race rather than eliding them glosses over criticisms of the Barnard conference specifically, and sex-radical feminism more generally, levied by feminists of color who were present at the Barnard conference and active in sex-radical feminist circles (184–85).

This habit of overlooking or minimizing the contributions of nonwhite women to the sex wars is consistent with a larger trend in histories of feminist politics and theory. Feminists of color are often cited in what Holland has called "a discretionary vacuum," cordoning them off from fields of contestation and inquiry that they, in fact, helped produce (2011, 91).[2] My goal in this chapter is to release at least a handful of Black and third world feminists, as many nonwhite feminists referred to themselves in the 1970s and 1980s, from this discretionary vacuum and restore them to the center of the sex wars debates where they belong.[3] By foregrounding the work of scholars, artists, and activists like Patricia Hill Collins, Tracey Gardner, Audre Lorde, Rose Mason, Cherríe Moraga, Tina Portillo, Karen Sims, Barbara Smith, Luisah Teish, Mirtha Quintanales, and Alice Walker, I aim to show that, contra Rubin and other scholars of the period, feminists of color did in fact intervene in the sex wars, and that they did so in diverse, complex, and significant ways.[4] Far from simply choosing sides in a preexisting white feminist debate or abstaining from the sex wars fracas altogether, Black and third world feminists articulated their own distinct analyses of pornography, S&M, and other sex-related issues, often confounding or exceeding the terms in which white feminists were analyzing these issues at the time.

By recentering the contributions of Black and third world feminists to the sex wars, I also hope to build on the work of scholars like Benita Roth, whose research on Black and Chicana feminist activism has helped replace a "white-washed" and singular model of second-wave feminism with "a picture of second-wave-feminisms, feminisms that were plural and characterized by racial/ethnic organizational distinctiveness" (2004, 1–2). This insight into the racially/ethnically differentiated character of second-wave feminisms, in the plural, has yet to permeate sex wars historiography. In fact, it remains commonplace in both scholarly and popular feminist circles to depict the sex wars as a straightforward, two-sided catfight pitting sex-negative and presumptively white feminists on one side against sex-positive and presumptively white feminists on the other. By highlighting the various ways in which Black and third world feminists fail to fit comfortably within the binary framework of this catfight narrative, I also intend to continue the work undertaken in the book's previous three chapters: pressing contemporary understandings of the sex wars beyond Barnard—that is, beyond an image of the sex wars as coextensive with the dramatic conflict that erupted between antipornography and sex-radical feminists at "The Scholar and the Feminist 9" conference in spring 1982. The debates that transpired during the sex wars were much more complex than the Barnard-centric catfight narrative lets on. Considering the contributions of Black and third world feminists to the sex wars can help us appreciate more fully this richness and complexity.

Finally, and perhaps most importantly, I hope the careful analysis of Black and third world feminist contributions to the sex wars offered in this chapter will shed some much-needed historical and theoretical light on the questions that I raised at the end of the previous chapter. How was liberalism, which started the sex wars as the foil and political opponent of both antipornography and sex-radical feminism, able to so swiftly and thoroughly overtake these feminist projects by the sex wars' end? Why were feminist–liberal amalgamations like antipornography liberalism and anti-censorship/pro-sex feminism able to so successfully supplant earlier and more radical approaches to feminist sexual politics? As I will argue in this chapter, it was the failure of white antipornography and sex-radical feminists to heed the calls of their Black and third world feminist allies to exchange their monistic and unidimensional analyses of sexual politics for intersectional alternatives that smoothed the way for the liberal appropriations and co-optations described in chapters 2 and 3. Had the Black and third world feminist voices surveyed in this chapter carried the day, the developments that ended up compromising antipornography and sex-radical feminism in their original forms may have been avoided and the terrain of contemporary feminist sexual politics thoroughly transformed.

DISRUPTING MONISM: THE SEXUAL POLITICS
OF BLACK AND THIRD WORLD FEMINISM

Before discussing the specific interventions Black and third world feminists made into the sex wars debates, some brief remarks are in order about the relationship of Black and third world feminism to feminist sexual politics and thought more generally. As both the question put to Gayle Rubin by the anonymous audience member at the 2009 conference and Rubin's response to it described above indicate, Black and third world feminism are rarely thought of in relation to feminist sexual politics and thought. One pertinent example of this tendency to cordon off feminist engagements with race and class from feminist engagements with sex and sexuality appears in the popular documentary film, *She's Beautiful When She's Angry* (2014). In the film, which tells the story of the women's liberation movement in the United States from 1966 to 1971, Black feminism and lesbian feminism are portrayed as isolated offshoots of the main trunk of the women's liberation movement, and the stories of their emergence are told in completely separate acts. Furthermore, Black feminism is represented through the personal narratives of *straight* Black women like Frances Beale and Linda Burnham, while lesbian feminism is represented through the personal narratives of *white* lesbians like Rita Mae Brown, Karla Jay, and Ellen Shumsky. In the world according to *She's Beautiful When She's Angry,* all the feminists contesting racial oppression within the women's liberation movement were straight, and all the feminists contesting lesbian oppression within the liberation women's movement were white. However, even the most cursory glance at the actual history of the women's liberation movement shows that the rise of Black and third world feminism and the migration of issues pertaining to sex and sexuality, like lesbian identity, to the forefront of feminist political consciousness overlapped and intersected in many respects.

The most obvious connections between Black and third world feminism and feminist politicizations of sex and sexuality like lesbian feminism are evident at the level of personnel. For example, several key figures in the articulation of Black and third world feminism were also key figures in the articulation of lesbian feminism. Consider, for example, Barbara Smith, Cheryl Clarke, Audre Lorde, and other founding members of the Combahee River Collective. In their influential statement, the Combahee River Collective members identify themselves as "Black feminists and lesbians," declaring that, in contrast to straight feminists, white lesbian feminists, straight Black liberationists, and white gay liberationists, they are "actively committed to struggling against racial, sexual, heterosexual, and class oppression," and see as their "particular task the development of integrated analysis and practice based upon the fact that the major systems of oppression are interlocking" (Taylor 2017, 27, 15). This means that the Combahee River Collective's statement, rightfully hailed as a formative contribution to Black feminist politics and thought, is equally an important contribution to lesbian feminist politics and thought. It also means that other major works analyzing the intersections of racial, sexual, and class oppressions that were authored or edited by Combahee River Collective members like Barbara Smith and Akasha Gloria Hull's *All the Women Are White, All the Blacks Are Men, but Some of Us Are Brave: Black Women's Studies* (1982); Barbara Smith's *Home Girls: A Black Feminist Anthology* (1983); and Audre Lorde's *Zami: A New Spelling of My Name* (1982) merit distinction as significant contributions not only to Black feminism but also to lesbian feminism.[5]

Another influential contribution to Black and third world feminist politics and theory that is equally a contribution to lesbian feminism is the celebrated anthology *This Bridge Called My Back: Writings by Radical Women of Color* (1981). Edited by Cherríe Moraga and Gloria Anzaldúa, two activists, artists, and intellectuals who self-identify as Chicanas, third world women, and lesbian feminists, *This Bridge* was compiled in part as an immanent critique of lesbian feminism for its failure to live up to what the editors saw as its radical antiracist potential. As Moraga explains in the preface:

> Lesbianism is supposed to be about connection. What drew me to politics was my love of women. . . . I was so driven to work on this anthology . . . to deal with racism because I couldn't stand being separated from other women. Because I took my lesbianism that seriously. . . . The deepest political tragedy I have experienced is how with such grace, such blind faith, this commitment to women in the feminist movement grew to be exclusive and reactionary. I call out my white sisters on this. (1981, xiv, xvii)

The "white sisters" Moraga and Anzaldúa compiled *This Bridge* to "call out" are lesbian feminists:

Do I dare speak of the boredom setting in among the white sector of the feminist movement? What was once a cutting edge, growing dull in the too easy solution to our problems of hunger of soul and stomach. The lesbian separatist utopia? No thank you, sisters. I can't prepare myself a revolutionary packet that makes no sense when I leave the white suburbs of Watertown, Massachusetts and take the T-line to Black Roxbury. . . . I am a lesbian. I want a movement that helps me make some sense of the trip from Watertown to Roxbury, from white to black. I love women the entire way, beyond a doubt. (xiii–xiv)

As these passages make clear, the intersectional antiracist analysis for which *This Bridge* is rightly celebrated is inextricably bound up with what is named here as explicitly lesbian feminist desires and commitments. Like the Combahee River Collective statement, *This Bridge* is a groundbreaking contribution to Black and third world feminism as well as a critical intervention into the sexual politics of lesbian feminism.[6]

As these examples show, the tendency to treat Black and third world feminism as though they were somehow separate from feminist politicizations of sex and sexuality is ahistorical and misleading. Black and third world feminism and feminist sexual politics and thought are not discrete and isolable phenomenon. In fact, many Black and third world feminists were as deeply concerned with the politics of sex and sexuality as they were with the politics of race and class. For lesbian feminists of color like Gloria Anzaldúa, Cheryl Clarke, Audre Lorde, Cherríe Moraga, and Barbara Smith, their lesbian feminism animated and infused their antiracism, and vice versa. They repudiated lesbian separatism as an insufficient tactic for addressing interlocking oppressions of race, gender, sex, and class, but this should not be mistaken for a repudiation of lesbian feminism or sexual politics more generally. The lesbian feminism they envisioned was one in which a fiercely plenitudinous love for women spurred lesbians to fight against the oppressive structures that kept women of different races, classes, and sexual orientations apart, both sexually and politically. By theorizing the racist and classist limitations of lesbian separatism and formulating antiracist and anticapitalist alternatives, Black and third world feminists made vital contributions to lesbian feminism and feminist sexual politics and thought.

Now to move beyond these general observations to specifics. It is not only the case that linkages between Black and third world feminism and the sex wars are evident at the broad level that I have been describing; these currents in feminist politics and history also overlapped and intersected in much more clear-cut and straightforward ways. In fact, many Black and third world feminists—including leading luminaries like Patricia Hill Collins, Audre Lorde, Cherríe Moraga, Barbara Smith, and Alice Walker, as well as less familiar figures like Tracey Gardner, Rose Mason, Tina Portillo, Karen Sims, Luisah Teish, and Mirtha Quintanales—engaged directly in sex wars debates about pornography, S&M, butch/femme roles, and commercial sex. Some contributed to antipornography feminist anthologies. Some contributed to sex-radical feminist anthologies. Some participated in important sex wars–era conferences, workshops, and events, including the notorious Barnard conference. While their interventions have for the most part been set outside of the history of the sex wars by the catfight narrative, Black and third world feminists engaged directly in these debates in diverse and significant ways, staking out a variety of positions that exceed simplistic pro-sex/anti-sex, sex-positive/ sex-negative, or pleasure/danger frames.

Before proceeding to a detailed exploration of some specific Black and third world feminist interventions into the sex wars, I must pause to offer a point of clarification: I am not arguing here for the existence of some single Black and third world feminist position to which all feminists of color active in the sex wars debates subscribed. Just as the liberal theorists and activists described in previous chapters did not all cohere behind a single position or platform but rather engaged strategically and in a variety of distinctively liberal ways with both sex-radical and antipornography feminist ideas, so feminists of color during the sex wars did not unite behind any single position or platform. Rather, these heterogenous thinkers and activists offered analyses that differed in many respects, all the while retaining a distinctive concern with what we today call intersectionality but what feminists before 1989 knew by a variety of names, including "interlocking" or "simultaneous" oppressions, "multiple jeopardy," and "the many headed demon of oppression."[7] What Black and third world feminists brought to the sex wars, no matter where they fell on the pleasure/danger continuum that so dominates and distorts our contemporary thinking about these events, was a distinctive concern for the ways in which dynamics of race and class play out in the domain of sex and sexuality, as well as a heightened awareness of how women of color were being sidelined within discussions of sex and sexuality that were transpiring within the predominantly white women's movement at the time.

In this respect, my interpretation of Black and third world feminist involvement in the sex wars differs significantly from that offered by another scholar who has engaged with some of the same texts and interventions that I explore here, Celine Parreñas Shimizu. Shimizu argues that during the sex wars, feminists of color united behind a single position that she calls race positive sexuality. According to Shimizu, race positive sexuality "emerges from the literature of Cherríe Moraga, Audre Lorde, and others who present pleasure, pain, and trauma simultaneously in ways that embrace the liberating possibilities of sexuality while also acknowledging the risks of reifying perversity and pathology traditionally ascribed to women of color in popular culture" (2007, 145). "Race positive sexuality," Shimizu continues, "connects gender and sexuality in pornography to slavery and colonial history while keeping open its anti-racist and sex-positive potentialities"; it "argues for the need to acknowledge how sexuality can be pleasurable, powerful, and painful simultaneously" (145). Race positive sexuality is, in short, a kind of third way or middle path that feminists of color staked out during the sex wars between the sex-negative and sex-positive poles occupied by white feminists.

While Shimizu's theory of race positive sexuality has much to offer contemporary feminist thinking about race, gender, and sexual representation, as a hermeneutics for interpreting the work of Black and third world feminists engaged in the sex wars, it is lacking. Consider Audre Lorde, for example, one of two feminists Shimizu directly credits for developing the position of race positive sexuality. Audre Lorde was a Black lesbian feminist poet, novelist, theorist, and activist. She was a member of the Combahee River Collective and a cofounder, along with Barbara Smith, Cherríe Moraga, and others, of Kitchen Table: Women of Color Press.

Lorde was also involved in feminist antiviolence work, helping to found the Women's Coalition of St. Croix, an organization serving survivors of intimate partner violence on the island of St. Croix in the U.S. Virgin Islands.

During the sex wars, Lorde played an active and influential role in the antipornography feminist movement. Her most important contribution to antipornography feminism is her essay "The Uses of the Erotic: The Erotic as Power." While Shimizu (2007) reads this essay as a rejection of antipornography feminism's categorical condemnation of pornography in favor of a more moderate view open to pornography's feminist and antiracist "potentialities," the essay's content as well as its context and reception militate against such a reading. For starters, Lorde presented "The Uses of the Erotic" at the first national Feminist Perspectives on Pornography conference held in San Francisco in November 1978.[8] Organized by Women Against Violence in Pornography and Media (WAVPM), this conference featured contributions from some of the antipornography feminist movement's leading theorists and intellectuals, including Kathleen Barry, Susan Brownmiller, and Andrea Dworkin. Lorde's essay was later anthologized in 1980 alongside contributions from these other figures in *Take Back the Night*. Lorde's decision to present her essay at a conference organized by an antipornography feminist organization and to then allow that essay to be anthologized alongside work by other antipornography feminists in a collection edited by the national coordinator of an antipornography feminist organization are strong indications that Lorde endorsed antipornography feminism's bold and unequivocal stance against pornography and eschewed the "race positive sexuality" Shimizu ascribes to her.[9]

The content of Lorde's essay offers further evidence that Lorde would have rejected Shimizu's efforts to locate some feminist and antiracist potential in pornography by way of the concept of race positive sexuality. "The Uses of the Erotic" begins with Lorde feting "the erotic" as a "source of power" that might supply "energy for change" to women and other oppressed people (1980, 295). However, as the essay unfolds, Lorde makes it clear that "the erotic," as she conceptualizes it, is something akin to a feeling of enjoyment and creative fulfillment that is not to be confused with what she calls "the superficially erotic," "sensation," "sex," and "the pornographic" (295–96). "The erotic," Lorde writes, "has often been misnamed by men and used against women. It has been made into the confused, the trivial, the psychotic, the plasticized sensation. For this reason, we have often turned away from the exploration and consideration of the erotic as a source of power and information, confusing it with its opposite, the pornographic. But pornography is a direct denial of the power of the erotic, for it represents the suppression of true feeling. Pornography emphasizes sensation without feeling" (296). As this passage makes clear, the erotic and the pornographic are distinct in Lorde's view—so distinct, in fact, that she goes on to characterize them as "two diametrically opposed uses of the sexual" (297). So bent is Lorde on distinguishing the erotic from the pornographic that she almost goes so far as to sever any connection between the erotic and the sexual whatsoever. For example, of the various "erotically satisfying experience[s]" Lorde describes in the essay (i.e., "dancing, building a bookcase, writing a poem, examining an idea," "painting a back fence," and engaging in the "deep participation" of political activism), virtually all of them are nonsexual in character (298–300). Emphasizing this capacity of the erotic to transcend the sexual, Lorde declares, "There is, for me, no difference between writing a good poem and moving into sunlight against the body of a woman I love" (299).[10]

As this brief look at Lorde's "The Uses of the Erotic" makes clear, characterizing Lorde as a theorist of race positive sexuality imputes to Lorde a perspective that she clearly would have rejected. Lorde's project was not to recuperate pornography for what Shimizu calls its "anti-racist and sex-positive potentialities"; her project was to criticize pornography as antithetical to true eroticism and the political, economic, sexual, and spiritual equality she believed it might engender if unleashed. Shimizu's concept of race positive sexuality is a better fit for Cherríe Moraga, the other feminist of color she credits specifically by name as one of the originators of this concept; I will explore Moraga's distinctive contributions to the sex wars later in this chapter. The point I want to emphasize here is that Black and third world feminists like Lorde and Moraga staked out substantially different positions during the sex wars, and any attempt to lump them together under the aegis of one single perspective is bound to confuse and obscure more than illuminate.

Rather than follow Shimizu in identifying a single Black and third world feminist position in the sex wars debates, my goal in this chapter is to attend to the full gamut of positions feminists of color occupied during the sex wars while simultaneously marking out what made these positions distinct from those of white feminists engaged in these debates. As I will show, whether they were critical of pornography and S&M like Patricia Hill Collins and Alice Walker, or whether they were willing to extend the benefit of the doubt to these controversial sexual practices like Cherríe Moraga and Mirtha Quintanales, Black and third world feminists stood apart from white feminists on all sides during the sex wars in one key respect: they rejected what Deborah King (1988) calls the monistic politics characteristic of many liberation movements, including feminism, and attempted to carve out space within feminist sexual politics for grappling with the intersections of gender, race, sex, and class that characterize the lives, including the sexual lives, of women of color.[11]

My effort to maintain this balance between recognizing the distinctiveness of Black and third world feminist contributions to the sex wars and refusing to impute to them a false and ahistorical homogeneity is informed by Chela Sandoval's theorization of Black and third world feminism as defined by a practice of differential consciousness. Sandoval describes "differential consciousness" as a mode of oppositional politics that is "mobile," "kinetic," "cinematographic," kaleidoscopic, and tactical (1991, 3). It refuses to limit itself to any single overarching oppositional strategy or approach, be it liberalism (appealing to the subordinate group's similarity to the dominant group), separatism (appealing to the subordinate group's difference from the dominant group), or supremacism (appealing to the subordinate group's moral, intellectual, spiritual, and physical superiority over the dominant group). Unlike resistance movements that rigidly commit themselves to only one of these oppositional strategies, Black and third world feminists practicing differential consciousness, Sandoval argues, shift between and creatively combine them as circumstances require. Like Machiavelli's Prince, whose *virtù* inheres in his flexibility, adaptability, and readiness to transform himself in response to the whims of *fortuna,* Sandoval's third world feminists are agile and resourceful, unrestrained by abstract doctrine or ideology. Embracing the Emersonian wisdom that "a foolish consistency is the hobgoblin of little minds," third world feminists are guided only by their desire to contest the intersecting oppressions confronting women of color in a capitalist, white-supremacist, and heteropatriarchal social order. Black and third world feminists' varied and even contradictory interventions into the sex wars are an almost ideal display of Sandovalian differential consciousness. Black and third world feminists did not limit themselves to one side or position in the sex wars; they did not align themselves uncritically with existing white feminist groups, positions, or platforms; they were not simply sex-positive or sex-negative, pro-sex or anti-sex, anti-pornography or sex radical. Rather, they intervened in the sex wars tactically and in a variety of ways, always with an eye to furthering their overarching goal of disrupting monism wherever it appeared and offering in its stead a sexual politics more attentive to the intersections of sex, gender, race, and class and the women of color who live their lives there.

BEYOND OBJECTIFICATION: TOWARD
AN INTERSECTIONAL ANTIPORNOGRAPHY FEMINISM

Having clarified my approach, I will proceed now to describing some specific instances of feminists of color intervening directly in the sex wars debates to disrupt the monism of both antipornography and sex-radical feminism. I will begin with the work of Black and third world antipornography feminists who pressed beyond antipornography feminism's monistic critique of pornography centered on pornography's gender-based harms to embrace an intersectional analysis equally attuned to pornography's role in bolstering white supremacy.

To appreciate the challenge feminists of color posed to monistic antipornography feminism, one must first appreciate just how prevalent monistic thinking about pornography's harms was among antipornography feminists during the sex wars. In *Battling Pornography,* Carolyn

Bronstein documents several instances of gender monism at work within the antipornography feminist movement. Perhaps the most vivid example Bronstein describes comes from an interview with Judith Reisman, then a graduate student and antipornography organizer in Ohio, published in the *NewsPage,* the official newsletter of WAVPM.[12] In this interview, Reisman encourages women to set aside their differences and focus on combatting their shared enemy: pornography. "A coalition of all women needs to be established, regardless of race, color, creed or political persuasion," Reisman insists. "Disagreements on other issues can be dealt with when fewer of us are being murdered, beaten, tortured and raped" (Bronstein 2011, 270). This statement is a textbook example of monistic antipornography feminism. By insisting that the sexual violence incited by pornography should be women's top priority and that action on "other issues" should be postponed, Reisman centers the perspectives of economically secure white women who are vulnerable to sexual violence, but far less vulnerable than poor women or women of color to "other issues" such as racism or poverty. Reisman's gender monism also shines forth in another part of this same *NewsPage* interview that Bronstein does not excerpt. "There are always those who need to dehumanize others and who will exploit the weakest group at hand," Reisman claims. "Since contemporary culture prohibits exploitation and denigration on the basis of race, creed, color or religion, it would appear that the only 'group' at hand is sexual—the female sex specifically" (1978, 76). Reisman's naive presumption here that racism is a thing of the past and that the group most vulnerable to exploitation and denigration today (Reisman said this in 1979) is "the female sex," who, she presumes, is targeted exclusively on the basis of gender, is monism at its most glaring and myopic.

Another example of antipornography feminist gender monism documented by Bronstein concerns the educational slide show produced by WAP. In a pre-Internet world in which pornography was far less accessible than it is today, slide shows featuring examples of pornography accompanied by scripts elucidating pornography's harms served as important consciousness-raising and recruitment tools for the antipornography feminist movement. In 1979 alone, WAP's slideshow was presented 225 times, reaching an audience of thousands all across the United States

(Bronstein 2011, 216). In 1982, WAP's national headquarters received a letter regarding their slide show from a woman who claimed to be "the only Black member" of the Cleveland chapter of Women Against Violence Against Women. For over a year, the letter writer explains, the Cleveland WAVAW had been presenting WAP's slide show all over northeastern Ohio. She was writing now to express her disappointment with the monistic analysis of pornography offered in WAP's official script. While WAP's slide show included five pornographic images featuring Black women, the script failed to question why Black women were represented almost exclusively in "hardcore," as opposed to "softcore," pornography, and why they are shown almost invariably as "base, brutal, sadistic, savage, and willing to submit to any sexual practice" (273). "Why," the Cleveland WAVAW member inquires, "does the slide show script avoid the implication of active white racism in the production as well as consumption of such materials?" (273). With an analysis only of pornography's sexism and not its racism, the Cleveland WAVAW member explains, WAP's slide show leaves attendees with the false impression that hard-core pornography featuring Black women is produced to cater to the baser and more extreme sexual appetites of Black men, when in fact its primary appeal is to white men's racist nostalgia for a time when they could inflict sexual humiliation onto the bodies of enslaved Black women with impunity. With its limited analysis of pornography only through the lens of gender and not race, WAP's slide show offers a textbook example of monistic antipornography feminist thinking.[13]

Not all antipornography feminists embraced a gender monism as egregious as that evident in these first two examples. Consider, for example, Andrea Dworkin. In *Pornography: Men Possessing Women* ([1981] 1991), Dworkin's essential statement of her antipornography feminist theory, Dworkin devotes a section of the concluding chapter, "Whores," to an analysis of representations of Black women in pornography.[14] This section opens with one of Dworkin's signature, numbingly detailed play-by-play summaries of a pornographic work. The work, a book entitled *Black Fashion Model,* tells the story of the sexual humiliation of the eponymous Black fashion model by a white man and his two accomplices, a white woman photographer and a Black police officer. Unlike many of her antipornography feminist peers, Dworkin is keenly attuned to the critical work race performs in this pornographic text. "All the sex in *Black Fashion Model* is the standard stuff of pornography: rape, bondage, humiliation, pain," Dworkin writes. "All the values are the standard values of pornography: the excitement of humiliation, the joy of pain, the pleasure of abuse. . . . The valuation of the woman is the standard valuation ('a wanton, lusty *woman!*'), except that her main sexual part is her skin, its color" ([1981] 1991, 215, emphasis added). According to Dworkin, pornographic representations of Black women differ from pornographic representations of white women because in pornography featuring Black women, "the genital shame of any woman is transferred to the black woman's skin" (216). "The black female's skin reveals her," Dworkin explains, "Her skin is cunt; it has that sexual value in and of itself. . . . She has no part that is not cunt. . . . As long as her skin shows, her cunt shows" (215–16). "This is the specific sexual value of the black woman in pornography in the United States, a race-bound society fanatically committed to the sexual devaluing of black skin perceived as a sex organ and a sexual nature," Dworkin concludes. Connecting the sexualization of Black women's skin in pornography to the entrenched racial hierarchies that have defined America since its founding, Dworkin pronounces, "The imperial United States cannot maintain its racist system without its black whores, its bottom, the carnal underclass. The sexualization of race within a racist system is a prime purpose and consequence of pornography" (216–17).

Two aspects of Dworkin's analysis of *Black Fashion Model* distinguish Dworkin from her more conspicuously monistic antipornography feminist peers. First, Dworkin perceives that the appeal of pornography does not derive solely from the fantasies of male dominance it indulges, but rather from the fantasies of a specifically racialized male dominance. *Black Fashion Model* works as pornography, Dworkin recognizes, not only because a woman is sexually humiliated by a man, but also because a Black woman is sexually humiliated by a white man. Race, in Dworkin's analysis, is not incidental to pornography; it is among its most potent elements.

A second move Dworkin makes that distinguishes her from more monistic strains of antipornography feminism is situating pornography in the context of histories, practices, and institutions of white supremacy.

For example, Dworkin identifies the peculiar sexualized devaluation of Black women's skin in pornography as a legacy not only of men's historic domination over women but also of race-based slavery and the social and economic marginalization of Black women in the present day. "This meaning of the black woman's skin [in pornography] is revealed in the historical usage of her, even as it developed from the historical usage of her," Dworkin writes. "This valuation of the black woman is real, especially vivid in urban areas where she is used as a street whore extravagantly and without conscience. Poverty forces her; but it is the sexual valuation of her skin that predetermines her poverty and permits the simple, righteous use of her as a whore" ([1981] 1991, 217). In Dworkin's analysis, racism and sexism work together in pornography and beyond to keep Black women impoverished, oppressed, and ripe for especially brutal forms of sexual exploitation by men of all races.

As her reading of *Black Fashion Model* shows, Dworkin displayed a cognizance of pornography's racial dynamics that eluded many of her white antipornography feminist peers. However, it remains clear that Dworkin's more race-conscious antipornography feminism never fully escaped the orbit of gender monism.[15] On the one hand, Dworkin explicitly connects representations of Black women in pornography to the maintenance of both male supremacy and white supremacy. This dual concern with multiple systems of oppression and how they interact and intertwine is a far cry from a monistic focus on only the oppression of women qua women. On the other hand, Dworkin insists that what distinguishes representations of Black women in pornography from representations of white women in pornography is the sexual value assigned to Black women's skin. In Dworkin's schema, the sexualization of white women in pornography is limited to specific body parts (e.g., breasts, buttocks, vulva) and is thus partial, and to some extent restrained. By contrast, the sexualization of Black women in pornography is all-pervasive. As Dworkin puts it, "The black model need not model naked to be sex; any display of her skin is sex" ([1981] 1991, 216). Within this emphasis on the sexualization of Black women in pornography—on the reduction of Black women's skin to "cunt," as Dworkin so bluntly puts it—traces of gender monism linger. What Dworkin is essentially saying is that the same thing that happens to white women in pornography (dehumanization through sexualization) happens to Black women too, but more harshly and more relentlessly. In Dworkin's framework, the difference between Black women's oppression and white women's oppression is one of degree, not kind. White women have it bad; Black women have it worse. In this way, Black women figure in Dworkin's antipornography feminist analysis as adjuncts and accessories. Their sexualization in pornography, compounded as it is by racism, is used as a sort of rhetorical flourish to underscore and accentuate the sexualization of all women (read: white women) in pornography. Thus, Dworkin's discussion of pornography's racial dynamics is ultimately in the service of her monistic goal of making pornography's oppressive gender dynamics all the more visible and atrocious.

For Dworkin, race in pornography is ultimately always really about gender. One can see this monistic thinking even more vividly in another examination of a pornographic work featuring nonwhite bodies that Dworkin offers in *Pornography: Men Possessing Women*. The work splayed out on Dworkin's dissection slab this time is a magazine spread. Putatively set in a Mexican jail, the spread features what the accompanying narration describes as a Mexican woman, Consuela, her "Yankee boyfriend," and a Mexican policeman ([1981] 1991, 151–52). In a series of ten photographs, Consuela is depicted having painful anal sex with the Mexican policeman in a bid to free her Anglo boyfriend, who is locked in a jail cell. Once the policeman passes in a stupor of drunkenness and sexual satiety, Consuela has tender and conventional vaginal sex with her boyfriend in his cell. According to Dworkin, these images are less about "the hot-blooded señorita" positioned prominently at their center and more about "the racial and sexual tension between the two men" (155–56). "The racially degraded male," which in this set of images is the Mexican policeman, Dworkin observes, is consistently depicted as superior to the white male "in terms of brute sexual force" (157). His alleged "brute and bestial" sexual nature, Dworkin continues, "is precisely what licenses violence against [the racially degraded male] in a racist value system" (156). This link between the savage, hypermasculine sexuality imposed on men of color and the racist violence perpetrated against them prompts for Dworkin the following question: Why do men of color accept the role of the Mexican policeman?

Why do they embrace the aggressive hypermasculinity assigned to them by white supremacy and collaborate with their oppressors in the degradation of women, including women of their own race? Dworkin's answer to this question is what she calls "the bribe" (157). "The racially degraded male collaborates in the degradation of women—all women," Dworkin explains, "—because he is offered something important for his complicity: an acknowledgement of a sexuality of which the racially superior male is envious" (158). The man of color, Dworkin continues, "cannot see his way clear to making an alliance with women—even the women of his peer group—based on sexual justice because he has accepted the bribe: masculinity belongs to him" (156–57).

Dworkin's concept of the bribe, the mechanism that rivets Black and brown men's loyalty to systems of both white supremacy and male supremacy, shows that in Dworkin's analysis, sex and gender ultimately trump race. The man of color accepts the bribe, Dworkin problematically assumes, because he ranks his manhood above all else, even his racial identity and dignity as a person of color. As was the case in Dworkin's analysis of *Black Fashion Model,* solidarity between the races on the basis of gender through sex (in the case of white and Black women, solidarity through their shared status as cunts and whores; in the case of white and Black men, solidarity through their shared status as omnipotent masculine purveyors of brute sexual force) is what this scene in the Mexican jail is really about. Race is present in Dworkin's variant of monistic antipornography feminism, but it is always cast in a secondary, supporting role. The real drama of pornography, on Dworkin's account, is a drama of sex and gender.

While Dworkin's analysis of race and pornography marks a significant advance over the work of many of her white antipornography feminist peers, Dworkin's antipornography feminism remains, in the final analysis, locked within the ambit of the same gender monism that bedeviled the antipornography feminist movement more generally. Pornography's racism was simply not Dworkin's primary concern. This is why, even in her magnum opus on pornography, she discusses it for only a few scattered pages and by way of only a handful of examples. Although Dworkin made important strides in thinking through pornography's racial dynamics, it would be left to antipornography feminists of color like Patricia Hill Collins, Tracey Gardner, Luisah Teish, and Alice Walker to fully divest antipornography feminism of its gender monism and place pornography's racism at the heart of antipornography feminist analysis.

That Black and third world feminists would align themselves with the cause of antipornography feminism is, on one level, surprising. When we survey some of the earliest statements by women of color engaged in the women's liberation movement, we find a profound skepticism, even wariness, of the very aspects of women's liberation that would eventually give rise to antipornography feminism. For example, in 1969, in a pathbreaking pamphlet entitled "Double Jeopardy: To Be Black and Female," Frances Beale, a founding member of the SNCC Women's Liberation Committee and the Third World Women's Alliance, criticizes white women's liberationists for their excessive concern with sexual objectification. "If the white [women's liberation] groups do not realize that they are in fact, fighting capitalism and racism, we do not have common bonds," Beale declares. "If they do not realize that the reasons for their condition lie in a debilitating economic and social system, and not simply that men get a vicarious pleasure out of 'consuming their bodies for exploitative reasons,' . . . then we cannot unite with them around common grievances or even discuss these groups in a serious manner, because they're completely irrelevant to black women in particular or to the black struggle in general" ([1969] 2008, 174–75). Beale's point here is that women, particularly women of color, are oppressed not only or even primarily through processes of sexual exploitation, but rather through exploitation as workers in the low-wage, low-status jobs to which they are relegated in a racist capitalist economy. Beale does not altogether dismiss sexual objectification and exploitation as legitimate feminist concerns. As she herself observes, the Black woman's "physical image has been maliciously maligned; she has been sexually molested and abused by the white colonizer" (168). However, Beale and other Black and third world women active in the women's liberation movement were wary of a monistic feminism too narrowly focused on sexual objectification at the expense of other forms of sexist oppression that primarily affect nonwhite working-class women.

The Black and third world feminists who eventually did take up the antipornography feminist cause did so with this characteristic wariness of feminism's gender monism in mind. Although they were unambiguously opposed to pornography, they refused to follow their monistic antipornography feminist peers in singling out sexual objectification as pornography's primary and universal harm to all women. Pornography, they insisted, harmed women in racially differentiated and specific ways. Reaching beyond Dworkin, who argued that Black women, like white women, were sexualized in pornography, but in a more totalizing and inescapable way because of their race, Black and third world antipornography feminists insisted that the oppression of Black women in pornography differed not merely in degree from that of white women, but also in kind. As artist and activist Luisah Teish puts it in "A Quiet Subversion," an essay she contributed to the anthology *Take Back the Night,* "The pornography industry's exploitation of the Black woman's body is qualitatively different from that of the white woman. While white women are pictured as pillow-soft pussy willows, the stereotype of the Black 'dominatrix' portrays the Black woman as ugly, sadistic, and animalistic, undeserving of human affection" (1980, 117). Alice Walker seconds Teish's point in a short story entitled "Coming Apart" included in the same anthology. "Where white women are depicted in pornography as 'objects,'" Walker writes, "Black women are depicted as animals. Where white women are at least depicted as human bodies if not beings, Black women are depicted as shit" (1980, 103).[16] When Black and third world feminists like Teish and Walker point to pornography's racist harms, they point to more than just the sexual objectification of nonwhite women; they indicate portrayals of nonwhite women in pornography as lower than sexual objects, as revolting and degraded subhuman beasts. As Patricia Hill Collins notes in her discussion of racism in pornography, "As [sexual] objects White women become creations of culture—in this case, the mind of White men—using the materials of nature—in this case, uncontrolled female sexuality. In contrast, as animals Black women receive no such redeeming dose of culture and remain open to the type of exploitation visited on nature overall" (1993, 367).

Members of the antipornography feminist collective Lesbians of Colour make a similar point in their contribution to *Good Girls/Bad Girls:*

Sex Trade Workers and Feminists Face to Face, an anthology that grew out of a conference held in Toronto in November 1985 entitled "Challenging Our Images: The Politics of Prostitution and Pornography." While some women are portrayed in pornography as the ultimate sex objects, Lesbians of Colour notes, others "have been so severely stereotyped as ugly, savage, poor, and drunk that the presentation of their beauty and attractiveness is inconceivable to the producers and consumers of pornography" (1987, 60). This is why, Lesbians of Colour continues, "*Penthouse* and *Playboy* do not include Native women" (60). Whereas a monistic antipornography feminism like Dworkin's perceives only the similarities and continuities in how white and nonwhite women are represented in pornography, Black and third world feminists like Lesbians of Colour emphasize the differences and discontinuities. Not all women are depicted in pornography as sex objects, these Black and third world antipornography feminists note; some are marked off by their race as too lowly and loathsome even for that. The figuration of nonwhite women as objects not of lust and desire but of disgust and revulsion is a harm that pornography visits uniquely on women of color. Only by breaking with the gender monism of mainstream antipornography feminism are Black and third world feminists able to see this race-specific harm and name it.

Another race-specific harm of pornography emphasized by Black and third world antipornography feminists concerns not only women but also men of color. In "Coming Apart," Alice Walker deftly unpacks how she and other Black and third world antipornography feminists believe Black men are harmed by the dehumanization of Black women in pornography. In this story, a Black woman initiates a conversation with her husband, a Black man, about his use of pornography. At first the husband is resistant to his wife's questioning. His enjoyment of images of "white blondes and brunettes . . . with elastic waists and inviting eyes" and "a brownskin woman" laying "twisted and contorted" at the feet of a "well-dressed Black man . . . so that she looks like a human turd" is harmless, he insists (1980 95–96). However, after reading and discussing with his wife the work of several Black and third world antipornography feminists, including Audre Lorde, Luisah Teish, and Tracey Gardner, the husband becomes more receptive to his wife's concerns. Walker describes the husband's shift in consciousness as he reflects on the connection Tracey Gardner posits between lynching and pornography as a tool for keeping "uppity" women in their place:

> [He] thinks, for the first time in his life, that when he is not thinking of fucking white women . . . , he is very often thinking of ways to degrade them. Then he thinks that, given his history as a Black man in America, it is not surprising that he has himself confused fucking them *with* degrading them. But what does that say about how he sees himself. . . . He begins to feel sick. For he realizes that he has bought some if not all of the advertisements about women, Black and white. And further, inevitably, he has bought the advertisements about himself. In pornography the Black man is portrayed as being capable of fucking anything . . . even a piece of shit. (1980, 103)

After this initial realization that pornography feeds his own internalized racism and misogyny, the husband has a second insight. Pornography, he realizes, has alienated him both sexually and politically from Black women, including his wife. Walker describes this slow-dawning epiphany: "Those movies and magazines (whose characters' and pursuits are irrelevant or antithetical to his concerns) . . . have insinuated themselves between him and his wife so that the totality of her, her entire corporeal reality is alien to him. . . . Even to clutch her in lust is to automatically shut his eyes. Shut his eyes, and . . . he chuckles bitterly . . . dream of England. For years he has been fucking himself" (103–4).

Walker's aim in "Coming Apart" is to dramatize the toll that dehumanizing representations of Black women in pornography exact on both Black women and Black men. This toll, as Walker represents it, is psychic, emotional, sexual, and also, importantly, political. Walker accentuates the political dimensions of pornography's racist and sexist messages in the following passage, where she records the husband's thoughts as he berates his wife for sympathizing with the antipornography feminist movement and being "a 'women's liber'" and "a 'white women's lackey'": "There is a way in which, in some firmly repressed corner of his mind, he considers his wife to be *still* Black, whereas he feels himself to have moved to some other plane. . . . He has detached himself from his own blackness in attempting to identify Black women only by their sex. . . . *Is it because he can now ogle white women in freedom and [his wife] has no similar outlet of expression that he thinks of her as still Black and himself as something else?*" (1980, 99–100). Walker's point here is subtle but significant, for it marks a key difference between her more intersectional antipornography feminism and the monistic antipornography feminism of a thinker like Andrea Dworkin. Among pornography's most consequential race-specific harms, Walker contends, is its subversion of intraracial, intergender political solidarity between Black men and Black women. By habituating Black men to view white women as sexual objects of great value and Black women as objects of disgust and disdain, pornography in effect detaches Black men from their blackness, destroying possibilities for political solidarity between Black men and women. As Frances Beale underscores, the destruction of this solidarity has dire consequences for the project of Black liberation, for neither Black men nor Black women can win the battle against white supremacy alone: "All the resources that the black community can muster up must be channeled into the struggle" ([1969] 1995, 176). This critical analysis of pornography as a threat to Black political solidarity and Black liberation is a distinctive contribution Black and third world feminists made to antipornography feminist politics and thought.[17]

Walker's conceptualization of pornography as "a race/gender system that entraps everyone," Black men and Black women alike, is echoed in the work of Lesbians of Colour (Collins 1993, 103). In the discussion of racist stereotypes typically found in pornography, Lesbians of Colour singles out for particularly close scrutiny the stereotypes pornography purveys about Black men. "Another stereotype we have to deal with is the Black man as rapist," Lesbians of Colour writes. "It's bad enough being male and not being able to resist a woman, but it's even worse when you're a Black male, because then you've got no hope of stopping yourself! And the flip side of that coin is how Black women's sexuality is portrayed. If they're saying that about Black men, what are they saying about Black women?" (1987, 59). Like Walker in "Coming Apart," Lesbians of Colour insists here that both Black women and Black men have a stake in pornography's racist and sexist representations. "Pornography is not just a battered image," Lesbians of Colour notes. "Pornography is about whether we have schools or not. It's about whether we are able to have access to jobs or not. These images promote stereotypes that get translated into very real situations. We are faced with stereotypes that Black people are lazy, that West Indians are lazy, that we only like parties, that we only like drinking rum, that we're not capable of organizing a high school, that the kids who come to it are going to steal, loot, and plunder" (1987, 63). Because pornography adversely affects communities of color as a whole, Lesbians of Colour envisions an intraracial, intergender coalition of Black women and Black men coming together to oppose pornography's racism and sexism. This vision is a far cry from the monistic antipornography feminism of a thinker like Dworkin. Such a broad-based coalition against pornography is impossible for Dworkin to imagine because she assumes that gender will always trump race and that men of color will always accept the bribe of hypermasculinity offered them within the racial/sexual imaginary of white supremacist patriarchy. During the sex wars, Black and third world antipornography feminists rejected this monistic analysis in favor of a critique of pornography that highlighted not only its sexism but also its racism, and that envisioned a place for both women and men of color in the struggle against it.

"PLAYED BETWEEN WHITE HANDS": TOWARD AN INTERSECTIONAL SEX-RADICAL FEMINISM

While some Black and third world feminists engaged in the sex wars to disrupt monistic thinking among the predominantly white antipornography feminist movement, others intervened to center the lives and concerns of women of color within sex-radical feminist contexts. To appreciate the monism that spurred this set of Black and third world feminist interventions, it is helpful to consider the work of one of sex-radical feminism's most influential theorists and activists: Gayle Rubin.

Before she was a cofounder of the San Francisco–based lesbian S&M group Samois, and before the publication of "Thinking Sex: Notes for a Radical Theory of the Politics of Sexuality" made her the intellectual lodestar of the sex-radical feminist movement, Gayle Rubin was an undergraduate student at the University of Michigan caught up in the radical political ferment engulfing that campus in the late 1960s.[18] Rubin's first forays into radical political activism centered on opposition to the Vietnam War, but in 1968, her work on draft resistance put her in contact with a network of radical women on the University of Michigan's campus who banded together to form the Thursday Night Group, an early women's liberation and consciousness-raising group. During this period of budding feminist consciousness, Rubin published an essay on women's liberation in the *Argus,* a biweekly underground newspaper published in Ann Arbor, Michigan, entitled "Woman as Nigger" (1969). As its title indicates, the essay is informed by a monistic vision of women as a homogenous group defined solely by their gender that was widespread among white women's liberationists of the period. Consider, for example, the following passage: "The basic premise of women's liberation is that women are an exploited class, like black people. . . . In other words, women suffer from some form of racism. . . . I started thinking seriously about the 'woman as nigger' . . . at a training session on racism held by People Against Racism. As the speaker explained the dynamics of black–white interaction, I kept substituting female for black, and was astonished by the similarities" (1969, 230–31). While each line of this passage relies on monistic assumptions (e.g., women are "like Black people," not Black people themselves; women "suffer from some form of racism," not the actual racism that Black people suffer from), Rubin's description of how she "kept substituting female for black, and was astonished by the similarities" in this passage is particularly revealing. By setting up the categories of "female" and "Black" as mutually exclusive, Rubin obscures the existence of Black women, who are, of course, both Black and female, and whose lives and experiences attest not only to the similarities or differences between oppression on account of one's gender and oppression on account of one's race, but to the intersecting and co-constitutive natures of these oppressions. Rubin's central claim in "Woman as Nigger" is not the intersectional feminist point that gender oppression and racial oppression are deeply intertwined and interrelated, inflected by and imbricated with one another in the lives of women of color; her claim is that gender oppression is like racial oppression, that being a "woman" is like being a "nigger." From the vantage point of Rubin's nascent and glaringly monistic feminism, all the women are white, all the Blacks are men, and racism is relevant to feminist analysis only insofar as it can be used as an analogy to illuminate the oppression of presumptively white women on account of their gender.

Rubin wrote "Woman as Nigger" during the earliest days of the women's liberation movement, while she was either a sophomore or a junior in college. Had Rubin abandoned the monistic thinking displayed in this early work as she matured intellectually and politically, it would hardly be relevant to the case for the monistic character of sex-radical feminist thought that I am building here. However, the monistic thinking evident in "Woman as Nigger" continues to operate even in Rubin's more developed work. For example, in what is arguably Rubin's most influential contribution to feminist theory, "The Traffic in Women: Notes on the Political Economy of Sex" (1975), Rubin offers an account of the origin of women's oppression that echoes the gender monism of "Woman as Nigger." Rejecting the biological determinism of some radical feminist theories and the economic determinism of more Marxist-influenced accounts, Rubin, by way of a syncretic reading of structuralist anthropology and psychoanalytic theory, traces the origins of women's oppression to what she calls the "sex/gender system" (1975, 32). The sex/gender system, Rubin explains, is the "set of arrangements by which the biological raw material of human sex and procreation is shaped by human social intervention, and satisfied in a conventional manner" (28). Just as any human group must "apply its activity to reshaping the natural world in order to clothe, feed, and warm itself," Rubin argues, so must it "reproduce itself from generation to generation" (21). Human groups do this, Rubin maintains, by way of the sex/gender system. While this system need not be "gender stratified" and "oppressive" to perform its vital function of socially coordinating human reproduction, most known examples of sex/gender systems, Rubin notes, have molded human sexuality to suit the imperatives of what she calls "the traffic in women," taking up "females as raw materials and fashion[ing] domesticated women as products" (28). Hence, Rubin concludes, the sex/gender system is "that part of social life which is the locus of the oppression of women" and "sexual minorities" and feminism's political task is to initiate "a revolution in kinship" that will end the "traffic in women" and "reorganize" the "sex/gender system . . . through political action" (33, 28, 52, 54).

The monism of the theory of women's oppression Rubin presents in "The Traffic in Women" (1975) is so conspicuous that Rubin herself would come to repudiate at least one aspect of it within a decade of the essay's original publication. In "Thinking Sex: Notes for a Radical Theory of the Politics of Sexuality" (1984), Rubin takes "The Traffic in Women" to task for subsuming sexuality into gender and making feminism out to be "the privileged site of a theory of sexuality" (307). "Feminism is the theory of gender oppression," Rubin of 1984 explains to Rubin of 1975, "To automatically assume that this makes it the theory of sexual oppression is to fail to distinguish between gender, on the one hand, and erotic desire, on the other" (307). Rubin's insistence in "Thinking Sex" on the distinctiveness of sexuality and gender presents a stark contrast with her claim in "Traffic in Women" that "the suppression of the homosexual component of human sexuality, and by corollary, the oppression of homosexuals, is . . . a product of the same system whose rules and relations oppress women" (1975, 40–41). As Rubin concedes, her earlier work "did not distinguish between lust and gender" but treated "both as modalities of the same underlying social process" (1984, 307). In "Thinking Sex," Rubin rejects this monistic impulse and strives "to separate gender and sexuality analytically to reflect more accurately their separate social existence" (307).[19]

While Rubin concedes the monistic limitations of "The Traffic in Women" with respect to its subsumption of sex into gender, there is another dimension to the monism at work in this essay that Rubin does not address in her later work. "The Traffic in Women" displays the same monistic inattentiveness to the intersections of gender oppression and racial oppression that characterized "Woman as Nigger." This inattentiveness is particularly evident in a passage like the following: "Women are given in marriage, taken in battle, exchanged for favors, sent as tribute, bought, and sold. . . . Men are of course also trafficked—but as slaves, hustlers, athletic stars, serfs, or as some other catastrophic social status, rather than as men. Women are transacted as slaves, serfs, prostitutes, but also simply as women" (1975, 38). The primary purpose of this passage is to highlight the unique gender-based disadvantage women face in a sex/gender system in which they are reduced to the status of objects to be exchanged among men. What this monistic focus on gender overlooks are the distinctive ways in which Black women have been implicated in the traffic in women. Unlike white women, whose experiences provide the tacit foundation for Rubin's analysis, Black women bear the dubious distinction of having been trafficked not "simply as women" (like white women) nor simply as slaves, but as slaves who were both Black and women, and who therefore served a specific function: the replenishment and increase of domestic slave populations through forced reproduction.[20] Rubin's essay-length description of the traffic in women never once mentions the fact that Black women were trafficked in a distinctive manner bound up with both their gender and their race for nearly four centuries. This oversight is a symptom of Rubin's monistic thinking, which marks gender oppression or the oppression of women off as separate and distinct from racial oppression, thereby obscuring the lives and experiences of women of color.

This inability to think gender oppression and racial oppression together as co-occurring and co-constitutive phenomenon is also evident in the feminist utopia Rubin sketches at the climax of "The Traffic in Women." "Ultimately," Rubin writes, "a thoroughgoing feminist revolution would liberate more than women. It would liberate forms of sexual expression, and it would liberate human personality from the straightjacket of gender" (1975, 52). Because "we are not only oppressed *as* women," but "*by having to be* women, or men as the case may be," Rubin continues, "the feminist movement must dream of even more than the elimination of the oppression of women. It must dream of the elimination of obligatory sexualities and sex roles" (54). "The dream I find most compelling," Rubin tells us, "is one of an androgynous and genderless (though not sexless) society, in which one's sexual anatomy is irrelevant to who one is, what one does, and with whom one makes love" (61). This dream of a genderless and polymorphously perverse feminist utopia is, without a doubt, radical. However, it is telling that so grandiose a feminist vision as this, which promises to liberate not only women but also men and sexual minorities from tyrannies as colossal as heteronormativity and the binary gender roles that underpin it, does not explicitly envision the abolition of racial oppression; nor does it broach the ways in which the norms of gender and sexuality it seeks to overthrow are entangled with racist ideas and histories. Even at her most utopian, Rubin fails to envision a world in which not only "the straightjacket of gender" but the braided ropes of all oppressions are loosed, and all are set free to live and love as they please.

It is ironic that an animating impulse of Rubin's "Traffic in Women" appears to have been a desire to escape what Rubin derisively calls "the attempt to extract all of the phenomena of social subordination from the first volume of *Capital*" (1975, 27). Rubin's distaste for the economic monism of Marxist theory propels her to "look for the ultimate locus of women's oppression within the traffic in women, rather than within the traffic merchandise" and to formulate "a conception of the women's movement as analogous to, rather than isomorphic with, the working-class movement, each addressing a different source of human discontent" (37). Unfortunately, in freeing herself from the grip of one form of monism, she plunged headlong into another. Focusing as it does primarily on the oppression women experience on account of their gender, which Rubin believes is intimately connected to the oppression both women and men experience on account of their sexuality, Rubin's "The Traffic in Women" ignores the oppression women experience on account of their race and overlooks the ways in which oppressions of gender, sex, and race intersect and intertwine, particularly in the lives of women of color.

The monism evident in "Woman as Nigger" and "The Traffic in Women" persists in Rubin's work right up through "Thinking Sex," in which Rubin draws an analytical distinction between "feminism," which she continues to define in gender-monist terms as "the theory of gender oppression," and a new "theory of sexual oppression" (1984, 307). Rubin's interest here is not the origins of women's oppression qua women as it was in "The Traffic in Women." Rather, her aim here is to theorize the structure and logic of what she calls "the system of sexual oppression," a "Kafkaesque nightmare" of laws, norms, and social practices designed to punish sexual desires and behaviors that fall outside "the charmed circle" of monogamous "vanilla" heterosexuality (1984, 293, 280–81).

With "Thinking Sex," Rubin effects a clear break with the gender monism that characterized her earlier work. Unfortunately, in disambiguating sex from gender, and in shifting her gaze deliberately away from gender oppression and toward sexual oppression, Rubin does not escape the pull of monism altogether. For example, in "Thinking Sex," Rubin makes the same problematic analogical move she made in "Woman as Nigger," likening the system of sexual oppression to racism and pushing out of view the experiences of sexual minorities of color who are affected not only by a system of sexual oppression that is like racism, but by racism itself. Here is the relevant passage in full:

> [A sexual morality that figures] promiscuous heterosexuality, sadomasochism, fetishism, transsexuality, and cross-generational encounters as unmodulated horrors . . . has more in common with ideologies of racism than with true ethics. . . . Progressives who would be ashamed to display cultural chauvinism in other areas routinely exhibit it toward sexual differences. We have learned to cherish different cultures as unique expressions of human inventiveness rather than as inferior or disgusting habits of savages. We need a similarly anthropological understanding of different sexual cultures. (1984, 283–84)

In this passage, Rubin once again relegates racism to the status of a helpful analogy used in the service of a liberatory project that does not explicitly address racism itself. This passage also exhibits a sanguineness about progress in the fight against "cultural chauvinism" that reflects Rubin's continued inattentiveness to the lives and experiences of people of color. In effect, what Rubin is saying here is that now that tolerance of different cultures, customs, and peoples has won the day, progressives should focus their energies on defending persecuted sexual minorities. Centering the lives and concerns of people of color might have led Rubin to a different conclusion. For example, she might have exchanged this multicultural Pollyannaism for a critical analysis of the ways in which the Kafkaesque system of sexual oppression overlays and overlaps with other oppressive systems, like racism and colonialism. Instead, in "Thinking Sex," Rubin merely exchanges the gender monism of her earlier work for a new sexual monism premised on the belief that tools forged in the struggles against racism and "cultural chauvinism" should be repurposed to fight for the liberation of presumptively white sexual minorities.

This idea that racial oppression could be used as an analogy to dramatize the plight of overwhelmingly white sexual minorities was widespread among sex-radical feminists in the late 1970s and early 1980s. One finds it clearly expressed, for instance, in Samois's *What Color Is Your Handkerchief?* "We believe," the authors proclaim, "that sadomasochists are an oppressed sexual minority. Our struggle deserves the recognition and support of other sexual minorities and oppressed groups" (Samois 1979, 2). Pat (now Patrick) Califia, a founding member of Samois, put forward a similar claim in an essay he published in the so-called sex issue of *Heresies* in spring 1981 entitled "Feminism and Sadomasochism." "Those feminists who accuse sadomasochists of mocking the oppressed by playing with dominance and submission," Califia writes, "forget that we are oppressed. We suffer police harassment, violence in the street, discrimination in housing and in employment. We are not treated the way our system treats its collaborators and supporters" (1981b, 32).

Not surprisingly, Black and third world feminists took umbrage at these portraits that predominantly white sex radicals painted of themselves as a persecuted minority that was owed support from other oppressed groups. For example, in an interview published in *Against Sadomasochism* (1982), Karen Sims, a self-identified Black lesbian feminist, argues that instead of drawing parallels between white sadomasochists and people of color, the differences in relative power and privilege between these two groups "ought to be pointed out" (Sims and Mason with Pagano 1982, 99). "I cannot align myself with anything that is not about the liberation of Black and Third World women," Sims explains, "and [defending S&M] does not speak to my needs, it does not speak to building a stronger movement of Third World women, it does not speak to the racism within the women's movement. It does not speak about the homophobia in the women's community—it doesn't progress us. And I do think it's a white women's issue. I really do. It comes out of a luxury I don't have" (99). Rose Mason, another Black lesbian feminist, extends Sims's critique. "I think it is racist," Mason declares, "for [sadomasochists] to even call themselves an oppressed minority. I am very insulted that they would align themselves with me as a Third World woman in terms of being oppressed. They don't know oppression. . . . I haven't seen . . . sadomasochists at all address themselves to any sort of racism and I have seen their pamphlets. I haven't seen classism, racism, or any of that dealt with" (101, 104). What both Sims and Mason highlight here is a lack of concern among predominately white sex-radical feminists with the actual racial oppression experienced by people of color despite their eagerness to use racial oppression as an analogy to paint themselves in a more sympathetic light. "I have a question to the people that are into sadomasochism and talking about dealing with their own struggles," Sims says. "How do they align themselves with the day-to-day struggles of Third World people?" (99). If white sadomasochists want to lay claim to the mantle of oppressed minority and demand support from people of color, then, these Black and third world feminists contend, they must act in kind. Absent some sort of political reciprocity—some effort to, in Sims's words, speak directly to "the day-to-day struggles of Third World people"—sex-radical feminists' claim that their fight was a fight shared by all oppressed people came across as little more than self-serving rhetoric.

Sex-radical feminists did not take these sorts of criticisms lying down. For example, in the same 1981 *Heresies* article referenced above, Pat (now Patrick) Califia offers a full-throated defense of S&M against charges of complicity with racism and racial oppression. Ironically, Califia's defense exhibits the very monistic inattentiveness to race of which he and his fellow sex radicals stood accused. "The key word to understanding S/M is fantasy," Califia writes:

> The system is unjust because it assigns privileges based on race, gender, and social class. During an S/M encounter, the participants select a particular role because it best expresses their sexual needs, how they feel about a particular partner, or which outfit is clean and ready to wear. . . . If you don't like being a top or a bottom, you switch your keys. Try doing that with your biological sex or your race or your socioeconomic status. The S/M subculture is affected by sexism, racism, and other fallout from the system, but the dynamic between a top and a bottom is quite different

from the dynamic between men and women, whites and Blacks, or upper- and working-class people. The roles are acquired and used in very different ways. (1981b, 32)

Califia's defense here hinges on the claim that an S&M scene is a space of pure fantasy that is somehow cordoned off from the oppressive forces prevalent in the system—that is, the world outside S&M fantasy. In the context of an S&M scene, Califia assumes, racial identities are like roles or outfits that one can simply slip into or out of as desire dictates. Of course, Califia is speaking here from the position of a white person for whom racial identity is much more likely to feel volitional—like a role or an outfit—than for a person of color. Had this defense come from a nonwhite woman active in the lesbian S&M scene of this era, it would be much more credible. Unfortunately, firsthand accounts of nonwhite women active in this scene are rare. This is partly a result of the paucity of women of color who participated in this scene—a paucity that is yet another reason to regard Califia's claim that S&M roles can be neatly disambiguated from the very real social hierarchies they sometimes invoke with skepticism.

One of the few firsthand accounts of a person of color active in the lesbian S&M scene of the 1980s provides further cause to doubt Califia's claim that S&M subcultures are somehow set apart from the oppressive dynamics that characterize more mainstream segments of society. Tina Portillo, a self-described "S/M dyke of color," describes her surprise upon realizing that "some white leather-dykes didn't want to play with me unless they were bottoming for me" (1991, 50). "For some reason (my naivete, I suppose)," Portillo continues, "I had reasoned that S/M people were above *all* kinds of prejudices, and certainly all sexual hang-ups and taboos" (50). Portillo's remarks here indicate that racial identity in the context of an S&M fantasy scene was for her, a Black woman, more than just a role or outfit. Because she was Black, she was in demand in the predominantly white S&M dyke community as a top, but she had difficulty finding white partners who were willing to top for her. "If someone desires a scenario such as plantation slave and master, or cowboy and Indian, as long as it is mutual and done in a loving spirit, that's all that matters and all I care about," Portillo writes (51). Unfortunately, this was clearly not the case for Portillo's white partners, who were unwilling to enact certain sexual scenarios with Portillo on account of her race. While white S&M lesbians like Califia may have experienced S&M subcultures as exceptional spaces in which racial and other hierarchies could be rendered amenable to experimentation and play, nonwhite S&M lesbians like Portillo clearly had a different experience.

By the time the Barnard conference rolled around in spring 1982, sex-radical feminism's blind spot concerning race had garnered enough critical attention that leading sex-radical feminists were ready to take concrete steps toward ameliorating it. This shift away from the posture of defensiveness exhibited in Califia's writings on the topic and toward a more constructive response is evident in the program of the Barnard conference itself. For example, while the twenty-five-member planning committee for the Barnard conference included only one woman of color, Barnard professor Quandra Prettyman Stadler, the conference program exhibited a fair amount of racial diversity.[21] Hortense Spillers, then a scholar of African American literature at Haverford College, presented a paper on the sexuality of Black women in the conference's opening session, Hattie Gossett and Cherríe Moraga read poetry as part of the conference's closing session, and Mirtha Quintanales, then a graduate student in anthropology at Ohio State University, and who also cofounded the Third World Women's Archives and contributed to *This Bridge Called My Back,* participated as a panelist in an afternoon workshop entitled "Politically Correct, Politically Incorrect Sexuality." While Jane Gerhard overstates the case in claiming that the Barnard conference "embodied the accomplishment of minority feminists," it is true that Black and third world feminists made important contributions at the Barnard conference. Foremost among these were their efforts both during and immediately after the conference to critically engage with sex radical feminism as white sex radicals had theorized it and to carve out space within the sex-radical feminist movement for the distinctive sexual and political concerns of women of color.

The first rumblings of the challenge Black and third world feminists posed to the monism prevalent within sex-radical feminist politics at the Barnard conference emerged during the conference's afternoon session on "Politically Correct and Politically Incorrect Sex." Mirtha Quintanales, one of the handful of women of color included in the conference's official program, was a panelist in this session. The other panelists were Dorothy Allison, acclaimed author and cofounder of the Lesbian Sex Mafia; Joan Nestle, cofounder of the Gay Academic Union and the Lesbian Her-story Archives; and anthropologist and psychoanalyst Muriel Diamond. Unfortunately, a complete transcript of the workshop is not available.[22] However, a detailed synopsis, including lengthy direct quotations from the panelists' remarks, is available in the coverage of the event published in the radical feminist periodical *off our backs*.

According to *off our backs*'s coverage, Dimen spoke first, followed by Nestle. Nestle spoke about her marginalization as a femme lesbian in both the lesbian bar scene of the 1950s and the lesbian feminist community of the present day. Her remarks were clearly colored by the fact that both she and another panelist, Dorothy Allison, had been singled out in the pamphlet circulated among conference attendees earlier that day by antipornography feminist picketers. As Nestle recounted her painful personal history of exclusion and invisibility within the lesbian feminist community, *off our backs* reports that Quintanales was crying visibly. When it came time for her to speak, according to *off our backs*, Quintanales began by saying that "she had been a little apprehensive from the time she got the invitation to speak at the workshop, had hoped that third world issues could be brought up, but realized now that it is not yet time for that kind of discussion, a discussion about how race, class, and ethnic background affects sexuality, because of the polarization imposed by the labels politically correct and politically incorrect sexuality" (Moira 1982a, 22). Expressing empathy as a woman of color with her copanelists, who were being vilified on account of their "politically incorrect" sexualities, Quintanales continues, "We have all been given this label because of presumed sexual preference or because we are women of color; we are all seen as outlaws. The idea of politically correct, politically incorrect sexuality is the same old thing—deviance and social control—delivered in feminist rhetoric. But the business of politics is to protect our right to personal, private, sexual lives" (22).

Having offered this sharp rebuke to the antipornography feminist picketers as well as a clear expression of support for the sex-radical feminists who had been targeted, Quintanales then shifts into a more critical mode. "The defining of people who do and don't fit in—how do we deal with this in the feminist community?" Quintanales asks (Moira 1982a, 22). Then, marking a clear distinction between her position as a third world woman and the position of white sex radicals like Nestle and Allison, Quintanales answers her own question:

> It seems we are struggling against feminist social control by yelling that deviance is good. Disclosure and affirmation of one's unacceptable sexual practices is presented as analysis, but it is not analysis, and that is what we need. As a Latina lesbian feminist, I have been a recalcitrant observer. What has it all to do with me? It tells me very little about my sexuality. I see I have two choices in the women's community: either to fight against sexuality or to accept and celebrate deviance. I cannot identify with either position and that keeps me quiet. You folks are worried about condemning and being condemned; I am worried about omission. (22)

Quintanales's intervention here highlights an important fissure between third world women sympathetic to the sex-radical feminist cause like herself and white sex-radical feminists like Nestle and Allison. For Nestle and Allison, sex-radical feminism was a monistic politics oriented around resisting sexual oppression; its aim was to affirm sexual minorities who are condemned by society at large as well as by influential factions within the women's movement. For Quintanales—and, later, we will see, for her third world feminist comrade at the Barnard conference, Cherríe Moraga—the goal of sex-radical feminism was larger than this. While Quintanales is clear that she opposes antipornography feminism's dogmatic and condemnatory stance on politically incorrect sexuality, and while she clearly sympathizes and sides with the sex-radical feminists who are being targeted, she also pleads here, "as a Latina lesbian feminist," for a sex-radical feminism that is better equipped to offer what she calls "analysis," "a discussion about how race, class, and ethnic background affects sexuality," and a space in which "third world issues could be brought up." What Quintanales came to the Barnard conference hoping to build was a sex-radical feminism committed to more than simply inverting the sexual order of things and uncritically "celebrat[ing] deviance." As Quintanales expressed poignantly through tears at this workshop, she wanted a sex-radical feminism capable of generating a sophisticated political inquiry into the sexual situations of women like her, whose identities, desires, and struggles are inflected not only by norms of the dominant white/Anglo culture but also by their own cultures, as well as the inequalities of race, gender, ethnicity, and class that structure virtually every aspect of the lives of third world women living in the United States. What Quintanales offered in these remarks at Barnard was a sympathetic yet nonetheless trenchant critique of sex-radical feminism: By focusing too intently on the particular forms of sexual oppression primarily affecting white women, white sex-radical feminists had failed to hold space in their movement for the sexual strivings and struggles of all women, including third world women.

Quintanales ended her remarks that afternoon by saying that as a third world woman, she was worried less about the conflict between antipornography feminists and sex-radical feminists that was playing out so dramatically at the Barnard conference that day—"condemning and being condemned," as she puts it—and more about "omission," that is, being overlooked altogether as a woman of color in feminist discussions and debates about sexuality. This worry, it turns out, was well founded, because as soon as Quintanales finished speaking, Dorothy Allison refocused the workshop's attention right back on the narrow set of concerns that, just moments before, Quintanales had urged her white sex-radical feminist allies to move beyond. "I got this flyer as I walked in," *off our backs* reports Allison told workshop attendees. The flyer Allison was referring to was, of course, the flyer circulated by WAP criticizing her personally by name. "You cannot do serious political work if you are trying constantly to watch your ass, if you're being terrorized, made an outlaw," Allison continues, "Sex is *not* the work I want to do but I won't lie about myself" (Moira 1982a, 22). Allison then proceeds to catalog each of the politically incorrect sexual preferences that had put her out of WAP's good graces: "I am a lesbian; I occasionally do S&M sex; I like anal sex; I like dildoes; I have two silk dresses and very high heels; I do public sex, fuck at night in bars, and come very loudly. You must face all these things and what they mean. I work in this movement and I'm here for the duration, so you have to talk with me" (22). Allison's remarks here embody precisely the sort of uncritical "yelling that deviance is good" that Quintanales had just finished explaining would not suffice for a sex-radical feminism attuned to the sexual needs and concerns of women of color. Quintanales's plea for "analysis" and "a discussion about how race, class, and ethnic background affects sexuality" had clearly fallen on deaf ears. Locked in a monistic battle against what Rubin would dub at this conference "the system of sexual oppression," all the white sex-radical feminists at Barnard could do was wage a war against their antipornography feminist foes from which third world women like Quintanales felt they had little to gain (Rubin 1984, 293).

Quintanales's struggle at the Barnard conference to open up space within sex-radical feminism for the voices and experiences of women of color continued at an event held the day after the conference formally ended. Organized by the Lesbian Sex Mafia, a New York–based sex-radical feminist consciousness-raising and support group, the "Speakout on Politically Incorrect Sex," as the event was billed, was not formally connected to the Barnard conference. It was, however, clearly designed to take advantage of the rare gathering of hundreds of women from all over the country interested in both feminism and "politically incorrect" sex that the Barnard conference had occasioned. Many individuals who participated in the Barnard conference also participated in the speak-out, including Dorothy Allison, Judith Butler, Amber Hollibaugh, Cherríe Moraga, Joan Nestle, Mirtha Quintanales, and Gayle Rubin. The speak-out was also designed to complement the Barnard conference in another way: By bringing together a racially diverse group of women to speak openly about their politically incorrect sexualities, the white sex-radical feminists who organized the speak-out hoped to rebut accusations voiced by Black and third world feminists like Karen Sims and Rose Mason that sex-radical feminism was a "white women's issue." As the event's lead organizer, Lesbian Sex Mafia cofounder Dorothy Allison, explained to the *off our backs* reporter covering the event, the goal of the speak-out was "to build coalitions between the disenfranchised, such as the 'radical perverts' in the Lesbian Sex Mafia and the women of color" (Moira 1982b, 23).[23] To this end, proceeds from the speak-out were to be donated to Kitchen

Table: Women of Color Press, which Barnard conference participants Cherríe Moraga and Hattie Gossett had recently cofounded. Also, *off our backs* reports, a packet was distributed at the speak-out containing an informational worksheet on the Family Protection Act, a congressional bill intended to stifle abortion and gay rights advocacy, and promotional flyers for Kitchen Table: Women of Color Press and Dykes Against Racism Everywhere, a Black lesbian feminist group formed in New York in 1980 to protest Ku Klux Klan rallies in the South (Moira 1982b, 23).

Given that the speak-out's organizers were touting solidarity with Black and third world women as one of the event's core aims, it is not surprising that the matter of sex-radical feminism's somewhat equivocal relationship to the political struggles of women of color was raised during the event. According to *off our backs*'s coverage, about halfway through the speak-out, a Black woman who is not identified by name in *off our backs*'s reporting took the stage to underscore the dearth of Black women active in sex-radical feminist circles.[24] The Black women in attendance at the Barnard conference on the previous day, the speaker told the audience, "could be counted on one hand." "For the black lesbian, for black women in general," the speaker continues, "sex is not talked about, and it wasn't talked about at the conference yesterday. I am a black woman who has named myself" (Moira 1982b, 23). While the intentions of this speaker cannot be discerned in any fulsome sense from the sparse report in *off our backs,* it is clear that, at a minimum, by these remarks, she sought to point out a deficiency she perceived in the Barnard conference, and by extension the sex-radical feminist project it embodied. Just as Quintanales had done the day before when she voiced her concerns about omission, so too did this speaker use her platform at the speak-out to highlight what she perceived to be a failure on the part of sex-radical feminism to provide a space for women of color like her to break their silence around sex.

As the speak-out drew to a close, Mirtha Quintanales and Cherríe Moraga took the stage together to make a similar point. "We expected there would be very few Latinas, so we came together," Quintanales said, prefacing her and Moraga's statements with an acknowledgment of sex-radical feminism's ethnic and cultural homogeneity. Quintanales then proceeded to reflect on her experiences at the conference the day before, calling it "a disturbing, terrifying day" (Moira 1982b, 24). "We need a dialogue on sexuality; we need to talk together, not to be identified as of a certain camp," she said, reiterating the criticism of labels like "politically correct" and "politically incorrect" she had offered at the workshop panel the day before (24). After expressing empathy for the sex-radical feminists singled out by the WAP flyer, Quintanales then pivoted, just as she had done the day before, into a more critical mode, sharing her experiences of discrimination within the lesbian feminist movement not only on account of her politically incorrect sexuality but also on account of her ethnic and cultural identity as a Latina. "When I came out," Quintanales explains, "I thought I could finally be what I was. But I could not be a Latina, a woman, I was always labeled politically incorrect. We need to have dialogues about S&M issues, not about what is 'politically correct, politically incorrect.' We are forced to spend all our time defending and celebrating deviance rather than exploring, analyzing what it is all about and our diversity" (24). Just as she had done during the workshop panel at the Barnard conference the day before, Quintanales stresses here that if sex-radical feminism is going to be relevant to women like her, then it must expand to become about more than "defending and celebrating deviance"; it must reach beyond a monistic focus on sexual oppression as it is experienced by sexually nonconforming white women, and engage with the more complexly textured lives, experiences, identities, and sexualities of third world women.

When Quintanales had finished speaking, Cherríe Moraga, who, *off our backs* reports, had been standing at Quintanales's side, clasping her hand as she spoke, took the mic. Picking up where Quintanales left off, Moraga began to describe how her own ethnic and cultural identity as a Chicana had inflected her sexuality and shaped her experiences of sexual oppression.[25] "Some of you might think that things have moved very far because we can have such a thing as [this speak-out] we're having now and I think that to some degree as well," Moraga (1982) says, "but I can't even begin to tell you how little Latinas, Indian women, my Black sisters . . . , Asian American women. . . . I think that it's very hard possibly for you to conceptualize how little it is not even safe for us to say we are Dykes to each other." According to *off our backs*'s reporting, Moraga "said this haltingly because she was crying" (Moira 1982b, 24). In the audio recording of the event preserved in the Lesbian Herstory Archives, Moraga can be heard choking back tears and promising to "fight like hell to keep from crying" (24). Moraga's emotional response here underscores the profound implications her words carry for sex-radical feminist politics. Proudly and publicly proclaiming one's politically incorrect sexuality was sex-radical feminism's core political project—its raison d'être—but what Moraga is suggesting here is that this tactic of "defending and celebrating deviance," as Quintanales had described it just moments earlier, is not a viable option for women like her. As Moraga (1982) explains,

> I am a sexual minority. I am a Chicana, Catholic-raised lesbian. My own particular relationship to being a sexual person and a radical stands up in direct contradiction and in violation of much of how I was raised. I can't keep looking to white folks to explain my sexuality. I am my own brand. The connection between my racial/cultural tradition, my sexuality, and my political activism is crucial. To be a *política,* a writer, and a lesbian are equal acts of disobedience against and for my mother, my grandmother, and my culture.

What Moraga calls attention to here are both the continuities and the discontinuities between her sexual identity as a lesbian and her racial/cultural identity as a Chicana. As a "Chicana, Catholic-raised lesbian," Moraga says, she cannot "keep looking to white folks to explain [her] sexuality"—that is, she cannot simply follow the white sex-radical feminist formula of rejecting her community of origin and embracing a new autonomous political identity as a radical pervert or sexual outlaw. Such an approach would require her to disavow communities that help sustain her and that she sees it as her duty to fight for and liberate. Unlike white women, Moraga stresses, women of color are never contending with only the system of sexual oppression. While queer women of color may be persecuted within their own racial, ethnic, and cultural communities on account of their politically incorrect sexualities, they also face hatred and discrimination on account of their race, ethnicity, and class from both the dominant culture as well as the queer subcultures with which they might choose to affiliate in the name of sexual liberation. To gird themselves against these multifarious forms of oppression, which are unknown to white/Anglo women, even to those who have been cast out of what Gayle Rubin dubbed at this conference the "charmed circle" of sexual normativity, queer women of color, Moraga insists, need to be in community and political solidarity with other women of color who face similar oppressions (Rubin 1984, 280–81). Sex-radical feminism's monistic strategy of defiantly defending and celebrating sexual deviance simply will not do for women like her who are positioned at the intersections of multiple oppressions.

After offering this incisive critique of sex-radical feminism's monistic approach to the project of sexual liberation, Moraga proceeds to express her empathy for the women who had been targeted by the WAP flyer the day before. As she explains, the condemnation she saw these women incur and the fear she saw it provoke in them reminded her of her own experiences with racism. "I felt at the conference yesterday and saw in the faces of my friends that same panic I have always felt as a minority. I feel it in my gut—my guts tell me—this is familiar, this is like racism" (Moira 1982b, 24). Moraga (1982) then follows this generous expression of compassion and solidarity with a challenge:

> What my intuition always tells me in [situations like the one at the conference yesterday] is that when people are that afraid, then that is the thing that's got to be broken up. Now, I have to tell you the truth, I don't know when you break it up what that means. I agree with Amber [Hollibaugh] when she says, "I'm not really particularly interested at this point to figure out what my sexuality is going to be 25 millenniums from now, this is who I am now." I feel like we have to work for each other to have the right to be who we are now, but I have to say that I am not convinced that who we are now is where it's at.

The subtle yet searching critique of sex-radical feminism Moraga offers here is strikingly similar to the one Quintanales had offered the day before at the Barnard conference. Like Quintanales, Moraga presses her fellow sex-radical feminists for a sexual politics that is more than simply an uncritical struggle "to have the right to be who we are now." As a lesbian and a Chicana aligned not only with her fellow queers in a fight for sexual freedom but also with her fellow Chicanos and other people of color in struggles against racism, sexism, and colonialism, Moraga is seeking a sex-radical feminism that is open to the possibility that "who we are now" sexually is not authentic, just, or whole, but rather the product of multiple and intersecting forms of oppression. Like Quintanales, Moraga supports white sex-radical feminists in their struggle against those segments of the feminist movement that so cruelly shame them on account of their sexualities. Nevertheless, Moraga's dissatisfaction with the monistic manner in which white sex-radical feminists have been prosecuting their struggle for sexual liberation is undeniable. Moraga had come to Barnard hoping to build a sex-radical feminism that encompassed the needs and desires of women of color—women for whom being "a *politica,* a writer, and a lesbian are equal acts of disobedience against and for" their mothers, their grandmothers, and their cultures (Moraga 1982). Unfortunately, the most Moraga was able to do at this event was name herself as one of the many women of color that a monistic sex-radical feminism was currently failing.

At the Barnard conference and the associated Lesbian Sex Mafia speak-out, a cleavage within sex-radical feminism between the monistic approaches of figures like Rubin, Califia, Nestle, and Allison and the intersectional approaches of third world feminists like Quintanales and Moraga had clearly begun to emerge. In the war of words that followed on the heels of the Barnard conference in the back matter of the radical feminist periodical *off our backs,* this cleavage expanded into a full-blown rupture. *off our backs* had covered the Barnard conference extensively, but this coverage was by no means favorable. For example, *off our backs* reporter Carole Anne Douglass writes that she "was deeply disturbed by the conference" and the "attack[s]" she witnessed there against "radical feminists and lesbian feminists . . . without any defense presented" (Douglass and Henry 1982, 4). Fran Moira, the *off our backs* reporter who covered both the conference and the Lesbian Sex Mafia's speak-out, was similarly ill-disposed, as her gloss of Amber Hollibaugh's plenary address at the Barnard conference conveys: "Stripped of the language of sexual freedom and the right to fulfill one's desires, it seemed to me that the bottom line of that closing address was that the brave new world would allow today's children to assume their positions as beaters and the beaten without shame" (1982c, 24).

In response to *off our backs*'s unsympathetic coverage of the Barnard conference, several attendees, including Frances Doughty, Amber Hollibaugh, Cherríe Moraga, Esther Newton, Gayle Rubin, and Shirley Walton, wrote letters to the editor that were then published in *off our back*'s back matter. Most of these letters criticized *off our backs* for openly siding with the antipornography feminist movement and for failing to give sex-radical feminists a fair shake. Cherríe Moraga's letter, however, took a different tack. Published under the headline "Played between White Hands," Moraga's letter levies charges implicating far more than just *off our backs* and the antipornography feminists with whom it so clearly sympathized. In one of the most significant and overlooked contributions to the sex wars debates, Moraga takes to task both leading feminist factions in the sex wars for exploiting women of color to win a battle from which women of color themselves had little to gain. As she puts it in the rhetorical climax of this withering letter, "The way the movement is breaking down around sex makes me feel that women of color are being played between two white (sector's) hands" (Moraga and Moira 1982, 23).

From the letter's opening lines, Moraga's alienation from and mistrust of both antipornography feminists and sex-radical feminists is unmistakable:

> I am driven, finally, to address the feminist community about matters which, for some time, I have been hoping to reserve for my own people— Chicanos, other women of color. I thought for a time I could opt out of the white feminist debate around sexuality, knowing that what I needed to explore would not be found in the feminist lesbian bedroom, but more likely in the mostly heterosexual bedrooms of South Texas, L.A., or even Sonora, Mexico. Further, I came to realize that the boundaries white feminists confined themselves to in describing sexuality were based in white-rooted interpretations of dominance, submission, power-exchanges, etc.; and, although they are part of the psychosexual lives of women of

color, these boundaries would have to be expanded and translated to fit my people, in particular, the women in my family. And, I am tired always of these acts of translation. (Moraga and Moira 1982, 23)

Having voiced these feelings of exhaustion and frustration with the monistic sexual politics permeating what she tellingly characterizes as "the white feminist debate around sexuality," Moraga continues, "But I write here because despite my desire to wait and remain silent to gather my strength, thoughts, and memories into print, I am forced to speak, fearing that my words and body have already been used, not against me and my people, but more significantly, not for. And, I write here knowing even these words will be used against us" (23).

After making it clear that she does not see an authentic place for herself in the internecine struggle between antipornography feminists and sex-radical feminists and that she is offering the remarks in this letter reluctantly and under duress, Moraga then turns to address the specific ways in which she believes that the white feminist combatants in the sex wars have exploited and misrepresented her as a third world woman. She begins with the antipornography feminist sympathizers who covered the Barnard conference for *off our backs*. "In reading Fran Moira's coverage of 'A Speak-out on Politically Incorrect Sex,' sponsored by the Lesbian Sex Mafia, I was struck," Moraga writes, "by the flatness of her interpretation of the event, as well as the workshop [on 'Politically Correct, Politically Incorrect Sexuality'] at Barnard the day before" (Moraga and Moira 1982, 23). What Moraga had personally experienced as events with great "richness and complexity" were collapsed in *off our backs*'s coverage, she alleges, "into an across-the-board endorsement of s/m" (23). Moreover, Moraga continues, both she and Mirtha Quintanales had been portrayed by *off our backs* as something akin to third world feminist mascots for lesbian S&M. While reading Moira's article, Moraga writes:

It hit me, solidly in the pit of my stomach, that through white feminist eyes, Mirtha Quintanales and I are Latinas, and nothing but, Latinas. We are used throughout the article as representatives of our culture (Latin), our organizations (The Third World Women's Archives and

Kitchen Table Press, respectively; even though we never publicly an-
nounced these affiliations at the Speakout), and our politics (Third World
Feminism). . . . When we are depicted by a white-controlled medium at
white-conceived and white-run events, we are simply not allowed our
lives and our individual choices. (23)

Moraga's overarching critique here is that, through a combination of
fixating on the most salacious aspects of the Barnard conference and
fetishizing Moraga's and Quintanales's ethnic identities at Latinas, *off our
backs* had deliberately tried to drive a political wedge between feminists
of color and sex-radical feminists, threatening the precarious standing of
both within the broader feminist movement. As she puts it, "Did Moira,
through her innuendos, hope to force us, women of color, to publicly dis-
sociate ourselves from 'deviant' women in order to save political face. . . .
Since Kitchen Table is the only women-of-color organization of its kind,
so fragile in its first year of development, one would hope that the author
would have considered how her negative and inaccurate characterization
of the Speak-out might possibly affect the Press. . . . This is the feminist
media, where women of color . . . have little or no control of what goes
into it. You get to decide how we're gonna look" (23).

Having trained her first volley of criticism squarely on *off our backs*
for what she viewed as their cynical exploitation of third world women to
strike a blow against their rivals in what she views as "the white feminist
debate around sexuality," Moraga's letter goes on to criticize the sex-radical
feminists who organized the postconference speak-out of doing exactly
the same thing. "For the record," Moraga explains, clarifying the nature
and extent of her involvement with the Lesbian Sex Mafia's speak-out,
"Kitchen Table Press was approached about our being beneficiaries, along
with Dykes Against Racism Everywhere, of funds raised at the Speak-out
and those of us available to respond, agreed, understanding the event to
be a speak-out where women, including women of color, would be free to
discuss 'the everyday reality of our lives as women and as sexual beings'"
(23). "It is my impression," Moraga continues, "that the organizers of the
Speak-out, in soliciting some speakers for the event, laid low on the s/m
content, for example, making no mention of it in their statement" (23).

The speak-out's organizers may have been motivated to engage in this kind of duplicity, Moraga speculates, because "many of us, especially women of color, might have been reluctant to commit ourselves to public statements at an event that was being billed visually as an s/m event" (23).

In essence, what Moraga is saying here is that members of the Lesbian Sex Mafia lied to representatives of Kitchen Table: Women of Color Press and Dykes Against Racism Everywhere, inviting them to participate in a wide-ranging discussion of women's diverse sexualities that was, in fact, a pro-S&M pep rally tailored to the needs and concerns of white women. Moraga cannily observes that the mere presence of women of color can, when filtered through "a white feminist medium," give "legitimacy to individuals and events because as 'published' Third World women we become 'politically correct' entities" (Moraga and Moira 1982, 23). However, she also generously grants the less-than-forthcoming members of the Lesbian Sex Mafia the benefit of the doubt, suggesting that their dishonesty may have been well intentioned—a sort of Platonic "noble lie" told for the sake of realizing their "vision of having a diverse group of women speak about their varied sex lives" (23). Moraga then poses what she calls a "painful question": "Did the Speak-out organizers, in their eagerness to make political connections with women of color around sex issues, not truly take into account our already disenfranchised position in the women's movement at large? And, therefore, did they ultimately serve to put us in an even more vulnerable position, politically?" (23). In other words, did some combination of ambition and willful ignorance on the part of the speak-out's organizers set the stage for *off our backs*'s exploitative misrepresentation of Moraga, Quintanales, Kitchen Table: Women of Color Press, and Dykes Against Racism Everywhere in their subsequent coverage? This is what Moraga means when she says that she feels she is "being played between two white (sector's) hands." The fight between white antipornography feminists and white sex-radical feminists is not her fight, yet first at the Barnard conference itself and then again in *off our backs*'s coverage of the conference and speak-out, she finds herself conscripted into it on both sides against her will.

Moraga concludes her letter with an astute analysis of how the dynamics generated by "the white feminist debate around sexuality" work to marginalize the more complex and multifaceted explorations of sex and power that third world feminists like her were interested in. According to Moraga, "the terror" inspired on all sides of the sex wars by topics like "s/m, 'pornographic' fantasies, butch/fem roles, pedophilia, [and] prostitution" causes "communication networks to breakdown and tactical political mistakes to take place" (Moraga and Moira 1982, 23). This is precisely what Moraga believes transpired at the Barnard conference, where white antipornography feminists squared off against white sex-radical feminists, with the voices of third world feminists like her drowned out by the crossfire. These fear-driven dynamics, Moraga continues, are fed by both white antipornography feminists, whose "reductive thinking" demonizes sexual difference, and white sex-radical feminists, who respond to antipornography feminist attacks with "what looks like a 'civil libertarian' stand," demanding "the right of s/m lesbians to speak, call themselves feminists, and have sex as they like it," but nothing more (23). "I'm tired of this mess," Moraga exclaims. "Is it any wonder under these conditions that a deeper analysis has been slow to appear?" (23).

This "deeper analysis" is precisely what Moraga had pressed her white sex-radical feminist allies for at the Barnard conference. When Moraga (1982) addressed the audience at the Lesbian Sex Mafia's speak-out, she stressed the need to "break up" fear and explore the possibility that "who we are now" is not "where it's at." In her *off our backs* letter, Moraga reprises this call for critical self-reflection, enumerating a whole host of questions that the defensive and monistic posture of white sex-radical feminists had made it virtually impossible to explore. "Lesbian s/m has never been critically examined in any sensitive and realistic way," Moraga writes, "which could be useful to its feminist practitioners and to other feminists who simply want a right to their sexual desire, and at the same time, understand what that desire means in a racist/sexist and violent culture" (Moraga and Moira 1982, 23). "What does it mean," Moraga continues,

> that some images and acts of s/m sex mirror actual acts of violence visited upon people of color, Jews, and women as a group—and that some Jewish women and women of color are sexually stimulated by these? Do images

mean anything in relation to life? Does sex influence non-sexual behavior? If so, what do we do about this, sexually? Can a class analysis provide us with any useful insights into the inefficacy of feminist sex theory to date? And finally, is sex separate from politics and if so, does it only become political when the "sex deviant" is denied his/her civil rights? (23)

"For three years now," Moraga laments, "I have been hoping for someone(s), including women who do s/m, to come up with some analysis of what it all means, accepting as a given that the anti-porn line is inadequate . . . ," but "for three years now, this last question," the one geared around the "civil rights" of "sex deviants, "reflects as far as the sexual debate has gone" (23). "Until people agree to lay down their guns"— that is, until white feminists agree to stop attacking each other and start listening to the third world women within their own ranks—Moraga concludes, "we'll see little in the way of advanced thinking. But maybe it is this deeper analysis that women on both sides fear, not knowing what it will divulge" (23).

In light of the history excavated in the first three chapters of *Why We Lost the Sex Wars,* the connection Moraga draws here between antipornography feminists' and sex-radical feminists' inattentiveness to the voices of the women of color within their own ranks calling for "deeper analysis" and the fixation of white sex-radical feminists on a narrow set of concerns centered on the "civil rights" of "sex deviants" is significant. What Moraga is suggesting here is that the failures of both white sex-radical feminists and white antipornography feminists to heed the calls of their Black and third world feminist allies and exchange their monistic sexual politics for something more multidimensional and intersectional set the stage for the liberal appropriations and attenuations of antipornography feminism and sex-radical feminism described in chapters 2 and 3. I will return to this suggestion in the conclusion. For now, suffice it to say that Moraga's insight that a monistic focus on the sexual needs, experiences, and desires of white women may have blunted the radicalism of both antipornography feminism and sex-radical feminism, leaving them more vulnerable to liberal co-optation than they otherwise would have been, may

THIRD WORLD FEMINISM AND THE SEX WARS   179

be the single most valuable insight the historical excavation undertaken in *Why We Lost the Sex Wars* has generated.

Taken as a whole, then, Moraga's letter—right down to its signature, which reads, "By Cherríe Moraga, who represents no one but herself"—is a stern rebuke of the monism that was prevalent among both antipornography and sex-radical feminists during the sex wars. As this chapter has shown, Moraga was far from alone in her efforts to make visible the sexual needs, desires, and concerns of women of color during this period. Like Moraga, each of the Black and third world feminists highlighted in this chapter resisted the compulsion to choose sides in a sex war oriented around the experiences of white women. Instead, this heterogenous group of writers, artists, and activists intervened strategically on all sides of the sex wars, disrupting monistic thinking wherever they found it and insisting that the experiences of women of color be made foundational to feminist sexual politics. One of the catfight narrative's most regrettable consequences is that, in forcing the history of the sex wars down onto its procrustean bed, it truncates and distorts the vital contributions these Black and third world feminists made during this pivotal and politically and theoretically fecund moment in feminist history. It is my hope that this chapter has helped restore to these contributions at least a portion of their originality and sophistication. Appreciating the critical work of Black and third world feminist sex warriors is important not only for the sake of historical accuracy, but, as I will argue in the conclusion, for the sake of prudently navigating the complex terrain of contemporary feminist sexual politics and resisting the increasingly powerful allure of carceral feminism in the #MeToo moment.

Conclusion

THE LIBERAL ROOTS OF CARCERAL FEMINISM

I began the present work with an invitation to consider the sex wars beyond Barnard—that is, to rethink the sex wars as something other than
a straightforward, two-sided catfight between sex-positive feminists on
one side and sex-negative feminists on the other. Accepting this invitation, I promised, would disclose aspects of the sex wars that are rarely
considered, including a rich history of contestation and collaboration
between antipornography feminists, sex-radical feminists, and liberals
of various stripes, as well as potent challenges Black and third world
feminists posed to the political and theoretical monism prevalent among
both white antipornography and white sex-radical feminists during the
sex wars. Now, having recovered this history and placed it squarely in our
view, I would like to extend one final invitation. Let us reflect on some
of the implications the counternarrative of the sex wars presented across
the last four chapters has for our view of the landscape of contemporary
feminist sexual politics.

SEX WARS, SLUTWALKS, AND CARCERAL FEMINISM

In recent years, a body of scholarship has emerged identifying a political formation that mobilizes the emancipatory energies of feminism in
the service of the expansion of the carceral state.[1] Carceral feminism, as
sociologist Elizabeth Bernstein has dubbed it, figures criminalization,
policing, prosecution, and incarceration as integral to women's liberation,
constructing gender justice as a matter of criminal justice. Within this

scholarship, carceral feminism is portrayed as primarily a product of the confluence of feminist and conservative energies. For example, in her study of contemporary antitrafficking activism, Bernstein associates the antitrafficking movement's embrace of carceral paradigms of justice with "a rightward shift" and "feminist-conservative alliances" formed between feminists and organizations like the Hudson Institute (2010, 47, 53).[2] Kristen Bumiller has offered a similar genealogy of carceral feminism, arguing that "reactionary" and "neoliberal forces" "appropriated" the feminist movement against sexual violence in the 1980s, giving rise to "a direct alliance between feminist activists and legislators, prosecutors, and other elected officials" demanding "more punitive action by the state" (2008, 5–7). Similarly, Mimi E. Kim has attributed the anti–domestic violence movement's turn toward "punitive carceral policies" to strategic decisions made by anti–domestic violence activists to ally themselves with a conservative politics of law and order in an effort to "feminize" and "control" the criminal justice system (2015, 5).

While there is no denying that the feminist–conservative conjunctions highlighted in this scholarship have contributed to the rise of carceral feminism, my research concerning the convergence of antipornography feminism, sex-radical feminism, and liberalism during the sex wars indicates an alternative genealogy for feminism's carceral turn. Consider, for example, the liberal appropriations of antipornography feminism described in chapter 2. According to my research, before the emergence of antipornography liberalism in the mid-1980s, antipornography feminists figured pornography as harmful in ways that challenged traditional liberal conceptions of harm, liberty, and the public and the private. They did not, however, advocate or pursue criminal legal solutions to the problem of pornography. This is because antipornography feminists tended to view the carceral state as an extension of the patriarchal rape culture they sought to dismantle. Recall Susan Brownmiller's remarks on this score: "A police department, like a prison or an army, is by nature and structure a traditionally male, authoritarian institution. . . . Operating through sanctioned force, the local police precinct has always been a bastion of male attitudes and responses that are inimical to women" (1975, 270). Also, recall that Catharine MacKinnon, the antipornography feminist who was perhaps most eager to wield the law in the service of feminist ends, advocated only a civil remedy for pornography's harms; indeed, she adamantly opposed efforts to regulate pornography through criminal law, including extant obscenity law. As MacKinnon explains, "Obscenity law helps keep pornography sexy by putting state power—force, hierarchy—behind its purported prohibition on what men can have sexual access to. . . . Suppressing obscenity criminally has enhanced its value, made it more attractive and more expensive and a violation to get, therefore more valuable and more sexually exciting" (1983b, 245). MacKinnon's antipornography feminism wanted no part of this patriarchal dynamic. As she herself puts it, "I have no particular interest in increasing the power of the *state* over sexuality or speech. I do not have that kind of faith in government. It has largely operated from the same perspective that *Playboy* does—that is, the male point of view" (1987a, 140). Because the ultimate goal of MacKinnon's antipornography feminism was "to increase women's power over sexuality, hence over our social definition and treatment," she sought to shift the problem of pornography away from "criminal law," which "empowers the state," and toward "civil law," which "empowers the people" (MacKinnon 1987a, 140; [1993] 1995, 302).

With the advent of antipornography liberalism, this reluctance to use criminal law and the power of the carceral state to address the problem of pornography all but vanished. Intent on doing something to address pornography's harmful effects, but wary of the sweeping regulations on speech that broad and deeply politicized conceptions of pornography's harms like "silencing" and "objectification" could be used to justify, antipornography liberals like Cass Sunstein opted to describe pornography's harms in terms of "violence," "crime," and "illegal conduct." While such narrow descriptions certainly lessened the likelihood that the sort of wholesale regulation of sexually explicit speech that the Dworkin–MacKinnon ordinance embodied and that liberals so feared would occur, they also tacitly endorsed criminal law as the most justifiable means for responding to and mitigating pornography's harms.

One sees this paradoxical logic at work vividly in the antipornography legislative proposals put forward by Elena Kagan in 1993 at the University of Chicago School of Law conference, "Speech, Equality, and Harm:

Feminist Legal Perspectives on Pornography and Hate Propaganda."
In her zeal to ameliorate the undesirable effects of pornography and
hate speech while remaining faithful to the liberal principle of viewpoint
neutrality and preserving the sanctity of the private realm of thought and
belief, Kagan advocates stepping up the regulation of various acts through
criminal law. Specifically, she calls for stricter enforcement of existing
hate crimes laws as well as the enactment of new criminal prohibitions on
both pornography whose production involved violence or coercion, and
certain kinds of harassment, threats, and intimidation (Kagan 1995, 204).
By translating the antipornography feminist critique of pornography into
a liberal idiom in which harm equals crime, and crime warrants coercive
government action to ensure the preservation of individual liberty, antipornography liberals like Kagan infused antipornography feminism with
an unmistakably carceral flavor.

My account of the emergence of anti-censorship/pro-sex feminism out
of the strategic alliances formed by sex-radical feminists and civil libertarians to fight the Dworkin–MacKinnon ordinance in the mid-1980s also
points toward a possible liberal genealogy for carceral feminism. Consider,
for example, the carceral thrust of the anti-censorship/pro-sex feminist
arguments put forward by the ACLU in its official report on the findings
and recommendations of the Meese Commission discussed in chapter
3. While the report offers a bold defense of sexual expression qua sexual
expression and alerts readers to the adverse effects of censorship on sexual
minorities—all largely untrodden terrain for anticensorship liberals up to
this point—it also advocates the criminalization of a variety of forms of
sexual conduct, including prostitution, pandering, and intergenerational
sex, as well as child pornography broadly defined. Once again, we see
how a conjunction with liberalism transformed a radical and insistently
anticarceral feminist project—sex-radical feminism—into a sexual politics that frames the criminalization of sexuality as an appropriate means
toward the fulfillment of feminist ends.

While it may seem counterintuitive to claim that liberalism, with its
emphasis on individual liberty and limited government, helped to forge
a feminist politics that figures the "carceral state" as the "enforcement
apparatus of feminist goals," this is precisely what seems to have occurred

in the case of both of the liberal–feminist hybrids that emerged out of the sex wars (Bernstein 2010, 56; 2007, 143). In the case of antipornography liberalism, a dogged commitment to the inviolability of expressive freedom led to calls for criminal antipornography statutes targeting conduct rather than speech. In the case of anti-censorship/pro-sex feminism, a similarly dogged commitment to expressive freedom supplanted sex-radical feminism's broader vision of sexual freedom and led to the endorsement of a variety of criminal laws regulating sexual conduct. In both of these cases, the carceral thrust, if you will, derived not from some latent conservative impulses or ill-advised conservative alliances but from consummately liberal commitments to privacy, freedom of speech and conscience, and limited government. This indicates that feminism's carceral turn may not be exclusively or even primarily a product of conservative or right-wing influence. Liberal inducements were clearly operative here as well.

Further evidence of carceral feminism's roots in the liberal–feminist convergences of the sex wars is clearly visible today in the transnational antirape movement SlutWalk. The SlutWalk movement began on April 3, 2011, in Toronto, Ontario, Canada, when some fifteen hundred people, mostly women, donned miniskirts, fishnet tights, go-go boots, and other "slutty" attire and marched to the downtown headquarters of the Toronto Police Service. Billed by organizers as SlutWalk Toronto, the purpose of the march was to protest a Toronto Police Service officer's remark at a public forum that, in order not to be raped, women "should avoid dressing like sluts."[3] Given these precipitating circumstances, one might imagine SlutWalk Toronto carried a bold anticarceral message, highlighting instances of the criminal justice system's complicity in sexual violence and injustice such as prison rape, sexual assault by law enforcement officers, and police harassment of sex workers and sexual minorities.[4] However, this was not the case. As SlutWalk Toronto's website explains, the aim of the march was to "call foul" on the Toronto Police Service for engaging in the sort of "slut-shaming" that deters survivors from reporting their victimization and to demand that police "take serious steps" to make survivors, "slut or otherwise," "feel respected and protected." The goal, in other words, was more vigorous law enforcement on behalf of "sluts." Within a year, SlutWalk Toronto had inspired similar events in approximately two hundred cities around the world, and a global grassroots SlutWalk movement had emerged.[5]

While SlutWalk's rise from local demonstration to transnational phenomenon has elicited some criticism from feminist quarters, many prominent feminists have embraced the movement.[6] For example, according to popular author and blogger Jessica Valenti (2011), SlutWalks "herald a new day in feminist organizing . . . when women's anger begins online but takes to the street [and] when a local step makes global waves." Similarly, veteran socialist–feminist activist Selma James (2011) hails SlutWalk as "the new women's movement . . . , born of student protests and Arab revolutions . . . , tearing up the past before our very eyes." Philosopher Judith Butler's assessment is equally sanguine. When asked about the SlutWalk marches, Butler (2011) describes them as exemplifying a new kind of public assembly that harnesses "a sense of vulnerability and injurability on the streets" to engender "modes of solidarity" that resist the limitations of identity politics while contesting neoliberal conditions of precarity. Butler has more recently reaffirmed this position, describing SlutWalks as a "public and courageous takeover of public space" (2016, 227).

Perhaps the highest praise garnered by the SlutWalk movement has come from scholars who frame the movement as a long-awaited resolution of feminism's sex wars. To scholars who know the sex wars only through the prism of the catfight narrative, SlutWalk's pairing of audacious assertions of feminine sexuality with strident denunciations of gender-based violence signals a long-awaited "sex détente" (Walters 2016, 4). As legal scholar Deborah Tuerkheimer observes, "By taking aim at rape while expressly promoting the virtues of female sexuality, SlutWalk situates itself where anti-rape and pro-sex norms converge" (2014, 1455–56). Joetta Carr has seconded this analysis, praising "SlutWalkers" for "speaking in a voice that deplores sexual violence while embracing sex positivity" (2013, 31).

In a superficial sense at least, these scholars are right. Certain affinities do exist between the SlutWalk movement and the preliberal variants of both antipornography feminism and sex-radical feminism that predominated during the sex wars' earliest phase. For instance, SlutWalk's resemblance to the Take Back the Night marches pioneered in the late

1970s by WAVPM is undeniable.[7] Equally undeniable is the SlutWalk movement's continuity, in at least some respects, with the audacious spirit of public sexual assertion characteristic of many sex-radical feminist undertakings, such as the Lesbian Sex Mafia's post–Barnard conference "Speakout on Politically Incorrect Sex." However, casting SlutWalk as some sort of Hegelian synthesis of sex wars antinomies ignores many of the complexities that my counternarrative has brought to light and leaves many of the SlutWalk movement's most important facets unaccounted for and unexplained.

For example, in her study of the SlutWalk movement, Kaitlynn Mendes notes that in addition to challenging "rape culture," one of the movement's central priorities has been combatting "slut-shaming" by promoting "respect for the individual and the variety of choices they make (including the freedom to dress how they want)." SlutWalk Toronto's cofounder, Heather Jarvis, has foregrounded this facet of the movement. When asked in an interview about SlutWalk Toronto's controversial decision to "re-appropriate" the word "slut," Jarvis explains that while she "completely respect[s]" people who have criticized her effort to "reclaim" the charged term, using the word "slut" in a "positive context" is "a choice for some people," and she "want[s] more choice, not less" (Mistry 2011). This emphasis on self-expression and personal choice, especially as it pertains to the conventionally feminine and heterosexual women who bear the brunt of the slut stigma, certainly distinguishes SlutWalk from the sexual politics of sex-radical feminism. Before their strategic appropriation of liberal anticensorship rhetoric in the mid-1980s, sex-radical feminists vindicated an expansive vision of sexual freedom. They demanded not merely more space for individual women to enact fairly conventional forms of feminine heterosexuality but also an end to all legal and extralegal methods of enforcing erotic conformity, including statutory rape laws, child pornography laws, laws prohibiting public sex, psychiatric diagnoses pathologizing sexual nonconformity, family violence, employment and housing discrimination, and any and all hegemonic norms that punish the sexually "perverse" and reward the sexually "normal" (Rubin 1984, 294, 292, 289, 295). In contrast, the SlutWalk movement shows little interest in addressing these multifarious forms of sexual oppression. In fact, rather than critically interrogating the erotic conformity enacted by SlutWalkers parading around in matching bra-and-panty sets calling themselves sluts as the ambivalent effect of a system of sexual oppression that makes alternative erotic possibilities virtually unthinkable, the SlutWalk movement valorizes these performances of a commonplace, even hackneyed, feminine (hetero)sexuality as hard-won products of individual struggle and choice.[8]

Such disregard for sexual oppression broadly conceived signals not only the SlutWalk movement's discontinuity with sex-radical feminism but also its continuity with anti-censorship/pro-sex feminism. For anti-censorship/pro-sex feminists like Nadine Strossen, sexual freedom was not "the freedom to be as queer, as perverted on the street and on the job as [you are] in [your] dungeon," but the freedom to express conventional ideas about sex and gender without being subject to state censorship. This narrow conception of sexual freedom is very much akin to the sexual freedom sought by the SlutWalk movement: the freedom to "dress how [you] want," "be sexual in your own way," and publicly perform a normative feminine (hetero)sexuality without being judged or sanctioned.

The SlutWalk movement's investment in a narrow and individualistic vision of sexual freedom fuels another aspect of the movement that marks a stark departure from both sex-radical feminism and antipornography feminism in their preliberal variants. As I have already noted, the SlutWalk movement seeks not just to combat sexual assault, but to do so in a way that celebrates (rather than critically interrogates the limits of) women's freedom to express their sexuality in whatever ways they choose. Honoring these dual commitments requires the SlutWalk movement to respond to the problem of sexual violence without engaging in critiques of normative scripts of (hetero)sexuality and gender that might have a chilling effect on individual choice and expression. Faced with this quandary of resisting sexual violence while refraining from questioning the norms that support it, the SlutWalk movement falls back on a strikingly carceral solution. In its rhetoric and messaging, SlutWalk places virtually all responsibility for sexual assault on individual perpetrators and figures the carceral state as the guarantor of women's sexual freedom.

The carceral thrust of the SlutWalk movement has been evident from its advent in Toronto. Even though the original SlutWalk was inspired by outrage at police complicity in rape culture, its primary message was an appeal to police for protection and respect. "We want Toronto Police Services to take serious steps to regain our trust," SlutWalk Toronto demanded via its website. "We want to feel that we will be respected and protected should we ever need them, but more importantly be certain that those charged with our safety have a true understanding of what it is to be a survivor of sexual assault—slut or otherwise."[9] A similar appeal emanated from a SlutWalk march in New York City in October 2011. Even though the protest occurred only a few months after the acquittal of two NYPD officers accused of raping a woman while on duty, and only one day after reports surfaced that police investigating a series of rapes in Brooklyn's Park Slope neighborhood were warning women against wearing skirts or dresses because they provide "easy access," SlutWalk New York figured police as agents of sexual and gender justice (Anderson 2011). Carrying signs bearing messages like "Punish rapists not victims!" and "NYPD: Target Brooklyn rapist not women!!!" SlutWalk New York demonstrators called on police to use the full force of their powers on behalf of survivors to catch and punish rapists (Daily Mail 2011; Kirschner 2011). SlutWalk New York organizer Sammy Lifson even couched her critique of victim blaming and slut shaming in terms of police efficacy. "The cops in Park Slope have really stepped up their presence and they're trying to be helpful," Lifson told a reporter at the event, "But to focus on women isn't going to help catch the perpetrator" (Daily Mail 2011). As these remarks reveal, the goal of these North American SlutWalks was not to highlight police and law enforcement complicity in sexual violence and rape culture but to figure the slut as a supplicant before the law as deserving of its benevolent protection as any other citizen.

By framing the slut as a vulnerable subject entitled to the state's protection, the SlutWalk movement invokes what Iris Marion Young calls "the logic of masculinist protection." According to this logic, men are "gallantly masculine" protectors who "[face] the world's difficulties and dangers in order to shield women from harm," while women are submissive "objects of love and guardianship" who "adore [their] protector[s] and happily defer to [their] judgment in return for the promise of security" (2003, 4–5). When this gendered logic is extrapolated to the macro level of the modern state, the outcome is authoritarian. Cast in the role of benevolent masculine protector, the state's power to surveil, police, detain, and repress in the name of the security of its feminized citizenry is virtually limitless. While the SlutWalk movement challenges the logic of masculinist protection at the micro level by repudiating slut shaming and insisting that women be treated as autonomous sexual subjects regardless of their sexual choices, its macro level demand that police respect and protect sluts just as they would any other citizens bolsters the carceral state's image as masculine protector and aggrandizes its power.

The SlutWalk movement's faith in the carceral state's capacity to protect—and ultimately liberate—is not something it inherited from either its sex-radical or antipornography feminist forebears. As I have shown, before the strategic alliance of sex-radical feminists with anticensorship liberals in the mid-1980s, sex-radical feminists were pointedly critical of the criminal justice system. In Gayle Rubin's analysis, the carceral state was not an ally in the feminist struggle for sexual freedom but part of a vast, Kafkaesque system of sexual oppression. The same is true of the original antipornography feminists, who tended to view the carceral state not as an ally but as a mainstay of male supremacy, and therefore an obvious enemy. However, as both of these feminist projects resolved into more conventional liberal forms in the late 1980s and early 1990s, their critical orientations toward the carceral state all but vanished. Intent on vindicating certain feminist goals (e.g., more freedom for certain kinds of sexually explicit expression in the case of anti-censorship/pro-sex feminists, and fewer pornographic images produced using criminal means in the case of antipornography liberals), but wary of betraying liberalism's core tenets, antipornography liberals and anti-censorship/pro-sex feminists stood fast by the freedom of individuals to engage in conventional forms of sexual expression while simultaneously endorsing the use of criminal law to regulate broad swaths of sexual conduct. Both saw criminalization as a legitimate means for achieving feminist goals because both were committed above all else to remaining comfortably within the ambit of liberal legal and political orthodoxy.

SlutWalk, at least in its North American instantiations, is a clear descendant of these sex wars–era liberal–feminist convergences. As such, it provides a concrete and vivid example of how the influence of liberalism can help forge a feminist politics that sees the aggrandizement of the carceral state as a viable means for achieving feminist goals. Committed to a narrow conception of sexual freedom qua expressive freedom, and reluctant to impose itself on the "private" realm of personal choice by criticizing norms, roles, and scripts that enable rape and sexual assault, the SlutWalk movement holds up the punitive power of the carceral state as the key to that great feminist desideratum: sexual freedom. Constrained by its liberal aims, the SlutWalk movement fails to address a variety of grievous sexual injustices in which the carceral state is complicit (e.g., the widespread sexual abuse of prisoners and the harassment of sex workers and queer, trans, and gender-nonconforming people by police), or to advance remedies that decenter and resist the power of the carceral state, such as restorative justice, transformative justice, community accountability, and liberatory abolitionism.[10]

The SlutWalk movement's failures on these fronts lends credence to Cherríe Moraga's insight, discussed in chapter 4, that a connection exists between a monistic focus on the needs, experiences, and desires of white women and a fixation on a narrow set of liberal concerns that fail to advance the cause of sexual freedom for all women, especially women of color. As I showed in chapter 4, during the sex wars, Black and third world feminists rejected the political and theoretical monism of their white allies and theorized intersectional variants of antipornography and sex-radical feminism that framed the fight for sexual freedom as a multidimensional struggle against sexism, racism, colonialism, heteronormativity, and economic exploitation. Given the fact that carceral responses to sexual injustice disproportionately negatively effect poor communities and communities of color, it stands to reason that, had antipornography feminists and sex-radical feminists exchanged their monistic approaches for these intersectional alternatives, feminist sexual politics both during the sex wars and beyond would have been far less susceptible to liberal co-optation and its concomitant carceral drift. The free-speech-friendly, law-and-order-oriented antipornography liberalism of Elena Kagan and Cass Sunstein did little to address the sexist and racist harms of pornography identified by Alice Walker and Patricia Hill Collins, such as the denigration and dehumanization of nonwhite bodies and the undermining of intraracial and intergender political solidarity between women and men of color. Similarly, the narrow defenses of sexual freedom qua expressive freedom offered by anti-censorship/pro-sex feminists like Nadine Strossen and the 1986 ACLU report *Polluting the Censorship Debate* did little to address the demands of Cherríe Moraga and Mirtha Quintanales for a sexual freedom struggle that would complement, rather that compete with and detract from, the antiracist, anticapitalist, and anticolonial struggles of Chicanas and other people of color. Thus, had white antipornography and sex-radical feminists heeded the calls of their Black and third world feminist allies and transformed their projects in explicitly antiracist and antisexist directions, they would have been far better equipped to resist liberal co-optation, thereby retaining their original radical and anticarceral orientations. Had the efforts of Black and third world feminists to build a truly intersectional feminist sexual politics centered on the needs and experiences of women of color during the sex wars succeeded, the trajectory of feminist sexual politics would have been dramatically altered, culminating in something far less beholden to liberalism and its attendant carceral logics than contemporary movements like SlutWalk. As critic and journalist Aura Bogado has suggested, SlutWalk's carceral orientation has everything to do with its origins in the narrow experiences and concerns of privileged white women.[11] A movement against sexual oppression and for sexual freedom framed along the lines proposed by Black and third world feminists during the sex wars would look quite different, placing far less emphasis on personal expression and the apprehension, prosecution, and punishment of criminals and far more emphasis on addressing the myriad forms of sexual injustice perpetrated by the carceral state.

THE TROUBLE WITH TRIGGER WARNINGS

As the foregoing discussion has shown, the convergence of antipornography feminism, sex-radical feminism, and liberalism during the sex wars gave rise to new liberal–feminist hybrids that were far less critically oriented toward the carceral power of the state than their unadulterated feminist predecessors had been. Nevertheless, the carceral thrust of antipornography liberalism, anti-censorship/pro-sex feminism, and their present-day descendants should not obscure the fact that these projects are, at bottom, creatures of liberalism, and as such are jealous of individual liberty, suspicious of state power, and deeply invested in the public/private distinction. Indeed, as I have argued, it is these consummately liberal commitments that seem to have propelled these liberal–feminist hybrids in unanticipated carceral directions. To more fully illuminate the dynamic by which an increasingly liberal feminism fuels an increasingly carceral feminism, I will turn now to what may strike some as a rather unlikely place: the modest, consummately liberal, and scrupulously nonpunitive trigger warning.

Originating in feminist spaces on the Internet, trigger warnings, as their advocates describe them, are "minimalistic description[s] that tag articles, literature, and other works of art for traumatic content" (Wythe 2014). According to a resolution to "Mandate Warnings for Triggering Content in Academic Settings" enacted by the University of California, Santa Barbara's, student senate in spring 2014, examples of trigger warnings include "Rape, Sexual Assault, Abuse, Self-Injurious Behavior, Suicide, Graphic Violence, Pornography, Kidnapping, and Graphic Depictions of Gore" (Calderon and Wakefield 2014). Affixing labels of this sort to potentially "triggering" materials, advocates argue, enables survivors of sexual assault and other trauma to "protect themselves" from content that might elicit "memories or flashbacks," "cause . . . severe emotional, mental, and even physical distress," and adversely "affect a student's ability to perform academically" (Wythe 2014; Diamba 2014; Calderon and Wakefield 2014).

While critics denounce trigger warnings as encroachments on academic freedom and freedom of speech, advocates insist that they are nothing of the sort.[12] For instance, according to the aforementioned University of California, Santa Barbara, student senate resolution, "Including trigger warnings is not a form of criticism or censorship of content. . . . It . . . simply requests the respect and acknowledgment of the effect of triggering content on students with PTSD, both diagnosed and undiagnosed" (Calderon and Wakefield 2014). The architect of a controversial trigger warning policy at Oberlin College makes a similar point, insisting that the policy outlined in the college's sexual offense resource guide "values academic freedom *and* support for survivors of sexualized violence" (Flaherty 2014). Likewise, in an op-ed urging professors to incorporate trigger warnings into course syllabi, Rutgers University student Phillip Wythe (2014) praises "trauma trigger warnings" as "a safety system that allows full artistic expression, as well as psychological protection for those who need it." Justin Peligri (2014), another student trigger warning advocate, has gone so far as to describe trigger warnings as a "liberal-minded attempt to promote sensitivity and respect."

As these arguments on behalf of trigger warnings indicate, trigger warnings are seen by their advocates as a means of addressing the potential harmfulness of depictions of sex and violence without interfering with the freedom of individuals to consider such depictions if they so choose. In this sense, trigger warnings appear to be the descendants of antipornography liberal proposals put forward in the 1980s and 1990s. Like the antipornography liberals described in chapter 2, proponents of trigger warnings eschew broad and deeply political conceptions of the harm brought about through sexually explicit or violent depictions (e.g., objectification, subordination, silencing), opting to speak instead in narrower, more individualized terms of harms such as emotional distress, physical discomfort, and psychological trauma. Such language is of course virtually identical to the language used in the antipornography liberal proposal offered up by Dorchen Leidholdt at the University of Chicago School of Law in 1993. Pornography in the workplace, Leidholdt argues, has the capacity to cause "psychological damage," "emotional distress," and "psychic trauma" so severe that it constitutes "a barrier to equal employment opportunities for women" (1995, 217, 218). The harm trigger warning advocates hope to obviate—debilitating psychic pain brought about through unwanted exposure to sexually explicit or violent depictions—is virtually identical to the harm that Leidholdt attempts to address through sexual harassment law.

While trigger warning advocates use descriptions of harm that are virtually identical to those used by antipornography liberals, the parallels between the trigger warning phenomenon and antipornography liberalism should not be overstated. For instance, despite their insistence that depictions of sex and violence have the power, in certain circumstances, to inflict acute and debilitating psychic pain, trigger warning advocates do not hitch this figuration of harm to policy prescriptions that seek to eliminate or curtail the availability of sexually explicit or violent depictions. Unlike antipornography liberals, who sought to regulate pornography as extensively as their various understandings of liberal principles would allow, trigger warning advocates do not seek to eliminate or restrain triggering expression at all. Rather, what they call for is the adoption of voluntary systems of content labels that enable individuals to make informed decisions about what to look at, listen to, or participate in.[13] As trigger warning advocate and editor in chief of *Bitch* magazine Kjerstin Johnson puts it, trigger warnings "center around a central tenet of feminism—choice. They're . . . a two-word announcement for people to choose to read on or pass over depending on their preference" (Johnson 2010). Such warnings are a far cry even from the attenuated version of the Dworkin–MacKinnon antipornography civil rights ordinance advocated by Sunstein, the criminal ban on materials whose production involved coercion or violence advocated by Kagan, and the sexual harassment approach to pornography in the workplace advocated by Leidholdt. In fact, insofar as they take unreconstructed liberal notions of choice, privacy, and expressive freedom as indispensable feminist values, trigger warnings appear to be the descendants not of antipornography liberalism but of anti-censorship/pro-sex feminism.

An op-ed written in support of trigger warnings by members of the Multicultural Affairs Advisory Board (MAAB) at Columbia University conveys the anti-censorship/pro-sex feminist dimensions of the trigger warning phenomenon plainly. After describing the experience of a student and sexual assault survivor who was triggered by an assigned reading in a mandatory general education course, the MAAB members urge the Center for the Core Curriculum, the body that oversees the general education program at Columbia, to act on three recommendations. First, they call on the center to "issue a letter to faculty about potential trigger warnings and suggestions for how to support triggered students" (Johnson et al. 2015). Second, they call for the creation of "a mechanism for students to communicate their concerns to professors anonymously" as well as "a mediation mechanism for students who have identity-based disagreements with professors." Finally, the MAAB members suggest that the center "create a training program for all professors . . . which will enable them to constructively facilitate conversations that embrace all identities, share best practices, and think critically about how the Core Curriculum is framed for their students." "Our vision for this training," the MAAB members emphasize, "is not to infringe upon the instructors' academic freedom. . . . Rather, it is a means of providing them with effective strategies to engage with potential conflicts and confrontations in the classroom, whether they are between students or in response to the material itself." As a *Washington Post* report on the Columbia trigger warning controversy observes, the goal of the students advocating trigger warnings is "more discussion, not less" (Miller 2015).

A more consummately liberal response to the problem of allegedly harmful expression is difficult to imagine. In fact, apart from their concern about the potential harmfulness of sexually explicit or violent representations and their vaguely feminist interest in accommodating survivors of sexual assault and "embrac[ing] all identities," MAAB members defend a position akin to the strict civil libertarian position on sexually explicit or otherwise offensive expression that predominated before the curious couplings of liberalism and feminism during the sex wars. Consider, for example, the following bit of cold comfort Herald Price Fahringer, defense attorney for unrepentant triggerers Al Goldstein and Larry Flynt, offers antipornography feminists at the New York University School of Law in 1978: "No one is compelled to either see or read what is repulsive to him or her. Those who are appalled by these materials can ignore them" (1979, 251). Today, in the aftermath of antipornography feminism's and sex-radical feminism's all but complete subsumption into liberalism, feminists who are earnestly concerned about the potentially harmful effects of certain sexually explicit representations are demanding little more than the tools necessary to allow individuals to act on Fahringer's advice.

Prima facie, trigger warning policies like those I have just described appear to undercut my earlier point regarding the liberal genealogy of feminism's carceral turn. After all, if the offspring begotten by the various conjunctions of liberalism and feminism during the sex wars are as feeble and benign as a voluntary system of content labels designed to facilitate individual self-protection and choice, then where is the impetus toward the aggrandizement of carceral power in that? Aren't trigger warnings prime evidence that the relationship between liberalism and carcerality is an inverse relationship? That the more authentically liberal a policy, the less susceptible it is to carceral drift? Ironically, this very assumption underlies civil libertarian critiques of trigger warnings, which cast the modest content labels as part of a nascent totalitarian feminist regime of thought control. On this account, the carceral feminist potential of trigger warnings inheres not in trigger warnings' liberalism, which these critics consider specious, but in their illiberalism, which these critics take to be a natural upshot of their feminism. My contention here is precisely the opposite. The relationship between liberalism and carcerality as I am theorizing it here is not inverse but direct, and the carceral feminist potential of policies like trigger warnings inheres not in their lack of liberalism but in their surfeit of it.

Allow me to explain. When confronted with the realities of sexual injustice like rape, sexual assault, sexual harassment, or other forms of sexual abuse, oppression, and exploitation, the menu of responses that liberalism permits itself to offer is remarkably limited. If it can be determined, according to the rigorous standards of due process that liberalism requires, that a crime has been committed, then liberals will afford victims of sexual injustice sweeping carceral remedies like indictments, prosecutions, and potentially punishment by imprisonment.[14] However, if a particular sexual injustice cannot be construed as a criminal act or cannot pass the high procedural bar set by liberal due-process standards, then the only remedies liberalism has to offer are toothless and insubstantial trifles like trigger warnings. Liberals will grudgingly, and with the utmost reluctance and caution, countenance these paltry, second-tier remedies because they leave undisturbed all relations, dynamics, norms, structures, events, and actions that occur within the sacrosanct prepolitical "private" realm of unconstrained individual liberty. Of course, the very sexual injustices for which these remedies are prescribed are also located within this private realm, thereby calling into question the status of these remedies as remedies at all. This incapacity, endemic to liberal politics and theory, to address sexual injustice in any meaningful way short of criminalization and punishment creates a vacuum that carceral feminism stands ready to fill. Unlike liberalism, feminism is a politics defined by a deep concern for sexual injustice. When feminism is not subordinated to the political preoccupations and priorities of liberalism, it is capable of addressing this injustice in a variety of ways. The struggles between antipornography feminists, sex-radical feminists, and Black and third world feminists during the sex wars are a testament to the wide range of sexual political possibilities open to a feminism that is not hedged round by liberal constraints. However, when feminism is made an adjunct of liberalism as it was during the sex wars' later phases, and as it has largely remained since, its ability to address sexual injustice is severely curtailed. Conceptually impoverished and politically hamstrung, the only remedies a thoroughly liberalized feminism has to offer are as feeble as trigger warnings or as grave as SlutWalk's dystopic vision of policing and prosecuting our way to sexual liberation. Confronted with these choices, those who are inclined to take sexual injustice seriously and who seek a remedy that is proportionate to the gravity of the harm will find the more substantial carceral option difficult to resist. It is in this way that liberalism propels feminism in carceral directions.

This observation regarding liberalism's propensity to galvanize carceral feminist energies connects back to my earlier observations in the introduction regarding the peculiar convergence of antifeminist conservatives and sex-positive feminists and progressives in the current #MeToo moment. If the relationship between liberalism and carceral feminism that I have just theorized holds true in this case, then sex-positive feminist framings of #MeToo as a threat to individual liberty, due process, and personal privacy are feeding into a dynamic that stands to increase the already powerful appeal of carceral feminism in our present political moment.[15] By stymieing efforts undertaken via #MeToo to politicize forms of sexual injustice that are quotidian, banal, and simply part of the furniture of everyday life for people who are situated at the losing end of any number of unjust social hierarchies, sex-positive feminists and progressives create a vacuum that carceral feminism stands ready to fill. If the sexual politics of liberalism carries the day and substantive remedies are made available for only the most egregious and extraordinary forms of sexual injustice, then the claims that are currently finding expression via #MeToo must go somewhere. A fast-food worker who endures unwanted sexual advances from her boss at work, only to be passed over for management trainings and promotions, has suffered a wrong and deserves a remedy. A hotel housekeeper who reports her boss for making unwanted sexual advances at work, only to have her work hours reduced and her job threatened, has suffered a wrong and deserves a remedy.[16] A woman whose date initiates sexual activity insistently and repeatedly, with no regard for her obvious lack of interest or desire, has suffered a wrong and deserves a remedy. A teenager who is corralled into a bedroom and groped clumsily over her clothes by a young man who will, decades later, be appointed to the Supreme Court of the United States has suffered a wrong and deserves a remedy.[17] Those aggrieved by sexual injustice that falls short of the threshold of criminality but that works to sustain unjust systems of sexual, racial, and economic subordination just the same must go somewhere. Where no crimes have been committed, sexual injustice may still have occurred, and if feminism is ever to be anything other than carceral feminism, then it must look beyond the attenuated sexual politics of liberalism and toward alternatives in which potent, public, political, and, most importantly, anticarceral responses to sexual injustice are at least conceivable.

As *Why We Lost the Sex Wars* has endeavored to show, the history of the feminist sex wars is brimming with such alternatives. Whether it was antipornography feminists challenging anticensorship liberals to take seriously women's subordination and the insidious "private" and "apolitical" dynamics through which it is effected, sex-radical feminists reaching beyond the ambivalent sexual politics of postwar liberalism to pursue an expansive program of sexual liberation that subverted the boundaries between the public and the private and the perverse and the normal, or Black and third world feminists pressing both antipornography and sex-radical feminists to realize the full radical potential of their sexual politics by centering the lives and experiences of women of color, feminists of virtually all stripes during the sex wars understood that a sexual politics hemmed in by liberal preoccupations and concerns was insufficient for the achievement of sexual justice. Unfortunately, the distortions of the catfight narrative have pushed much of this history from view and driven substantial swaths of contemporary feminism into an uncritical embrace of the false and politically paralyzing belief that engaging with sex in a critical way as a political practice that is often employed to maintain systems of subordination is repressive, sex-negative prudery. This sex-positive feminism, which likens #MeToo to the Cosa Nostra and joins with classical liberals and conservatives in demurring from any robust, collective, and explicitly political effort to combat sexual injustice by contesting the structures and norms that sustain it, purports to reflect the hard-won wisdom of the feminist sex wars, but nothing could be further from the truth. During the sex wars, antipornography feminists, sex-radical feminists, and Black and third world feminists all roundly rejected a liberal sexual politics oriented around expressive freedom, personal privacy, and the frisson of conventional heterosexuality. By exploding the catfight narrative and recovering this history, *Why We Lost the Sex Wars* will, I hope, fire feminist imaginations and revivify something of the radical impulses that sparked the feminist sex wars, but unfortunately did not survive them.

Acknowledgments

As Roland Barthes has famously observed, "A text does not consist of a line of words, releasing a single 'theological' meaning (the 'message' of the Author-God), but is a space of many dimensions, in which are wedded and contested various kinds of writing, no one of which is original: the text is a tissue of citations, resulting from the thousand sources of culture. . . . The book itself is only a tissue of signs, a lost, infinitely remote imitation" (1977, 146–47). Nothing has brought me more to grips with the cogency of Barthes's insight here than actually having written a book myself. I say this, of course, not to evade responsibility for what I have written—especially its many flaws and shortcomings—but to convey the sense of humility I feel as I join the ranks of "the eternal copyists" who "can only imitate a gesture forever anterior, never original" and whose "only power is to combine" (147). Each person included in these acknowledgments makes up a vital part of the tissue of this book, and I am inexpressibly grateful for their contribution to the illusion of my authorship.

The University of Florida is where I incurred my first debts with respect to this project. Daniel I. O'Neill was a boundless source of encouragement and insight. His unwavering conviction that even the most obscure facets of history can be of urgent contemporary political value infuses the book from beginning to end. The trust and respect he showed me by supporting my decision to pursue a project like this is something I will never forget.

A similar expression of gratitude is owed to other mentors and colleagues at the University of Florida. Florence Babb, Lawrence Dodd, Laura Sjoberg, Daniel A. Smith, and Leslie Paul Thiele all shaped this project in fundamental ways. Anita Anantharam, Leslie Anderson, Michael Bernhard, Kendal Broad, Aida Hozic, Michael Martinez, Bonnie Moradi,

Ido Oren, Judith Page, Beth Rosenson, and Benjamin B. Smith all helped initiate me into a rich, diverse, and refreshingly interdisciplinary intellectual community.

This book would also not exist without the nourishment—both intellectual and professional—that I have received from a community of brilliant and generous feminist political theorists. Whether it was inviting me to their campus to share my work or inviting me to share a drink or a meal and a conversation at a conference; whether it was encouraging me to contribute to an edited volume for which they thought my work would be well suited or encouraging me to stick it out through a challenging period because they believed in me and the work I was doing, everyone listed here has made not only this book but my career as a political theorist possible. Thank you to Brooke Ackerly, Libby Anker, Cristina Beltrán, Nolan Bennett, Sandrine Bergés, Jocelyn Boryczka, Eileen Botting, Susan Burgess, Anand B. Commissiong, Madeline Cronin, Heath Fogg Davis, Shirin Deylami, Andrew Dilts, Lisa Disch, Kevin Duong, Kathy Ferguson, Kennan Ferguson, Michaele Ferguson, Megan Gallagher, Farah Godrej, Lilly Goren, Judith Grant, Cheryl Hall, Mary Hawkesworth, Nancy Hirschmann, Jennie Ikuta, Kristy King, Sina Kramer, Ainsley LeSure, Jill Locke, Farhana Loonat, Samantha Majic, Lori Marso, Annie Menzel, Laura Roost, Alisa Rosenthal, Sara Rushing, Nichole Shippen, Carisa Showden, Stacy Clifford Simplican, David Temin, Anna Terwiel, Nancy Wadsworth, Denise Walsh, and Karen Zivi.

Beyond this extensive intellectual and professional community, I am indebted to a number of colleagues I am also fortunate enough to call my friends. Mauro Caraccioli, Alec Dinnin, Manu Samnotra, Mitchell Sellers, and Seaton Tarrant have supported me personally and challenged me intellectually. Former colleagues Patrick Arnold, William Aviles, Joan Blauwkamp, Diane Duffin, Megan Hartman, Susan Honeyman, Peter Longo, Claude Louishomme, Satoshi Machida, Richard Mocarski, Chuck Rowling, Janet Steele, Will Stoutamire, Paul Twigg, David Vail, Linda Van Ingen, Michelle Warren, and Laurinda Weisse showed me warmth, grace, and kindness (with an emphasis on warmth!) when I needed it most. My longtime teachers, mentors, and friends Art Vanden Houten and Timothy Johnson have been pushing me to achieve things I could not have possibly imagined for myself since I was a precocious first-year student in their political science and philosophy and religion courses at Flagler College. Since joining the Flagler College faculty myself, many of my new colleagues have gone out of their way to make me feel welcome and supported. Leslie Robison's whimsical and provocative sculpture series "Honing Power" inspired the earliest visions I had of this book's cover and the staff at both the Proctor Library and the Jacksonville Public Library provided research support at crucial moments. I am grateful to be surrounded by such competence, talent, and creative energy.

Finally, I must acknowledge the intimate circle of family (biological and otherwise) whose support—material and spiritual, emotional and practical—made this work possible. Lana Bracewell, Michael Bracewell, Jeannette "J.M." Goldman, Johnny Rocket Ibanez, William Kelly, Jessica Lancia, Nicole Matuska, "Uncle" Patricia Walsh, Amy Wenditz, and P. J. "Pork and Jalapeños" Worth, you make my life worth living, and I promise, this is the only part of this book that I expect you to read. Paola Aguirre, it seems foolish to even attempt to recognize all that you've poured into this work. Whatever is best in it, I learned from conversations with you . . . or possibly from marginalia you scribbled in books I stole from you somewhere along the way. As proud as I am of having seen this project through to its completion, I am prouder still to be your wife.

Notes

1. According to data released by Facebook, within twenty-four hours of Milano's initial tweet, 4.7 million users had made some twelve million #MeToo-related posts, comments, and reactions on the platform (CBS News 2017).
2. The online news website Vox (https://www.vox.com/) kept a running tally of those accused under the auspices of #MeToo up through January 2019. Some of the most prominent among the accused to face meaningful consequences are Al Franken, who was forced to resign his seat in the U.S. Senate; Travis Kalanick, who was ousted from his position as the CEO of Uber; and actor and comedian Louis C.K., who saw a host of lucrative film and television deals cancelled. As for Harvey Weinstein, he was fired from his position at the Weinstein Company and in February 2020 was convicted on two felony sex crimes charges. Of course, not all of those accused have experienced sanctions of this substance and severity. For example, Donald Trump was elected president of the United States, Brett Kavanaugh was appointed an associate justice of the U.S. Supreme Court, and Joe Biden was selected as the Democratic Party's 2020 presidential nominee despite credible accusations of sexual assault.
3. Data are available from the EEOC on the number of sexual harassment complaints and charges filed (https://www.eeoc.gov/).
4. Both houses of the U.S. Congress have taken up legislation updating Congress's sexual harassment policies to lessen the burden on victims filing formal harassment complaints and to require individual lawmakers, rather than U.S. taxpayers, to pay for any harassment-related settlements they may enter into while in office. House Democrats in April 2019 also introduced the BE HEARD in the Workplace Act (https://www.congress.gov/bill/116th-congress/house-bill/2148/text), legislation that would, among other things, close loopholes in federal discrimination law that leave many domestic workers without legal protections from sexual

harassment, authorize grants to help low-income workers seek legal recourse if they are harassed, and eliminate the lower minimum wage for tipped workers. Helpful overviews of #MeToo-inspired legislation at the state level are provided by the Pew Charitable Trusts (https://www.pewtrusts.org/) and the American Bar Association (https://www.americanbar.org/).

5. MeToomentum (http://www.metoomentum.com/) provides a vivid graphical depiction of #MeToo's reach and impact.

6. Since these critiques first appeared, #MeToo has transcended its origins in the Hollywood elite to become a tool for labor activists in the service industries. For example, the working-class women of color currently spearheading the fight for higher wages and better working conditions at the McDonald's fast-food chain are doing so under the banner of #MeToo as part of the Fight for $15 campaign (https://fightfor15.org/).

7. This convergence of various species of conservatives, progressives, and feminists on familiar classical liberal terrain is not confined to the #MeToo backlash. One sees a similar alignment in "A Letter on Justice and Open Debate," an open letter published online by *Harper's Magazine* on July 7, 2020 (https://harpers.org/a-letter-on-justice-and-open-debate/). Born of anxiety surrounding calls to "cancel," or withdraw public support and attention from, public figures who engage in objectionable behavior or express undesirable views, this letter was signed by 153 writers and academics from across the political spectrum. Its most prominent signatories include identity-politics skeptic Thomas Chatterton Williams (the letter's main author); feminists Margaret Atwood, Laura Kipnis, and Gloria Steinem; neoconservatives David Frum and Francis Fukuyama; "race realist" Stephen Pinker; gender essentialist J. K. Rowling; anti–political correctness crusader Jonathan Haidt; and civil libertarians Wendy Kaminer and Nadine Strossen. The letter decries "censoriousness," an "intolerance of opposing views," and "a vogue for public shaming and ostracism" among those engaged in "protests for racial and social justice." As the letter states, "The forces of illiberalism are gaining strength throughout the world . . . But resistance must not be allowed to harden into its own brand of dogma or coercion—which right-wing demagogues are already exploiting. The democratic inclusion we want can be achieved only if we speak out against the intolerant climate that has set in on all sides." While the letter does not expressly mention #MeToo, its claims that "institutional leaders, in a spirit of panicked damage control, are delivering hasty and disproportionate punishments" and that "the heads of organizations are ousted for what

are sometimes just clumsy mistakes" reflect concerns virtually identical to those expressed by #MeToo's critics—and in fact at least three of the letter's signatories (Margaret Atwood, Jesse Singal, and Bari Weiss) also took public stances against what they viewed as the excesses of the #MeToo movement.

8. In characterizing our current sexual politics as "homochromous" and "claustrophobic," I have in mind Eve Sedgwick's notion of "Christmas Effects": "The depressing thing about the Christmas season—isn't it?—is that it's the time when all the institutions are speaking with one voice. The Church says what the Church says. But the State says the same thing: maybe not (in some ways it hardly matters) in the language of theology, but in the language the State talks: legal holidays, long school hiatus, special postage stamps and all. And the language of commerce more than chimes in, as consumer purchasing is organized ever more narrowly around the final weeks of the calendar year, the Dow Jones aquiver over Americans' 'holiday mood.' The media, in turn, fall in triumphally behind the Christmas phalanx: ad-swollen magazines have oozing turkeys on the cover, while for the news industry every question turns into the Christmas question—Will hostages be free *for Christmas?* What did that flash flood or mass murder (umpty-ump people killed and maimed) do to those families' *Christmas?* And meanwhile the pairing 'families/Christmas' becomes increasingly tautological, as families more and more constitute themselves according to the schedule, and in the endlessly iterated image, of the holiday itself constituted in the image of 'the' family. The thing hasn't, finally, so much to do with propaganda for Christianity as with propaganda for Christmas itself. They all— religion, state, capital, ideology, domesticity, the discourses of power and legitimacy—line up with each other so neatly once a year, and the monolith so created is a thing one can come to view with unhappy eyes" (1993, 5–6). Our contemporary sexual politics can often feel this way: an echo chamber of paeans to privacy, pleasure, choice, and personal freedom embellished with cautionary notes sounding from all directions warning against undertaking any action—even the most paltry, meager, symbolic, and insufficient—to challenge this sexual status quo.

9. As Gayle Rubin observes, "As yet, there is no comprehensive history of feminism's sex wars" (2011a, 27). There is, however, a substantial body of scholarship chronicling and reflecting on certain aspects of this contentious episode. See, for instance, Walters (2016), Bronstein and Strub (2016), Bronstein (2011), Rubin (2011b), Love (2011), Duggan and Hunter (2006), Gerhard (2001), Cornell (2000), Hollibaugh (2000),

Rosen (2000), Chancer (1998), Abrams (1995), Vance (1993a), Hamilton (1993), Echols (1989), and Rich (1986).

10. In addition to attending the conference, Butler participated in a postconference "Speakout on Politically Incorrect Sex" organized by the Lesbian Sex Mafia. A brief account of Butler's contribution can be found in *off our back*'s extensive coverage of the Barnard conference (Moira 1982a, 1982b, 1982c). Butler also signed a letter decrying the antipornography feminist protest against the Barnard conference published in *Feminist Studies* (Vance et al. 1983). Butler's participation in the Barnard conference and surrounding events is discussed at length in Corbman (2015).

11. The full text of the leaflet was reprinted in *Feminist Studies* nearly a year after the conference (Coalition for a Feminist Sexuality 1983). Lengthy excerpts from the leaflet were also reproduced in the June 1982 issue of *off our backs* as part of its extensive coverage of the Barnard conference.

12. According to Pat Califia, by the time of the Barnard conference, New York Radical Feminists existed "only as a post office box" (1983, 594). Lisa Orlando (1982), a former member of New York Radical Feminists, corroborates this in an article for *Gay Community News*. A chronicler of the antipornography feminist movement in the United States, Carolyn Bronstein, has also called into question WAVAW's involvement with the leaflet. According to Bronstein, at the time of the Barnard conference, WAVAW was in such a "state of disarray" that "any support for the leaflet could not be said to truly represent the views of a national membership" (2011, 305).

13. In fall 1983, a year before the publication of Ferguson's article, *Feminist Studies* published a letter from Gayle Rubin describing clashes between antipornography and sex-radical feminists as "sex wars" (600). Nevertheless, given the prominent placement of Ferguson's article in a special issue of the flagship journal of the field of women's studies devoted exclusively to the feminist sexuality debates, it seems reasonable and fair to credit Ferguson with coining the name.

14. Vance's concept paper was originally published in 1982 in the Barnard conference's program, *Diary of a Conference on Sexuality*. It was later included in *Pleasure and Danger: Exploring Female Sexuality* (1984), an edited volume that grew out of the conference.

15. Elizabeth Wilson also characterizes the opposition to the antipornography feminist movement as "libertarian" and accuses Gayle Rubin of "simply [restating] an unreconstructed libertarian position" (1983, 36, 38). I take issue with such descriptions in chapter 3.

16. Whether you view sex wars–era feminist critics of pornography as

"pro-censorship" and "anti-sex" bluenoses or "radical feminist" critics of "sexism" and male "dominance" depends, of course, on where you position yourself in the context of sex wars–era debates concerning the relationship of sex and sexual expression to gender-based violence and oppression. Similarly, whether you view sex wars–era feminist critics of antipornography feminism as "sex-positive" feminist freedom fighters or "pro-pornography" sellouts and "sexual liberals" depends on whether or not you find their positions compelling or agreeable. Doubtless the fact that present-day feminists are still at odds over many of the questions at the heart of the sex wars explains, at least in part, the proliferation of names for the sex wars' central combatants.

17. Several scholars have attempted to complicate the traditional narrative of the sex wars by arguing that the clash at Barnard was prefigured by earlier clashes between antipornography feminists and lesbian sadomasochists in San Francisco in the late 1970s. See, for instance, Vance (1993a) and Rubin (2011a). While these accounts are invaluable insofar as they extend the historical frame of reference for the sex wars back beyond the Barnard conference, they ultimately fail to challenge the notion that the sex wars were a simple, two-sided, internecine feminist affair and thus do little to displace the Barnard conference from the center of the sex wars narrative.

18. Perhaps the most compelling example of a radical feminist critic of antipornography feminism is Ellen Willis. As a cofounder of Redstockings, one of the first self-proclaimed radical feminist activist groups in the United States, Willis's radical feminist bona fides are beyond question. Her credentials as a critic of antipornography feminism are equally impeccable. As early as 1977, Willis is on record in a column in *Rolling Stone* magazine as an opponent of the antipornography feminist movement.

19. One potential downside of my decision to use the label "antipornography feminism" instead of other possible alternatives is that it risks obscuring other sex-related issues apart from pornography that were of great concern to "antipornography" feminists, such as rape, S&M, and commercial sex work—or, as antipornography feminists preferred to call it, prostitution. While widespread organized feminist opposition to pornography has by and large receded from its high-water mark in the 1980s, feminists inspired by antipornography feminist ideas are still mounting prominent campaigns in some of these other issue domains, particularly commercial sex work. For examples of contemporary feminist antiprostitution activism, see Moran (2015) and Bindel (2017). For

insightful and critical analysis of this activism, see Showden (2011) and Heath, Gouweloos, and Braimoh (2016).

20. In 1999, Patrick Califia began a process of gender transition and sexual reassignment and now identifies as a bisexual transman. Before 1999, however, Califia was known as Pat Califia and identified as a female lesbian. I note Califia's personal trajectory in this regard because it is vital to understanding his participation in lesbian feminist politics in the 1970s and 1980s.

21. I borrow this figure of speech from Gayle Rubin. See English, Hollibaugh, and Rubin (1982).

22. Amber Hollibaugh made this point with great eloquence and force in her closing remarks at the Barnard conference: "We are searching for ways to examine sexuality, consent and power. We want to expand what we understand about sexuality so that more of us can live the desires we envision. We must start from where we are right now, from the real bodies we live in, the real desires we feel" (2000, 102).

23. As Judith Grant has observed, despite her reputation as "the quintessential essentialist," social constructivist views of gender and sexuality are also evident throughout Andrea Dworkin's oeuvre (2006, 968).

24. It is important to stress that although antipornography feminists opposed heterosexuality as a specific political institution engineered to oppress women, they did not oppose heterosexual behavior or sex between people of different genders as such. Andrea Dworkin (1995) makes this distinction: "Most men and a good number of women experience sexual pleasure in inequality," she explains. "Since the paradigm for sex has been one of conquest, possession, and violation, I think many men believe they need an unfair advantage, which at its extreme would be called rape. I don't think they need it. I think both intercourse and sexual pleasure can and will survive equality."

25. Pornography as heterosexual propaganda is a recurring trope in antipornography feminist discourse. For example, Adrienne Rich describes pornography as part of the "cultural propaganda" that sustains the domination of women by men in the institution of heterosexuality (1980b, 141). Susan Brownmiller describes pornography as "the undiluted essence of anti-female propaganda" and "a male invention, designed to dehumanize women, to reduce the female to an object of sexual access" (1975, 394).

26. In a speech she delivered in November 1979 at WAP's March on Times Square that was later anthologized in *Take Back the Night* (1980), Charlotte Bunch, a founding member of the Furies, one of the earliest lesbian feminist groups in the United States, drew a straight line between the

antipornography feminist movement and the struggle for lesbian and gay liberation. "Last week at the National Gay Rights Rally in Washington," Bunch writes, "over 100,000 people marched to demand better of our society. We demanded the right to control our bodies, including our sexuality, and we demanded an end to social degradation and violence against lesbians and gay men. Today, many lesbians are here marching again to demand that same right as women—to control our bodies and to protect all women from the violence of pornography. The demands of these two rallies are two sides of the same coin. Both are about the absolute right of all people: to the dignity of our sexuality, to the control of our own bodies, and to an end to all forms of violence and degradation against us" (1980, 91–92).

27. Khan (2014) also helpfully underscores the lesbian feminist provenance of sex-radical feminism.

28. This difference raises serious questions about attempts to portray sex-radical feminism, particularly in its earliest articulations, as a species of libertarianism. I address this issue in detail in chapter 3.

29. As Judith Shklar observes, "Years of ideological conflict . . . have rendered [liberalism] so amorphous that it can now serve as an all-purpose word, whether of abuse or praise" (1998, 3). Duncan Bell echoes Shklar's observation, describing liberalism as "a hyper-inflated, multi-faceted, body of thought" and "a deep reservoir of ideological contradictions" (2014, 691).

30. On the centrality of the public/private distinction to liberal theory and practice, see Okin (1979, 1989), Elshtain (1981), and Pateman (1989b).

31. Rubin describes these descriptions as "erroneous and misleading" (2011b, 390). According to Rubin, while it is true that both sex-radical feminists and libertarians largely "agree on the pernicious qualities of state activity in" the area of consensual sex, the similarity between these two parties ends there. As Rubin explains, "Feminist sex radicals rely on concepts of systemic, socially structured inequalities, and differential powers. In this analysis, state regulation of sex is part of a more complex system of oppression that it reflects, enforces, and influences. The state also develops its own structures of interest, powers, and investments in sexual regulation" (390).

32. By describing the sexual politics of antipornography feminism and sex-radical feminism as monistic, I mean to convey their tendency to focus primarily on one form of oppression at the expense of others. For example, as I argue at length in chapter 4, white antipornography feminists were overwhelmingly concerned with pornography's role in

the oppression of women on account of their sex or gender, and often had less than illuminating things to say about pornography's role in oppressing women—and men for that matter—on account of their race. White sex-radical feminists were similarly myopic in their focus on sexual oppression, having little to offer in the way of thoughtful analysis of the complex political realities confronting women deemed deviant not only on account of their nonnormative sexualities but also on account of their nonnormative racial, ethnic, and cultural backgrounds. By using the term "monistic," I wish to highlight the failure of white antipornography and sex-radical feminists during the sex wars to offer a feminist sexual politics that was truly intersectional—that is to say, attentive to the ways in which interlocking and overlapping inequalities of race, gender, and class play out in the domain of sex and sexuality. For important contributions to the concept of intersectionality apart from King's (1988), see Beale (1995), Davis (1981), Crenshaw (1989, 1991, 2012), Collins (1990, 2000), Hancock (2016), and Cooper (2016).

1. "PORNOGRAPHY IS THE THEORY. RAPE IS THE PRACTICE."

1. As Joan DeJean (2002) notes, for centuries, *obscenus* and *obscenitas* were translated vaguely as "infamous" and "infamy." *Obscenity* did not take on its modern sexual connotation until the original Latinate meaning of these terms was recovered in seventeenth-century France.

2. The actual name of the Comstock Act was the Act for the Suppression of Trade in, and Circulation of, Obscene Literature and Articles of Immoral Use. Passed by Congress in 1873, the act endowed the U.S. Postal Service with the power to prosecute and punish anyone using the mails to disseminate obscene materials, including pornography, contraceptives, abortifacients, masturbatory aids, and information or advertisements concerning contraception. From his position as special agent of the U.S. Post Office, Anthony Comstock oversaw the implementation of the act for nearly forty years.

3. In an interview published in *Ms.* magazine in 1994, Andrea Dworkin and Norma Ramos call for the repeal of all obscenity laws (Dworkin et al. 1994). For a clear and concise statement of the antipornography feminist critique of obscenity, see MacKinnon (1983). On the distinction many (though not all) antipornography feminists draw between sexually explicit materials they find objectionable (pornography) and those they affirm (erotica), see Steinem (1980) and Brownmiller (1980). Not all

antipornography feminists embrace this distinction; see MacKinnon ([1981] 1987). On the close and sometimes fraught relationship between antipornography feminism and lesbian feminism, see Bronstein (2011), particularly chapters 2 and 7.

4. For a rich and illuminating discussion of the ambivalence regarding sex and sexual expression at the heart of postwar liberalism in the United States, see Strub (2011). I also develop this aspect of liberal sexual politics in chapter 3.

5. Defense attorney and outspoken civil libertarian Alan Dershowitz puts forward a similar charge: "Recognizing the reality that most Americans do not want to censor 'mere' violence or sexism . . . , but do want to censor explicit sex, some feminists have created an unholy alliance with some fundamentalists, puritans, and other opponents of sexuality for sexuality's sake" (2002, 167). MacKinnon and Dworkin (1997) catalog and respond to many instances of this charge.

6. This language comes from the pornography civil rights ordinance drafted by Andrea Dworkin and Catharine MacKinnon at the request of the city of Indianapolis in the early spring of 1984. I discuss the so-called Dworkin–MacKinnon ordinance in more detail below.

7. For accounts of the activities of these early liberal free-speech organizations, see Rabban (1997) and Horowitz (2002).

8. When the ACLU was first formed in 1920, its founders were reluctant to acknowledge Schroeder and the Free Speech League among its progenitors.

9. These words were not spoken by Thaddeus Wakeman but by his brother, Abram Wakeman, during the trial of D. M. Bennett on March 18, 1879. The Wakeman brothers served as co-counsel for Bennett, who was being prosecuted under the Comstock Act. That Thaddeus Wakeman shared the views expressed by his brother at Bennett's trial is made clear by comments he made on August 1, 1878, at an "indignation meeting" after the conviction of Ezra Heywood under the Comstock Act. "We are all agreed upon the question of obscenity; no one has a good word for that," Thaddeus Wakeman reassured the gathering of Heywood's supporters (Horowitz 2002, 423). Wakeman's contention was simply that the Comstock Act was an imprecise and overreaching obscenity regulation, and obscenity ought to be stamped out by some other means.

10. Although the laws themselves did not change, the common law standard by which judges and juries adjudged materials obscene, the so-called Hicklin test, was slightly modified. As Charles Rembar, an attorney who played a leading role in mid-twentieth-century liberal campaigns

against obscenity regulation, and who represented Grove Press during the *Lady Chatterley's Lover* litigation, explains, "By the end of the 1940s, the prevailing view was that a book should be judged as a whole, not on the basis of isolated passages" (1968, 22). Also, by this time works were no longer judged obscene on the basis of their tendency to "deprave and corrupt" a reader "whose mind is open to immoral influences" as the Hicklin test required, but by their effects on adult readers (22).

11. For detailed firsthand accounts of this campaign, see Rembar (1968) and de Grazia (1992). For briefer summaries, see Ellis (1988), Downs (1989), the documentary film O'Connor and Ortenberg (2007), and Glass (2013).

12. Rembar acknowledges Rosset's central role in the "the end of obscenity," writing that "Rosset is owed a debt of gratitude—or, if you happen to be on the other side of the fundamental issue, a deep reproach" (1968, 27).

13. The Supreme Court ruled *Tropic of Cancer* not obscene in 1964 in *Grove Press, Inc. v. Gerstein* (1964). Following the precedent set in this case and another in which the Supreme Court found the pornographic classic, John Clelland's *Memoirs of a Woman of Pleasure* (better known as *Fanny Hill*), not obscene, the Supreme Judicial Court of Massachusetts ruled *Naked Lunch* not obscene in 1966. For more detailed accounts of the trials surrounding the American publications of each of these works, see Rembar (1968), Lewis (1976), de Grazia (1969, 1992), Caffrey (1985), Ladenson (2006), and Boyer (2002).

14. United States v. A Motion Picture Film Entitled "I Am Curious—Yellow" 404 F.2d 196 (2d Cir. 1968).

15. *Byrne v. Karalexis,* 1969; see Dershowitz (1982).

16. For accounts of the Grove Press occupation, see Glass (2013), Morgan (2001), Gontarski (1998), and Rosen (2000).

17. Whitney Strub portrays the Grove occupation and other similar occupations undertaken by women's liberationists in the late 1960s and early 1970s as primarily anticapitalist gestures, and only secondarily protests against pornography. This is in the service of his thesis that, early on in the second wave, feminists viewed pornography as more of "an epiphenomenal annoyance" than "the root cause of women's oppression" (2011, 214). Although Strub is right to emphasize that feminist thought on pornography evolved between the earliest days of women's liberation and the heyday of WAP, I believe he understates the antipornography feminist dimensions of the Grove Press occupation. Not only does pornography figure centrally in the demands issued by the Grove Press occupiers, but Robin Morgan, one of the occupation's organizers, would

go on to describe the occupation as "the first time feminists declared pornography as an enemy" (1980, 268).

18. For details regarding the Women's Anti-Defamation League, see Brownmiller (1999) and Bronstein (2011).

19. Morgan's assertion is not entirely accurate. Before the Grove occupation, at least one feminist had openly declared pornography an enemy. In November 1969, in an article entitled "'Sexual Revolution': More of the Same," Cell 16 founder Roxanne Dunbar offers a trenchant feminist critique of pornography (collected in Echols 1989). Andrea Dworkin's description of the takeover of Grove Press as "the first antipornography feminist demonstration" is more accurate, although it does bear mentioning that in January 1970, women, some of whom identified as "women's liberationists," staged a takeover of one of the major "underground" newspapers of the New Left, *Rat* (Dworkin and MacKinnon 1997, 28). The *Rat* takeover was motivated, at least in part, by the paper's publication of sexually explicit images of women. It was also the occasion of Robin Morgan's famous diatribe, "Goodbye to All That," which criticizes *Rat* and other New Left publications for their "porny photos, sexist comic strips, and 'nude chickie' covers" (Morgan 1977, 122). Ruth Rosen (2000) describes an even earlier women's liberation action in the San Francisco Bay area against a radical newspaper, *Dock of the Bay*. The founders of *Dock of the Bay* planned to fund their endeavors through the publication of a pornographic magazine. Women's liberationists caught wind of their plans and sabotaged the plates from which the magazine was to be printed. The publication folded.

20. The impact and significance of Brownmiller's *Against Our Will* is difficult to overstate. In 1975, Brownmiller's book was featured on the cover of the *New York Times Book Review* as one of the best books of the year. In that same year, *Time* magazine hailed Brownmiller as a person of the year, making her one of very few women to have ever received that distinction. Two decades later, in 1995, the New York Public Library included *Against Our Will* in its Books of the Century exposition.

21. Brownmiller is not only the first president of WAP but also its cofounder and chief spokesperson, as well as the author of the script used by the organization in its now legendary porn tours of Manhattan's Times Square. Brownmiller's involvement with WAP is recounted in great detail in Bronstein (2011) and Brownmiller (1999).

22. Born of the entrenched perception that the accusation of rape is "easily to be made, hard to be proved, and harder to be defended," corroboration rules stipulated that a rape conviction could not be sustained based solely

on the basis of testimony of the "prosecutrix." In the 1970s, feminists successfully campaigned for the repeal of these rules. For more information on this and many other aspects of rape law reform in the United States, see Caringella (2009) and Corrigan (2013).

23. This controversy was reported in a series of articles in the university's student newspaper, the *Collegian*. See, for example, "Central Defeats Porno Movie," November 30, 1976a, by Rose Conway; "SW Must Have Sex, Race Programs," December 1, 1976, by Barbara Hoffman; "Central Govn't Debates Movies Guarantee," December 7, 1976b, by Rosemary Conway; and "SWA Votes to Permit Pornography," February 16, 1977, by Larry Cohen.

24. In August 1978, Dworkin's speech was reprinted in *Body Politic,* an influential Canadian gay liberation magazine (Hannon 1978). That winter, Dworkin was invited to deliver "Pornography: The New Terrorism" at a colloquium at the New York University School of Law. The speech was later published, along with a transcript of the colloquium, in the *New York University Review of Law and Social Change* (1979). Lengthy excerpts from Dworkin's speech also appear in a *New York Times* article on the colloquium (Klemesrud 1978).

25. An account of the day's events published in *off our backs* offers a particularly grim assessment. "As the day wore on," *off our backs* reports, "the conflict between feminists and civil libertarians, never exactly undercover, erupted into many bloody episodes, with feminists drawing most of the blood" (Brooke 1979).

26. Carolyn Bronstein has characterized the theoretical chasm on display at the colloquium as a conflict between "classical liberalism" represented by the civil libertarians and "a communitarian social position" represented by the antipornography feminists (2011, 181). While I think Bronstein's characterization of the civil libertarians' position is apt, I cannot say the same of her characterization of the antipornography feminists' position. The antipornography feminists at the colloquium did not assail the liberals for their universal aspirations, their atomized vision of the self, or their tendency to denigrate tradition and culture. In fact, several of them expressed what can only be described as anticommunitarian views. For instance, Florence Rush blamed traditional notions of marriage and family for the sexual abuse of children, and Andrea Dworkin impugned appeals to the common good as ideological ploys used to dupe women into defending a society in which "they have absolutely no stake" (Law 2011, 225, 242). For more on communitarian critiques of liberalism, see Bell (1993) and Delaney (1994).

27. Earlier that day, as Dworkin delivered her speech, "Pornography: The New Terrorism," Chevigny became so incensed that he stood up and left the room (Klemesrud 1978). This surely must have heightened the drama of Dworkin's response.

28. Phyllis Chesler, Leah Fritz, and Florence Rush had presented on the panel before Dworkin.

29. Chevigny's position here is reminiscent of John Stuart Mill's position in *On Liberty* concerning expressions of the opinion that "corn-dealers are starvers of the poor" (Mill [1869] 1989, 56). "When simply circulated through the press," Mill argues, this opinion "ought to be unmolested" (56). However, "when delivered orally to an excited mob assembled before the house of a corn-dealer, or when handed about among the same mob in the form of a placard," Mill contends, this opinion "may justly incur punishment" (56). What Mill means by this is that although accusations circulated through the press that corn dealers are starvers of the poor are likely to prove "disastrous to the interests" of corn dealers, merely "private" harms such as this cannot justify the imposition of a limit on the expression of an opinion (Jacobson 2000, 286). Only where the expression of an opinion can be shown to cause public harm of the sort likely to be brought about by an impassioned oration delivered to an angry mob can limits on speech be justly imposed in a Millian liberal view.

30. Recent sexual assault allegations against Dershowitz as well as his extensive involvement with Jeffrey Epstein, a wealthy financier who pled guilty in 2008 to a felony charge of solicitation of prostitution involving a minor and who was charged in 2019 with one count of sex trafficking of a minor and one count of conspiracy to commit sex trafficking, makes Dworkin's assessment of the masculinist sexual politics underpinning Dershowitz's rhapsodizing about the First Amendment seem prescient. For a detailed account of the allegations against Dershowitz and his decades-long friendship with Epstein, see Bruck (2019).

31. Later versions of the Dworkin–MacKinnon ordinance added a fifth cause of action, "defamation through pornography" (Dworkin and MacKinnon 1985, 140).

32. MacKinnon often juxtaposes the ordinance's civil rights approach with the criminal approach embodied in extant obscenity law. As she explains it, the ordinance "shifts [pornography] from the doctrine of offensive utterances to the doctrine of civil subordination, from the criminal law of morals regulation to the civil law of discrimination, from law that empowers the state to law that empowers the people [and] . . . redistribute[s]

power to citizens" (Lederer and Delgado 1995, 301–2). Robin Morgan makes a similar point in a letter to the editor of the *New York Times Book Review* defending the Dworkin–MacKinnon ordinance. "The 'law' drafted by Andrea Dworkin and Catharine MacKinnon," Morgan (1995) explains, "was in fact an ordinance permitting civil—not criminal—action toward obtaining relief from pornography's violent effects. This is a vital distinction. Having legal recourse to defend one's civil rights is a far cry from censorship. . . . I have never supported censorship (nor has Ms. Dworkin or Ms. MacKinnon)."

33. The ordinance provides that "the use of men, children, or transexuals in the place of women" in materials bearing the features it outlines would also qualify as pornographic and would thus be actionable under the ordinance (Dworkin and MacKinnon 1988, 101).

34. For a detailed account of the campaigns for and against the Dworkin–MacKinnon ordinance in Minneapolis, see Downs (1989). On the reasons behind Mayor Fraser's veto of the Minneapolis ordinance, see *New York Times* (1984).

35. Bronstein describes the decline of the antipornography feminist movement in the early 1980s. By the time the Dworkin–MacKinnon ordinance was introduced in 1983, WAP was the only national antipornography feminist organization left standing, and it "was a strong advocate for the MacKinnon Dworkin anti-pornography ordinances" (2011, 325). When the ordinance was defeated, Bronstein writes, "there was little to nothing left of the grassroots feminist anti-media violence movement to resuscitate" (329).

36. Consent functions in a similarly insidious manner, Pateman (1980) adds, in the laws and conventions concerning the employment and marriage contracts. These insights are more fully developed in Pateman (1988).

37. As we will see, Pateman (1988) echoes Brownmiller's quintessentially antipornography feminist claims regarding prostitution and pornography.

38. By 1980, the antipornography feminist movement had risen to national prominence in the United States. For instance, in July 1979, Brownmiller appeared on the *Phil Donahue Show* alongside WAP's other cofounder, Dolores Alexander, as well as the cofounder of WAVPM, Lynn Campbell. For a detailed description of their appearance, see Bronstein (2011).

39. On the distinction between "classical" and "modern" patriarchy, see Pateman (1989a).

40. Pateman's primary concern is women's subordination through the marriage, prostitution, and surrogacy contracts. However, she also explores

the subordination of both women and men through another contract concerning "property in the person," this time in the form of "labor power": the employment contract (1988, 148–53).

41. Despite the single-minded focus on pornography that their name implies, antipornography feminists were in fact concerned with many forms of what they considered violence against women, including pornography of course, but also rape, incest, wife battering, child abuse, sadomasochism, and prostitution. This wide array of concerns is reflected in many definitive antipornography feminist works, including Brownmiller (1975), Dworkin ([1981] 1991), Lederer (1980), and Barry (1979). Also, the name of the first antipornography feminist organization in the United States, Women Against Violence Against Women, points to the fact that antipornography feminist concerns extended far beyond pornography. Carolyn Bronstein (2011, chap. 2) discusses the influence of feminist antiviolence activism on the emergence of antipornography feminism at some length.

42. In 1976, Kathleen Barry cofounded WAVPM, a San Francisco–based antipornography feminist organization that organized the first national feminist conference on pornography.

43. It is interesting to note that Barry's *Female Sexual Slavery* (1979) is among the works that inspired Adrienne Rich to coin the phrase "the law of male sex right"—a phrase and concept that, as I have already discussed, figures prominently in Pateman's *Sexual Contract* (1988). Also, in the course of laying out her own critique of prostitution in *Sexual Contract*, Pateman cites Barry's *Female Sexual Slavery* (1979) directly.

44. Pateman cites and criticizes Califia's article, "Feminism and Sadomasochism" (1981b), which was written and published as a rebuttal to antipornography feminist critiques of sadomasochism. Pateman's (1988) comments read as a sort of antipornography feminist rejoinder to Califia's defense.

45. Pateman does disagree with MacKinnon's analysis of pornography at one crucial juncture: she does not believe that pornography "turns sex inequality into sexuality and turns male dominance into the sex difference" (1990, 406). In Pateman's view, sex difference is not "merely an artifact of power" but to some significant extent a natural fact (406). Also, according to Pateman, pornography is not to blame for the fact that sexual difference has come to mean political difference. The sexual contract, Pateman explains, established the meaning of "sex" as "men's mastery" long before pornography was even invented (406). This

important difference aside, Pateman is in broad agreement with MacKinnon that pornography does serious harm to women and that the rapid growth of the pornography industry should be a central feminist concern.

46. Note that the problems Pateman identifies with MacKinnon's legal approach are merely technical and administrative ones, as opposed to the deep-seated normative and political problems that Wendy Brown identifies with it.

47. Brown returns to this theme later in the review when she derides MacKinnon's "lawyer's mind" for "silencing the requisite inquiries of nuanced political theory" and figures MacKinnon as a knife-wielding, syllogism-spouting castrator as opposed to a proper political theorist (1989, 491, 492).

2. FREE SPEECH, CRIMINAL ACTS

1. Some liberals did concede that pornography was harmful in the ways antipornography feminists alleged, but they maintained that it was nevertheless deserving of First Amendment protection. For instance, at the 1978 New York University colloquium, "Obscenity: Degradation of Women versus Right of Free Speech," Ephraim London stakes out this position. I present London's position in detail in the main body.

2. WAVAW's boycott of the recording industry was inspired by a billboard advertisement for the Rolling Stones' album *Black and Blue*. The ad featured an image of a woman dressed in lingerie. Her bodice was torn to display her breasts, her hands were tied above her head with ropes, and her bruised legs were spread-eagled atop an image of the Stones, with her crotch hovering just above Mick Jagger's head. The tag line read, "I'm black and blue from the Rolling Stones and I love it!" For a detailed account of the campaign this ad inspired, see Bronstein (2011).

3. Wendy Kaminer offered a similar defense of private action against pornography. "The feminist movement against pornography must remain an anti-defamation movement, involved in education, consciousness-raising, and the development of private strategies against the industry" (1980a, 247).

4. Ephraim London was a well-known civil libertarian attorney who exonerated Roberto Rossellini's film *The Miracle* of obscenity charges in 1952. He also advised Barney Rosset and Grove Press concerning the publication of the unexpurgated edition of *Lady Chatterley's Lover*. For a detailed account of London's involvement with Rossett and Grove, see Glass (2013).

5. Sunstein explicitly distances himself from the traditional liberal position that "all speech stands on the same ground and that government has no business censoring speech merely because some people or some officials are puritanical or offended by it" (1993, 262). Sunstein calls this the "speech is speech position" (267). Instead, Sunstein advocates for a sort of antipornography liberalism that focuses on the regulation of violent pornography. In his view, the problem of pornography is the violence against women that it causes: "Sexually explicit speech should be regulated not when it is sexually explicit (the problem of obscenity) but instead when it merges sex with violence (the problem of pornography). The problem of pornography does not stem from offense, from free access to sexually explicit materials, from an unregulated erotic life, or from the violation of community standards. Instead it is a result of tangible real-world harms, produced by the portrayal of women and children as objects for the control and use of others, most prominently through sexual violence" (263–64).

6. Jeanne Schroeder makes a similar argument regarding Sunstein's project. "In the name of embracing and explicating MacKinnon's critique of pornography," Schroeder argues, "Sunstein rewrites and distorts it in such a way as to leave only a surface similarity, while excising its essential nature. A call for political and sexual revolution becomes an anticrime, antismut bill" (1992, 124). Sunstein, in Schroeder's view, "sincerely wants to be simultaneously both a feminist sympathizer and a good liberal working within respectable, mainstream jurisprudence" (124–25).

7. For detailed accounts of WAVAW's various campaigns, see Bronstein (2011), especially chap. 4.

8. As Bronstein has emphasized, WAVAW leaders were generally reluctant to use the term "pornography" to designate the field of materials to which they objected. "'Pornography,'" WAVAW's national newsletter stresses, "is not a useful word for naming what we are fighting" (2011, 125). It is, the newsletter continued, "both over-inclusive (pulling in erotica and merely sexually explicit materials) and grossly under-inclusive (since it appears to take the heat off of abusive mainstream commercial materials, such as record album advertising" (125). Bronstein makes much of this wariness regarding the word "pornography," arguing that it sets WAVAW apart from other organizations like WAVPM and WAP as an antimedia violence organization as opposed to an antipornography organization. In my view, Bronstein makes too much of this particular difference between WAVAW and WAVPM and WAP. As Bronstein herself notes,

WAVAW, WAVPM, and WAP understood themselves as "sister organizations that were part of the same movement, namely 'the struggle against commercial and cultural exploitation of violence against women'" (6). None of these organizations objected to materials merely on account of their sexual explicitness, and all three objected to materials that they believed contributed to women's subordination. What set WAVPM and WAP apart from WAVAW (besides their emphasis on public legal action as opposed to private consumer action) was their belief that a feminist redeployment of the term "pornography" was possible. While WAVPM and WAP struggled to use the term "pornography" in a novel way to refer to a broad swath of materials that eroticized the abuse and degradation of women, WAVAW chose not to contest the term, believing that doing so would only breed confusion and misunderstanding. This is quite a difference in strategy, but it is not the difference in substance that Bronstein makes it out to be.

9. The Dworkin–MacKinnon ordinance has often been portrayed, particularly by its critics, as an attempt to codify the sweeping definition of pornography embraced by the broader antipornography feminist movement at the time. For instance, in the *Washington Post,* Hans Bader (1992) accuses the Dworkin–MacKinnon ordinance of seeking "to ban French and Italian art films, avant-garde art and even Rolling Stones album covers." Similarly, in the *New York Times,* Michiko Kakutani (1993) criticizes MacKinnon for "lump[ing] magazines like *Penthouse* and *Playboy* together with snuff films, a stand that leaves the status of Madonna videos, Calvin Klein ads and movies like 'Basic Instinct' decidedly open to question."

10. Dworkin devoted an entire book, *Intercourse* (1987), to criticizing literary works, from Tolstoy's *The Kreutzer Sonata* to James Baldwin's *Another Country,* for sanctioning the sexual abuse and degradation of women. Similarly, MacKinnon often notes the troubling continuities she perceives between pornography and other types of media, as in this representative remark: "Pornography becomes difficult to distinguish from art and ads once it is clear that what is degrading to women is the same as what is compelling to the consumer" (1989, 113). Later, she adds, "Pornography converges with more conventionally acceptable depictions and descriptions just as rape does with intercourse, because both are acts within the same power relation" (203). As Schroeder observes, MacKinnon's use of the word "pornography" in this more expansive sense in her theoretical writings marks quite a contrast with her "narrower" and more "technical" use of the term in her ordinance (1992, 157).

11. The ensuing catalog of ways in which Dworkin and MacKinnon believe women are subordinated by and through pornography is based on discussions of pornography's harms found in MacKinnon (1985, 1987a, 1993), Dworkin and MacKinnon (1988), and MacKinnon and Dworkin (1997).

12. Although the plaintiffs, the amici, and the lower district court in *American Booksellers Ass'n, Inc. v. Hudnut* (1986) all took issue with the breadth of the ordinance's definition of pornography, ultimately this aspect of the ordinance was not decisive in its legal defeat. Rather, what sealed the ordinance's fate was the determination of the U.S. Court of Appeals for the Seventh Circuit that it amounted to a content-based regulation on speech that was not neutral in regard to viewpoint. As Judge Easterbrook, writing for the majority, explains, "Under the ordinance graphic sexually explicit speech is 'pornography' or not depending on the perspective the author adopts" (328). In the eyes of the *Hudnut* majority, that the ordinance defines pornography as "the graphic sexually explicit subordination of women" means that the ordinance makes actionable only graphic, sexually explicit speech that endorses a particular viewpoint: the viewpoint that women are inferior to men. Graphic, sexually explicit speech endorsing the opposing viewpoint, that women are equal to men, was left unactionable and untouched. In this sense, Judge Easterbrook argues, the ordinance establishes "an 'approved' view of women, of how they may react to sexual encounters, of how the sexes may relate to each other" and amounted to "thought control" (328). Having found the ordinance unconstitutional on these grounds, it was not necessary for the court to rule on the question of whether the definition of pornography provided by the ordinance was vague or overbroad. "It is the structure of the statute rather than the meaning of one of its terms," Judge Easterbrook concludes, "that leads to the constitutional problem" (327).

13. As Sunstein explains, under the U.S. Supreme Court's holding in *Miller v. California* (1973), "materials can be regulated as 'obscene' when they: (1) taken as a whole, appeal to the prurient interest, (2) portray sexual conduct in a patently offensive way, measured by 'contemporary community standards,' and (3) taken as a whole, lack serious social value, whether literary, artistic, political or scientific" (1986, 595).

14. In *American Booksellers Ass'n, Inc. v. Hudnut,* the Court of Appeals for the Seventh Circuit note the Dworkin–MacKinnon ordinance's failure to incorporate such traditional exemptions to the regulation of obscenity. "The Indianapolis ordinance does not refer to the prurient interest, to offensiveness, or to the standards of the community. It demands attention

to particular depictions not to the work judged as a whole. It is irrelevant under the ordinance whether the work has literary, artistic, political, or scientific value" (1986, 324–25). It should be noted, however, that the most expansive provision in the ordinance, the trafficking provision, did stipulate that "isolated passages or isolated parts shall not be actionable under this section" (Dworkin and MacKinnon 1988, 45). Under this provision, any woman, whether or not she had been individually harmed by pornography, could bring a complaint against producers, sellers, exhibitors, and distributors of pornography for subordinating women as a group.

15. In a later work, MacKinnon rebukes "significant social value" exemptions even more strongly: "Value can be found in anything, depending, I have come to think . . . on how much one is being paid. And never underestimate the power of an erection, these days termed 'entertainment,' to give a thing value" (1993, 88).

16. Although by no means a supporter of antipornography feminism, philosopher Sandra Bartky has described objectification in a way that sheds light on antipornography feminists' use of the term. In Bartky's view, objectification is "compulsive sexualization" (1990, 26). To be sexually objectified is "to be routinely perceived by others in a sexual light on occasions when such a perception is inappropriate" (26). As Bartky explains it, objectification functions socially as "a ritual of subjugation," "a way of maintaining dominance" and "fixing disadvantaged persons in their disadvantage" (27). This closely resembles the arguments of Dworkin, MacKinnon, and other antipornography feminists that objectification is one way in which pornography subordinates women. As MacKinnon once put it, "Pornography turns a woman into a thing to be acquired and used" (1989, 199).

17. Frank Michelman also calls attention to this aspect of Sunstein's approach: "Sunstein urges that not all harms are equal in fitness for First Amendment analysis. Specifically, Sunstein would keep 'silencing' and 'subordination' off the First Amendment radar. He does not exclude these categories from the field of harms that speech can cause, nor does he minimize their gravity, but still he would screen them out of consideration when it comes to a legal appraisal of restrictions on speech. I wonder whether this position is tenable" (1995, 272). For a detailed elaboration of why Michelman wonders if Sunstein's position is tenable, see Michelman (1988–89).

18. For MacKinnon's critique of liberal jurisprudence, see MacKinnon (1983a, 1985, 1989).

19. In "Is Porn Liberating?," Brownmiller expresses a more sanguine view of the First Amendment. The Supreme Court's decision in *Miller v. California*, which was universally reviled by liberals for relaxing obscenity standards and giving the government a freer hand to regulate sexually explicit materials, had given her hope in the possibility that the First Amendment might be made to work for women. "Creeping porn in the name of freedom, liberty and pursuit of the quick buck is symptomatic of disease within a body politic that has yet to come to terms with women," Brownmiller (1973) writes, and "in new respect for Mrs. Grundy," she confesses, "I'm frankly overjoyed that the Court has chosen to give relief." Despite the confidence she expressed in the new *Miller* standards in 1973, by 1979 Brownmiller was no longer convinced that they were sufficient for feminist purposes.

20. As Sheila Kennedy, an attorney who worked on behalf of the ordinance in Indianapolis, explains, the Dworkin–MacKinnon ordinance "is an attempt to *amend* the existing constitutional framework. This particular group of feminists is quite clear in briefs, etc., that we understand that the ordinance as framed is inconsistent with existing law. But we *want* existing law changed so that this approach would be acceptable" (qtd. in Downs 1989, 141).

21. I have found no evidence of Dworkin and MacKinnon directly responding to this passage, but it is easy to imagine the form their response might take: Sunstein, so narrow and literal in his use of terms like "violence" and "harm" in the course of formulating his arguments about pornography regulation, is prepared to use this language liberally, even metaphorically, when it comes to protecting conventional interpretations of the First Amendment that shore up rather than challenge male power.

22. In making this point, Sunstein cites Ronald Dworkin's "Two Concepts of Liberty" (1991b), an essay that is equal parts ode to Isaiah Berlin and critique of Catharine MacKinnon. Ronald Dworkin (1991a, 1991b, 1992, 1993b, 1994) published several other pieces criticizing MacKinnon in the *New York Review of Books*.

23. Schroeder has described Sunstein's approach as transforming Dworkin and MacKinnon's "call for political and sexual revolution" into "an anticrime, antismut bill" (1992, 124).

24. Dyzenhaus's unqualified endorsement of "coercive state action" to mitigate pornography's inequality producing effects seems to go beyond even what proponents of the Dworkin–MacKinnon ordinance called for. For instance, his definition of "censorship" makes no distinction between criminal bans, civil remedies, or wholly private efforts to curtail the

production and consumption of pornography. "Although [antipornography] feminists set no store by conventional methods of censorship, I use 'censorship' here as a shorthand for any coercion, whether state initiated or by dint of informal public pressure, aimed at suppressing production, distribution, and consumption of pornography" (1992, 534). This willingness to use criminal law to address the problem of pornography anticipates the approach to pornography regulation proposed by Elena Kagan.

25. This description of the conference is from the conference's prospectus, excerpted in *off our backs* 23, no. 4. (1993).

26. For instance, both Catharine MacKinnon and Andrea Dworkin offered defenses of their now decade-old ordinance at the conference. Also, critical race theorist Kimberlé Williams Crenshaw delivered a paper criticizing objections to hate-speech regulation that relied on "a particular descriptive and normative image of social relations" in which people "in the absence of state interference" are thought to be "formally equal with one another, . . . interacting on a free plane, a space open to all, where any inequalities are the products of competition" (1995, 170). Such an image, Crenshaw argues, is "insufficiently attuned to social reality" and constitutes a "wholesale denial of the social context of racial domination" (175, 170).

27. For instance, conference organizers Laura Lederer and Richard Delgado highlight two of Kagan's reform proposals, hate crimes laws and laws criminalizing racist and sexist threats or "fighting words," as potentially effective solutions to the problems of pornography and hate speech (1995, 8–10).

28. Leidholdt had been active in the antipornography feminist movement virtually from its inception. She was a founding member of the New York chapter of WAVAW and a participant in that organization's boycott of the recording industry in the late 1970s. In the early 1980s, she became a leader of WAP. In this capacity, she organized protests against *Playboy* magazine and drummed up support for the Dworkin–MacKinnon ordinance in cities throughout the United States. See Bronstein (2011).

29. Leidholdt criticizes the liberal contention that "[human freedom] flourishes as long as the power of the state over the individual is kept in check" (Leidholdt and Raymond 1990, xii). "Although this philosophy accurately describes the situation of white men in this country," Leidholdt claims, "it has never been applicable to the situation of minorities and women" (xii).

30. Catharine MacKinnon actually called attention to this aspect of

Leidholdt's approach during her presentation at this same conference, remarking that although there may be a civil rights law prohibiting "a hostile working environment," "there is no law against a hostile living environment, so everywhere [besides the workplace, pornography] is protected speech" ([1993] 1995, 311).

31. Nussbaum credits Barbara Herman (1993) for prompting her to think about MacKinnon as a Kantian of sorts.

32. "The law of obscenity . . . has literally nothing in common with [the antipornography feminist] critique," MacKinnon insists in what is perhaps her most forceful engagement with criminal obscenity law, an essay entitled "Not a Moral Issue" originally published in the *Yale Law and Policy Review* in 1983. "Their obscenity is not our pornography. . . . Obscenity law helps keep pornography sexy by putting state power—force, hierarchy—behind its purported prohibition on what men can have sexual access to. The law of obscenity is to pornography as pornography is to sex: a map that purports to be a mirror, a legitimization and authorization and set of directions and guiding controls that project themselves onto social reality, while purporting merely to reflect the image of what is already there" (1983b, 345).

33. For example, Whitney Strub (2011) writes at length of the conservative "co-optation" of antipornography feminism. Additionally, many sex-radical feminist critics of antipornography feminism, including Carole Vance, Gayle Rubin, and Pat (now Patrick) Califia, have pointed to the ease with which conservatives adopted the antipornography feminist language of degradation and subordination to paint antipornography feminists as complicit in bolstering a reactionary and antifeminist sexual political agenda. See, for example, Califia (1980b), Vance (1993b), and Rubin (1993). Pro-sex/anti-censorship feminist Nadine Strossen has accused antipornography feminists of forging "frighteningly effective alliances with traditional political and religious conservatives who staunchly oppose women's rights, but who also seek to suppress pornography" (1995, 13). That these analyses of antipornography feminism's relationship to the politics of conservative backlash in the 1980s and 1990s fail to acknowledge or grapple with antipornography feminism's improbable liberal trajectories is truly regrettable, as there are many important questions that could be raised and engaged in light of the more complicated view of antipornography feminism's legacies that I am arguing for here. For example, did liberals prove more amenable to antipornography feminist ideas in the 1980s and 1990s than they had in the 1970s because they were eager to gain feminist allies in their fight

against their new formidable opponent, the New Right? Or did liberals adopt a more critical and oppositional stance toward pornography in the 1980s and 1990s as a way to remain politically relevant in a moment of conservative ascendancy by distancing themselves from the caricature the New Right had successfully painted of them as libidinous libertines? I raise these questions in the hope that future scholarship will explore them, thereby deepening our understanding of the scope and intensity of the politics of conservative backlash in this period.

3. AMBIVALENT LIBERALS, SEX-RADICAL FEMINISTS

1. Glass has emphasized the central role played by "experts" in legitimating not only the publication of sexually explicit texts, but in "the academic canonization of modernism" and the invention of the "modern classic" (2013, 103).

2. The Second Court of Appeals was ultimately persuaded by Rembar's reasoning. According to the majority opinion, "the predominant appeal of *Lady Chatterley's Lover* . . . is demonstrably not 'prurient interest'" and the work's "thesis" is the same one "pressed continuously in the modern marriage-counseling and doctors' books written with apparently quite worthy objectives and advertised steadily in our most sober journals and magazines" (*Grove Press, Inc. v. Christenberry,* 1960).

3. Interestingly, D. H. Lawrence appears to have shared these views: "The right sort of sex stimulus is invaluable to human daily life . . . but even I would censor genuine pornography, rigorously." "It would not be very difficult," Lawrence explains, "In the first place, genuine pornography is almost always underworld, it doesn't come into the open. In the second, you can recognize it by the insult it offers, invariably, to sex, and to the human spirit. Pornography is the attempt to insult sex, to do dirt on it. This is unpardonable" ([1930] 2004, 240–41).

4. Rembar's employer, Grove Press owner Barney Rosset, appears to have shared this view. In the late 1960s, Rosset, the publisher of numerous sexually explicit works, including an entire catalog's worth of Victorian and Edwardian pornography, criticized Al Goldstein, the publisher of *Screw,* for printing material that was "too dirty" (O'Connor and Ortenberg 2007). Goldstein retaliated by putting Rosset on his magazine's infamous "Shitlist."

5. The following discussion of sex-radical feminism's critical engagement with liberalism focuses on the writings and activism of Samois not

because Samois was the only sex-radical feminist organization active in this political space at this time, but because Samois and its members left behind the most thorough and accessible record of their activities and the political ideas that motivated them. Other sex-radical feminist groups active during this period include the Lesbian Sex Mafia, which was founded in New York City in 1981, and Cardea, a small discussion group for women that was housed within the larger, mixed-gender San Francisco–based S&M group, the Society of Janus. After Samois dissolved in 1983, its former members went on to found other similar organizations, including the Outcasts, which existed until 1997, and the Exiles. More information about these organizations can be found in Califia (1981a), Rubin (1991), Weymouth and Society of Janus (1999), and Warner (2012). Verta Taylor and Leila J. Rupp (1998) also briefly discuss the activities of Briar Rose, a lesbian S&M group based out of Columbus, Ohio. As this scanty source base shows, there is still much important historical work to be done documenting the sex-radical feminist activism of this period.

6. For Ti-Grace Atkinson's views on S&M, see Atkinson (1982).

7. Califia (1980a, 1981a) provides critiques of antipornography feminism. Bronstein (2014) has also done excellent work situating Califia's erotic fiction, particularly his 1988 *Macho Sluts* collection, in the context of his critical engagement with the antipornography feminist movement.

8. Even Califia's opposition to censorship differed fundamentally from the conventional liberal opposition. For Califia, "battles over freedom of expression . . . have implications far beyond the mere ability of print to circulate without being hampered by agents of the state" (1994d, 19). At stake in these battles, as Califia understands them, is the power of marginalized sexual minorities to counter the dominant culture's inaccurate and harmful messages about their sexualities and "to say what [their] sex means." "The line between word and deed is a thin one," Califia observes, and "a desire that cannot be named or described is a desire that cannot be valued, acted upon, or used as the basis for an identity" (19). Thus, in Califia's view, the freedom of sexual expression is not an end in itself but a crucial aspect of a broader politics of sexual resistance and liberation. For more on Califia's thinking about sexual freedom, see Sigel (1999).

9. Janet Schrim adopts a similar stance vis-à-vis sex law. "No one, I repeat, no one," Schrim declares, "is going to tell me what I can or can't, should or shouldn't do with my sexuality so long as I act with mutual consent

and a regard for personal safety. No feminist, no politician, no right-wing hero, no church—no one!" (1979, 23).

10. Gayle Rubin makes a similar observation: "The label 'libertarian feminist' or 'sexual libertarian' continues to be used as a shorthand for feminist sex radicals. The label is erroneous and misleading. . . . Feminist sex radicals rely on concepts of systemic, socially structured inequalities, and differential powers. In this analysis, state regulation of sex is part of a more complex system of oppression which it reflects, enforces, and influences. The state also develops its own structures of interest, powers, and investments in sexual regulation" (2011b, 390).

11. In a brief historical overview of Samois, Rubin (2004) emphasizes the social, cultural, and community-building facets of Samois's political work. "In its brief five-year history," Rubin writes, "Samois facilitated the establishment of social worlds for lesbian sadomasochists; helped inaugurate the feminist sex wars; developed innovative critiques of sexual oppression; and fundamentally changed the lesbian community, the feminist movement, and the politics of sexuality. It was one of the most influential lesbian organizations of its era."

12. Samois's struggles for access to all these spaces are recounted in Califia (1981a). See also Rubin (1991) and Warner (2012).

13. For a detailed account of the Dworkin–MacKinnon ordinance's career in Indianapolis, see Downs (1989).

14. Vance was the academic coordinator for "The Scholar and the Feminist IX: Towards a Politics of Sexuality," a conference held at Barnard College in the spring of 1982 that brought together leading sex-radical feminist theorists and activists from across the country to critically engage the sexual politics and ideology of antipornography feminism. She was also the editor of *Pleasure and Danger: Exploring Female Sexuality* (1985), a collection of essays that is widely considered one of sex-radical feminism's foundational texts.

15. While Suffolk County's antipornography ordinance borrowed language from the version of the Dworkin–MacKinnon ordinance enacted by the city of Indianapolis, it departed significantly from Dworkin and MacKinnon's original design. For example, according to county legislator Michael D'Andre, a Republican who opposed the Equal Rights Amendment but enthusiastically supported Suffolk County's antipornography ordinance, "The bill was an outgrowth of a move to the right by the country and of a conservative tide that last week propelled President Reagan to his landslide election victory" (Gruson 1984). "We've had too many liberals on the Supreme Court," D'Andre told the *New York Times,* "But we're

swinging the other way now. We're tired of children being ruined. For us to survive as a society, we need laws, we need morality. . . . I don't want to tell anybody what to do as long as they live by the 10 Commandments. I'm telling people what they can print only if it's immoral, only if it's filth, only if it's dehumanizing" (Gruson 1984). Noting the substantial modifications that had been made to her model ordinance as well as the general antifeminist tenor of its local support, MacKinnon denounced the Suffolk County ordinance as "bastardized" and worked to defeat it (MacKinnon and Dworkin 1997, 5).

16. For a transcript of testimony offered by FACT members at various hearings for the Dworkin–MacKinnon ordinance, see MacKinnon and Dworkin (1997). For a description of FACT's protest against the 1986 Attorney General's Commission on Pornography, see English (1987).

17. It has often been mistaken for such. See, for example, Leidholdt and Raymond (1990), Lee (2000), Larson (1993), and Delgado and Stefancic (1992).

18. As Kathryn Abrams notes, the FACT brief "was animated by many of the concerns that inspired the sex radicals" (1995, 321). FACT cofounder and influential sex-radical feminist Carole Vance has also emphasized the continuities between FACT and sex-radical feminism more broadly. "Anti-pornography feminists," Vance recounts, "denounced FACT and its allies as 'sexual liberals' and 'libertarians,'" but "feminist sex radicals . . . were almost never liberals or libertarians in terms of their political philosophy or analysis and rejected these terms, whether used by anti-porn feminists or thoughtless bystanders, as an attempt to misrepresent their intentions and positions" (1993a, 304).

19. The FACT brief was not the only or even the first time sex-radical feminists engaged in what might be thought of as a kind of strategic civil libertarianism in response to antipornography feminist attacks. For example, Cherríe Moraga refers to this tactic in a letter she wrote in the aftermath of the Barnard conference that was published in the back matter of *off our backs*. "Three or so years ago," Moraga writes, "at a 'forum' about s/m, members of WAVPM in the San Francisco Bay Area publicly humiliated Samois members who were in their very presence. I have seldom experienced such a rabid display of intolerance and disrespect for other human beings, even among the most ardent homophobes. Since that time, many women have spoken up for the right of s/m lesbians to speak, call themselves feminists, and have sex as they like it. . . . The WAP attack on the Barnard Conference was a replay of the attack on Samois by WAVPM, where once again many of

us were forced into the position of taking what looks like a 'civil libertarian' stand while anti-porn activists are attempting to destroy livelihood and reputations" (1982, 23). I discuss Moraga's letter and her incisive critique of sex-radical feminism's defensive civil libertarian posture in more detail in chapter 4.

20. My reading of FACT's strategy and its consequences differs from those of other commentators. For instance, in repudiating attempts to paint FACT and its allies as sexual liberals or libertarians, Vance (1993a) makes no mention of FACT's strategic deployment of liberal rhetoric. Deirdre English (1995), in contrast, represents FACT as a consummately liberal organization founded by women who "didn't like having [male civil libertarians] do the fighting for them." On this account, the only distinction between FACT and liberal anticensorship groups were the genders of their members. Finally, Kathryn Abrams (1995) portrays FACT as a largely failed effort on the part of sex-radical feminists to influence liberal thinking concerning women's agency and subjectivity. I am persuaded by Abrams that FACT did indeed fail to influence liberal thinking in this one respect, but I am also persuaded that FACT succeeded in influencing liberal thinking in other important respects that Abrams's account neglects.

21. Other key figures include Wendy Kaminer, Leanne Katz, Thelma McCormack, Wendy McElroy, and Alison Assiter. See, for instance, Kaminer (1980b, 1992), Katz (1993), McCormack (1985), McElroy (1982, 1995), and Assiter (1989).

22. In the summer of 1986, the U.S. Supreme Court summarily affirmed the ruling of the U.S. Court of Appeals for the Seventh Circuit in *American Booksellers Ass'n, Inc. v. Hudnut*. In *Hudnut,* the appellate court held that the version of the Dworkin–MacKinnon ordinance enacted by the city of Indianapolis was a content-based regulation of speech that was not neutral in regard to viewpoint and violated the First Amendment. The ruling referenced the FACT brief approvingly.

23. The essay the ACLU report quotes is "Mass Market Romance: Porn for Women Is Different." It is anthologized in *Powers of Desire,* an edited volume including contributions from other seminal sex-radical feminist thinkers such as Amber Hollibaugh, Cherríe Moraga, Dierdre English, Ellen Willis, Joan Nestle, and Carole Vance. Snitow (1986) also contributed an essay to FACT's *Caught Looking* and coauthored two short pieces with leading sex-radical feminists Carole Vance and Lisa Duggan (Vance and Snitow 1984; Duggan and Snitow 1984).

24. All in all, the 1986 ACLU report endorses thirty-two of the commission's

recommendations pertaining to the regulation of child pornography, including recommendations that state legislatures amend existing laws "to eliminate the requirement that the prosecution identify or procure testimony from the child who is depicted if proof of age can otherwise be established" and "to make child pornography in the possession of an alleged child abuser which depicts that person engaged in sexual conduct with a minor sufficient evidence of child molestation for use in prosecuting that individual, whether or not the child involved is found or is able to testify" (158–59).

4. THIRD WORLD FEMINISM AND THE SEX WARS

1. Bronstein rightly notes that some feminists of color "wanted the predominantly white anti-pornography movement to recognize that women of color experience pornography as a contemporary manifestation of an historic form of oppression, one that gave white men unlimited opportunity to sexually exploit their bodies" (2011, 245). To support this claim, she cites two works: an essay entitled "Racism in Pornography" by Lesbians of Colour included in the edited volume *Good Girls/Bad Girls* (1987); and a chapter from Patricia Hill Collins's *Black Feminist Thought* (1990, 2000) entitled "Pornography and Black Women's Bodies." As I demonstrate in this chapter, the universe of Black and third world feminist writings on pornography is much broader than these two citations, and not all of it is positioned as emanating from outside the antipornography feminist movement as Bronstein represents it. For example, some of the most prominent feminists of color of the era, including Collins, Audre Lorde, Ntozake Shange, and Alice Walker, chose to affiliate with the antipornography feminist movement. They published writings in movement anthologies and participated in movement activities, all the while calling attention to the movement's limitations in regard to diagnosing and responding to what they viewed as pornography's racist harms. The fact that "few women of color elected to join" antipornography feminist organizations like those that are the focus of Bronstein's study does not override the fact that many leading Black feminists were aligned with the antipornography feminist movement in explicit and significant ways.

2. Chicana sociologist Maxine Baca Zinn has made a similar observation, noting that work by U.S. feminists of color "is often tacked on, its significance for feminist knowledge still unrecognized and unregarded" (1986, 296).

3. During the period under consideration, the term "third world feminists" referred to feminists of color—not only Black feminists, but also Chicana, Latinx, and Asian feminists—located primarily in the United States who saw their social, political, and economic fates as linked with those of other nonwhite women in the so-called third world. One early example of third world feminism in action is the Third World Women's Alliance. Founded in New York in 1970 as an outgrowth of the Black Women's Liberation Committee, the TWWA was a revolutionary socialist organization composed of Black and Puerto Rican women who saw the struggles against capitalism, colonialism, racism, and sexism as interconnected and as integral to the liberation of women around the world. The third world feminism that TWWA pioneered proved influential, and by the early 1980s, prominent American feminists of color like Frances Beale, Audre Lorde, Barbara Smith, Gloria Anzaldúa, and Cherríe Moraga were identifying themselves as and with third world women. While the label has fallen into disuse, the legacy of third world feminism endures in what we know today as decolonial, postcolonial, intersectional, and transnational feminisms.

4. Other feminists of color whose contributions to the sex wars merit further examination, but who I have not included here, are Norma Ramos and Ntozake Shange. For a glimpse of their distinctive approaches to antipornography feminism, see Dworkin et al. (1994).

5. Barbara Smith's 1983 *Home Girls* anthology even devotes an entire section to Black lesbian politics and identity entitled "Black Lesbians—Who Will Fight for Our Lives but Us."

6. That *This Bridge Called My Back* was intended to intervene simultaneously into the politics of race, class, and sex is also made clear in the collection's introduction: "We envision the book being used as a required text in most women's studies courses. And we don't mean just special courses on Third World Women or Racism, but also courses dealing with sexual politics, feminist thought, women's spirituality, etc." (Moraga and Anzaldúa 1981, xxvi). Just over a decade after the publication of *This Bridge,* Moraga would go on to coedit, with Norma Alarcón and Ana Castillo, another groundbreaking contribution to feminist racial and sexual thought, an anthology of short stories, poetry, essays, art, and drama by thirty-seven Latina contributors entitled *The Sexuality of Latinas* (1989).

7. Crenshaw introduces the term "intersectionality" in a pair of now canonical articles: "Demarginalizing the Intersection of Race and Sex: A Black Feminist Critique of Antidiscrimination Doctrine, Feminist

Theory, and Antiracist Politics" (1989) and "Mapping the Margins: Intersectionality, Identity Politics, and Violence against Women of Color" (1991). As Crenshaw readily acknowledges, the concept has many antecedents in Black and third world feminist thought. The language of "interlocking" and "simultaneous" systems of oppression comes from Combahee River Collective's "A Black Feminist Statement" (2014). The language of "multiple jeopardy" comes from King (1988). The frightful image of "the many-headed demon of oppression" comes from Gloria Anzaldúa's introduction to the final section of *This Bridge Called My Back*, "El Mundo Zurdo: The Vision." Other forerunners of the concept of intersectionality can be found in Anna Julia Cooper's *A Voice from the South* (1892), Sojourner Truth's "Ain't I a Woman?" (1852), Angela Davis's *Women, Race, and Class* (1981), bell hooks's *Feminist Theory: From Margin to Center* (1984), and numerous other works by feminists of color. For a brilliant history of intersectionality as a political concept, see Hancock (2016).

8. It is unclear whether Lorde composed the essay specifically for the Feminist Perspectives on Pornography conference. Lorde had presented the essay one time previously, on August 25, 1978, at the Fourth Berkshire Conference on the History of Women at Mount Holyoke College. The essay was later included as a chapter in Lorde's *Sister Outsider* (1984). Audio of Lorde presenting "The Uses of the Erotic" at the Feminist Perspectives on Pornography conference is available at www.pacificaradioarchives.org. It should also be noted that Lorde was just one of several feminists of color who attended and participated in the Feminist Perspectives on Pornography conference. Lilia Medina served as moderator for the conference's opening session, and Tracey Gardner led a session at the conference on pornography and racism. For an overview of the conference, including the contributions of these feminists of color, see Friendman (1979).

9. An interview with Lorde was also included in another antipornography feminist anthology, *Against Sadomasochism: A Radical Feminist Analysis* (1982), coedited by WAVPM leader and cofounder Diana Russell.

10. Distinctions between the pornographic and the erotic were a commonplace of antipornography feminist thought. For example, in "Erotica and Pornography: A Clear and Present Difference," an essay first published in *Ms.* magazine and reproduced alongside Lorde's "The Uses of the Erotic" in the anthology *Take Back the Night,* Gloria Steinem explains the distinction in this way: "'Erotica' is rooted in 'eros' or passionate love, and thus in the idea of positive choice, free will, the yearning for a

particular person.... 'Pornography' begins with the root 'porno,' meaning
'prostitution' or 'female captives, thus letting us know that the subject
is not mutual love, or love at all, but domination and violence against
women.... It ends with a root 'graphos,' meaning 'writing about' or 'description of,' which puts even more distance between subject and object,
and replaces a spontaneous yearning for closeness with objectification
and voyeurism. The difference is clear in the words" (1980, 37).

11. By describing the politics of liberation movements as "monistic," Deborah
King means to convey the tendency of feminism, Black nationalism, and
socialism to focus primarily on one form of oppression—sexism, racism,
and classism, respectively—at the expense of others. As King explains,
"To the extent that any politic is monistic, the actual victims of racism,
sexism, or classism may be absent from, invisible within, or seen as
antagonistic to that politic. Thus, prejudicial attitudes and discriminatory actions may be overt, subtle, or covert; and they may have various
manifestations through ideological statements, policies and strategies,
and interpersonal relations. That is, black and/or poor women may be
marginal to monistic feminism, women's concerns may be excluded from
nationalistic activism, and indifference to race and gender may pervade
class politics" (1988, 52–53). I find King's concept of "monism" and
her language of "monistic feminism" accessible and illuminating, and I
use it to highlight the tendency prevalent among white feminists on all
sides of the sex wars to theorize on the bases of their own narrow sexual
experiences and to neglect the unique sexual situations and identities of
nonwhite women.

12. I cannot resist noting that Dr. Judith Reisman, once an antipornography feminist activist prominent enough to be featured in the WAVPM
newsletter, is now a faculty member at the Liberty University School
of Law. The dedication to her latest book, a monograph purporting to
proffer evidence that famed sexologist Alfred Kinsey was "a secret sexual
psychopath" entitled *Sexual Sabotage: How One Mad Scientist Unleashed
a Plague of Corruption and Contagion on America* (2010), reads as follows:
"In praise and gratitude to our moral and honorable Judeo-Christian
Greatest Generation to redress their libeled historical record. And to
United States Supreme Court Justice Antonin Scalia who assured me
decades ago that authoritative evidence might reverse our scientifically
fraudulent sex laws."

13. While Bronstein deserves immense credit for recovering this important
letter from the archive and including it in her text, she also deserves criticism for failing to see how the very existence of a letter like this belies

her claim that pornography was an exclusively white feminist concern. The author of this letter, like the other, more prominent Black feminists discussed in this chapter who allied themselves with the antipornography feminist movement, clearly viewed the fight against pornography as highly relevant to the fight against the oppression of Black women. Although antipornography feminism may have left some, or even most, nonwhite women cold, it incited and engaged the political energies of many others who viewed pornography as a key site of racist and sexist exploitation.

14. For a reading that emphasizes more intersectional currents and possibilities in Andrea Dworkin's political thought, see Whisnant (2016).

15. Collins has also pointed out the monistic character of Dworkin's analysis, noting, "Those Black Feminist intellectuals investigating sexual politics imply that the situation is much more complicated than that advanced by some prominent white feminists (e.g., Dworkin, 1981) in which 'men oppress women' because they are men" (1993, 103).

16. Alice Walker was an especially prolific Black and third world feminist (or "womanist," as she described herself) critic of pornography. She contributed essays and pieces of short fiction to two prominent anthologies of antipornography feminist writing, *Take Back the Night* (1980) and *Against Sadomasochism* (1982). She also included a short piece on pornography entitled "Porn" in *You Can't Keep a Good Woman Down* (1981), a collection of her own essays and short fiction.

17. Collins has also drawn attention to this distinctive aspect of Walker's antipornography feminism: "Walker conceptualizes pornography as a mechanism within intersecting oppressions that entraps everyone. But by exploring an African American *man*'s struggle to understand his participation in pornography, Walker suggests that a changed consciousness is essential to social change" (2000, 141).

18. For a discussion of Rubin's radical political activities at the University of Michigan during this period, see Rubin (1997–98).

19. Rubin's "Thinking Sex" (1984) actually trades in one form of monism for another. Even as "Thinking Sex" criticizes the gender monism of "Traffic in Women" (1975), the "radical theory of the politics of sexuality" it oulines reflects a sexual monism that is just as inattentive to intersections of gender, race, sex, and class.

20. Angela Davis calls attention to the unique position of enslaved Black women at the intersection of race and gender. "Where work was concerned," Davis writes, "strength and productivity under the threat of the whip outweighed considerations of sex. In this sense, the oppression of

women was identical to the oppression of men. But women suffered in different ways as well, for they were victims of sexual abuse and other barbarous mistreatment that could only be inflicted on women. Expediency governed the slaveholders' posture toward female slaves: when it was profitable to exploit them as if they were men, they were regarded, in effect, as genderless, but when they could be exploited, punished and repressed in ways suited only for women, they were locked into their exclusively female roles" (1981, 2).

21. The minutes of the Barnard conference planning committee's meetings, which were published in the conference's program, *Diary of a Conference on Sexuality,* indicate that the committee's analysis of issues pertaining to the intersections of race, gender, class, and sexuality may have suffered on account of the absence of meaningful numbers of women of color. For example, in an entry entitled "Dear Diary, Tues., Nov. 3," the minutes record a discussion among committee members about Black women and sexuality. "Part of the reluctance or difficulty Black women experience in talking about sexuality, especially with White women," the minutes state, "may stem from their experience of sexuality in a context of violence and oppression. One experience: adult Black women students found a discussion of the Hite Report on women's sexual frustration to be interesting, but not about their experience. Does this mean that there is no problem, or don't they want to talk about it in public?" (Vance 1982, 24). That the minutes attribute Black women's reluctance to discuss sex in public with white women to Black women's "experience of sexuality in a context of violence and oppression" is telling. The possibility that this reluctance stems not from some peculiarly negative attribute of Black women's sexual experience but rather from their distrust of white women on account of a long and painful history of being mistreated and oppressed at their hands does not occur to the overwhelmingly white planning committee. Another revealing moment in the minutes comes during a discussion of problems of racial exclusion within the antipornography feminist movement. "The interest in the anti-pornography movement has not been great in the Black community," the minutes read, "in part because the anti-porn analysis does not include the experience and motivation of young Black women working in pornography or on 42nd Street" (Vance 1982, 24). While the committee here displays some awareness of the possible intersectional limitations of antipornography feminism, it also perpetrates a highly problematic conflation of race and class by assuming that Black women would be more interested in antipornography feminism if it placed more emphasis on the experiences

of women engaged in street-level sex work. This attempt on the part of the committee to highlight how out of touch their antipornography feminist foes are with women of color actually ends up highlighting the limitations in this regard of the committee itself.

22. An audio recording of the workshop is preserved in the Lesbian Herstory Archives. The description and analysis offered here are based solely on the account of the workshop provided by *off our backs*.

23. In Allison's contribution to *Pleasure and Danger*, Allison explains the almost natural connection she perceived between the work of the Lesbian Sex Mafia and the work of Black and third world feminists like Barbara Smith and Cherríe Moraga. Citing *This Bridge Called My Back*, Allison explains that the model offered there for thinking through racial difference alerted her to sexual differences feminists were also failing to acknowledge: "In a very real sense, *Bridge* gave me a new way to look at my life because it was so full of the lives of women who, while they were very different from me, voice the same hopes, the same desperate desire to change what any of us is allowed. . . . Most of all it offered a vision that struggle between white women and women of color did not have to be framed in terms of betrayal, that, just as Barbara Smith had put it, we might 'emerge from this not broken.' If we could hope for this across the barriers of color and class, why not across sexuality and gender" (1984, 110). "When Cherríe Moraga spoke of how 'with such grace, such blind faith, this commitment to women in the feminist movement grew to be exclusive and reactionary,'" Allison continues, "she was speaking specifically about racism, and the tendency to ignore or misinterpret the lives of women of color. But her words not only made me look at my own fears, avoidance, and racism but they made me also see that I had the same criticisms of the movement around the issues of class and sex. Moreover, just as I was terrified of addressing my own racism, so too other women were afraid of stepping into the deep and messy waters of class and sexual desire" (110). Cherríe Moraga's and Mirtha Quintanales's remarks at the Lesbian Sex Mafia's post-Barnard speak-out, as I discuss, indicate that third world women themselves may have been less sanguine about the prospects of the interracial sex-radical alliance Allison so clearly wanted to achieve.

24. In a published response to Cherríe Moraga's letter to the editor of *off our backs* critiquing the periodical's coverage of the Barnard conference and the subsequent speak-out, Fran Moira, the reporter who covered the speak-out for *off our backs*, claims that "every single speaker indicated at the outset whether she could be photographed, quoted, or named. Only

one woman said she wanted no mention of her or what she said in any article" (1982d, 23). This leads me to believe that Moira did not name this speaker in her story because the speaker had requested anonymity.

25. Many of the direct quotations included in this section are taken from my transcription of an audio recording of Cherríe Moraga's remarks at the speak-out. The audio recording is preserved in the Lesbian Herstory Archive. A digital copy of the original audio recording was shared with me in a tremendous act of intellectual generosity by Rachel Corbman.

CONCLUSION

1. See, for instance, Critical Resistance and Incite! (2003), Gottschalk (2006), Simon (2007), Bernstein (2007, 2010, 2012), Bumiller (2008), Lancaster (2011), Kim (2015), Heiner and Tyson (2017), and Terwiel (2019).

2. Bernstein also highlights several examples of "center-left" feminists embracing the carceral politics of the antitrafficking movement (2010, 54). Unfortunately, instead of asking what distinctive political commitments may be driving these liberal feminists in carceral directions, she simply describes them as "eager partners to conservative feminist anti-trafficking campaigns" (54).

3. SlutWalk cofounder Sonya Barnett has also identified a Manitoba judge's decision to give the defendant in a sexual assault case a reduced sentence "merely because the victim was wearing a tube top with no bra" as an impetus for the original SlutWalk (Szakowski 2011).

4. According to U.S. Bureau of Justice Statistics studies, in 2011 and 2012, 3.2 percent of all people in jail, 4 percent of state and federal prisoners, and 9.5 percent of those held in juvenile detention in the United States reported having been sexually abused in their current facility in the preceding year (Kaiser and Stannow 2013). Although data on sexual abuse in Canadian prisons are more difficult to obtain, scholars claim that rates are likely similar to U.S. rates (Ellenbogen 2009). Regarding sexual abuse and harassment perpetrated by the carceral state beyond the walls of the prison, a 2015 report by the University of California's Williams Institute documents extensive police harassment of LGBTQ people. For example, according to a 2012 survey of more than 300 residents of Queens, New York, 54 percent of all LGBTQ respondents reported being stopped by police, compared to 28 percent of non-LGBTQ respondents. "Among those individuals who reported being stopped by

police," the report explains, "51 per cent of all LGBTQ respondents and 61 per cent of just transgender respondents reported that they had been physically or verbally harassed by the police during the stop, compared with 33 per cent of non-LGBTQ respondents. Some respondents also reported 'sexual abuse perpetrated . . . by police officers,' including individuals who reported that they were 'forced to perform sexual acts under threat of arrest'" (Mallory, Hasenbush, and Sears 2015, 7–8).

5. The focus of the analysis offered here are SlutWalks in the United States and Canada. On the movement's transnational peregrinations, see Leach (2013), Carr (2013), Lim and Fanghanel (2013), Kapur (2012), Mitra (2012), and Borah and Subhalakshmi (2012).

6. Journalists Gail Dines and Wendy Murphy (2011) accuse SlutWalk of contributing to the "pornification" of women and girls. Bonnie Dow and Julia Wood express concern that SlutWalk "negate[s] or pathologize[s] queerness" (2014, 30). Kathy Miriam criticizes SlutWalk for relying on a neoliberal discourse of self-determination that willfully ignores "the matrices of social relations through which [women's] choices are structured" (2012, 263). Perhaps the most influential critique of SlutWalk has been that it marginalizes women of color; see, for example, Crawford (2011) and Bogado (2011).

7. Deborah Tuerkheimer has noted this similarity. "Like the Take Back the Night rallies before it," she writes, "SlutWalk seeks to spread awareness— to women who have been raped and to others—of the prevalence and harm of rape" (2014, 1461). Tuerkheimer also notes "important differences in emphasis between the two protests." "In contrast to SlutWalk," she observes, "Take Back the Night largely targeted stranger rape and related sexual dangers associated with public spaces" (1461).

8. In this respect, the SlutWalk movement is a paradigmatic example of so-called choice feminism (Kirkpatrick 2010).

9. SlutWalk Toronto, "Why? Because We've Had Enough!, " 2011, archived at https://web.archive.org/web/20110522042925/http://www.SlutWalkToronto.com/about/why.

10. On these anticarceral feminist approaches, see Kelly (2010–11), Ritchie (2012), Patterson (2016), Chen et al. (2011), Whalley and Hacket (2017), Russo (2018), and Dixon et al. (2020).

11. Reclaiming the word "slut," journalist Aura Bogado (2011) writes, "will not stop the criminalization of black women . . . , nor will it stop one woman from being potentially deported after she calls the police subsequent to being raped. SlutWalk completely ignores the way institutional violence is leveled against women of color. The event highlights its origins

from a privileged position of relative power, replete with an entitlement of assumed safety that women of color would never even dream of."

12. For critical responses to the trigger warning phenomenon, see Halberstam (2017), Jarvie (2014), Goldberg (2014), the *Los Angeles Times* Editorial Board (2014), and Lukianoff and Haidt (2015).

13. While some trigger warning advocates have demanded that their use be mandatory, most express a preference for policies that simply encourage, advise, or recommend their use. The guidelines for the use of trigger warnings laid out in Oberlin College's Sexual Offense Resource Guide are an example of one such voluntary trigger warning policy (Falherty 2014).

14. Consider, for example, the severe criminal sentences handed down to Larry Nasser, the former USA Gymnastics national team doctor who sexually assaulted an estimated 250 young women and girls. After pleading guilty to federal child pornography charges in July 2017, Nassar was sentenced to 60 years in federal prison. Then, on January 24, 2018, after pleading guilty to seven counts of sexual assault of minors, Nassar was sentenced by the state of Michigan to 175 years in state prison. Finally, on February 5, 2018, Nassar was sentenced to an additional 40 to 125 years in prison after pleading guilty to three additional counts of sexual assault. The carceral remedies liberalism affords victims of sexual injustice that meet its exceedingly high threshold of criminality are awesome indeed.

15. Reactions by several prominent feminists to the recent convictions of Harvey Weinstein offer a telling glimpse of carceral feminism's contemporary appeal. "The convictions of the once-powerful movie producer certainly bring a measure of validation to his many accusers, both in and out of the courtroom," writes Tuerkheimer (2020), "But this outcome is not an endpoint. While there may never be another prosecution quite like the one of Mr. Weinstein, increasingly we'll see others that resemble it. This alone counts as real progress." Journalist Irin Carmon (2020) is even less reserved in her praise for the Weinstein verdict, calling it "radical," "an indictment of all of society," and a rejection of the "long-standing ordering of society" that "has required women to stay on the correct side of male power."

16. Of course, under current U.S. law, civil remedies do exist for victims of the sort of sexual harassment described in these first two examples. The reason for this is that, throughout the 1970s, feminist activists and attorneys, including Catharine MacKinnon, argued these remedies into existence over the opposition of civil libertarian naysayers. For a history of this feminist struggle, see Baker (2007). For the first legal formulation

of sexual harassment as a form of sex discrimination prohibited under Title VII of the Civil Rights Act of 1964, see MacKinnon (1979). For a recent interview with MacKinnon reflecting on her early work on sexual harassment, see MacKinnon and Mitra (2018).

17. These examples are based on the stories of Maribel Hoyos, a former employee at a McDonald's restaurant in Tuscon, Arizona (Campbell 2019); Sandra Pezqueda, a former employee at the Terranea Resort in Ranchos Pallos Verdes, California (Sainato 2018); an anonymous woman using the pseudonym Grace, who shared her experience of an unwanted sexual encounter with actor Aziz Ansari (Way 2018); and the testimony Dr. Christine Blasey Ford offered before the Senate Judiciary Committee during the confirmation hearings for Associate Justice Brett M. Kavanaugh (Brown 2018).

Bibliography

Abrams, Kathryn. 1995. "Sex Wars Redux: Agency and Coercion in Feminist Legal Theory." *Columbia Law Review* 95 (2): 304–76.

ACLU. 1986. *Polluting the Censorship Debate: A Summary and Critique of the Final Report of the Attorney General's Commission on Pornography.* By Barry W. Lynn. Washington, D.C.: American Civil Liberties Union.

Adams, Don. 2002. "Can Pornography Cause Rape?" *Journal of Social Philosophy* 31 (1): 1–43.

Alarcón, Norma, Ana Castillo, and Cherríe Moraga, eds. 1989. *The Sexuality of Latinas.* Berkeley, Calif.: Third Woman Press.

Allison, Dorothy. 1984. "Public Silence, Private Terror." In *Pleasure and Danger: Exploring Female Sexuality,* edited by Carole S. Vance, 103–14. Boston: Routledge & K. Paul.

American Booksellers Ass'n, Inc. v. Hudnut. 1986. 771 F.2d 323 (7th Cir. 1985), aff'd mem., 475 U.S. 1001 (1986).

Anderson, M. 2011. "SlutWalk New York City Preparing to Take Over Union Square." *Village Voice,* October 1, 2011. https://www.villagevoice.com/.

Assiter, Alison. 1989. *Pornography, Feminism, and the Individual.* London: Pluto Press.

Atkinson, Ti-Grace. 1982. "Why I'm against S/M Liberation." In Linden et al. 1982, 90–92.

Atwood, Margaret. 2018. "Am I a Bad Feminist?" *Globe and Mail,* January 13, 2018. https://www.theglobeandmail.com/.

Audience Member. 1979. Remarks in "Panel Discussion: Effects of Violent Pornography." *New York University Review of Law and Social Change* 8:225–45.

Bader, Hans. 1992. "Portrait of the New Puritanism." *Washington Post,* February 2, 1992. https://www.washingtonpost.com/.

Baker, Carrie N. 2007. *The Women's Movement against Sexual Harassment.* Cambridge: Cambridge University Press.

Bar On, Bat-Ami. 1982. "Feminism and Sadomasochism: Self-Critical Notes." In Linden et al. 1982, 72–82.

Barry, Kathleen. 1979. *Female Sexual Slavery*. Englewood Cliffs, N.J.:
Prentice-Hall.

Barthes, Roland. 1977. "The Death of the Author." In *Image–Music–Text*,
142–48. New York: Hill & Wang.

Bartky, Sandra Lee. 1990. *Femininity and Domination: Studies in the Phe-
nomenology of Oppression*. New York: Routledge.

Bazelon, Emily. 2015. "The Return of the Sex Wars." *New York Times
Magazine*, September 13, 2015. https://www.nytimes.com/.

Beale, Frances M. (1969) 2008. "Double Jeopardy: To Be Black and Female." *Meridians* 8 (2): 166–76.

Bell, Daniel. 1993. *Communitarianism and Its Critics*. Oxford: Oxford
University Press.

Bell, Duncan. 2014. "What Is Liberalism?" *Political Theory* 42 (6):
682–715.

Bernstein, Elizabeth. 2007. "The Sexual Politics of the 'New Abolitionism.'" *differences* 18 (3): 129–51.

Bernstein, Elizabeth. 2010. "Militarized Humanitarianism Meets Carceral
Feminism: The Politics of Sex, Rights, and Freedom in Contemporary
Antitrafficking Campaigns." *Signs* 36 (1): 45–71.

Bernstein, Elizabeth. 2012. "Carceral Politics as Gender Justice? The
'Traffic in Women' and Neoliberal Circuits of Crime, Sex, and Rights."
Theory and Society 41:233–59.

Bindel, Julie. 2017. *The Pimping of Prostitution: Abolishing the Sex Work
Myth*. London: Palgrave Macmillan.

Body Politic. 1982. "Feminists Split on 'Correct' Sex." *Body Politic*, July/
August 1982.

Bogado, Aura. 2011. "SlutWalk: A Stroll through White Supremacy." To
the Curb (blog), May 13, 2011. https://tothecurb.wordpress.com/.

Borah, Rituparna, and Nandi Subhalakshmi. 2012. "Reclaiming the Feminist Politics of SlutWalk." *International Feminist Journal of Politics* 14 (3):
415–21.

Boyer, Paul S. 2002. *Purity in Print: Book Censorship in America from the
Gilded Age to the Computer Age*. Madison: University of Wisconsin Press.

Brake, Elizabeth. 2004. "Rawls and Feminism: What Should Feminists
Make of Liberal Neutrality?" *Journal of Moral Philosophy* 1 (3): 293–309.

Bronstein, Carolyn. 2011. *Battling Pornography: The American Feminist
Anti-pornography Movement, 1976–1986*. Cambridge: Cambridge University Press.

Bronstein, Carolyn. 2014. "The Political Uses of Lesbian Romance Fiction: Reading Patrick Califia's *Macho Sluts* as a Response to 1980s Anti-pornography Feminism." *Journal of Popular Romance Studies* 4 (1): 1–20.

Bronstein, Carolyn, and Whitney Strub, eds. 2016. *Porno Chic and the Sex Wars: American Sexual Representation in the 1970s.* Amherst: University of Massachusetts Press.

Brooke. 1979. "Life, Liberty, and the Pursuit of Porn." *off our backs* 9 (1).

Brown, Emma. 2018. "California Professor, Writer of Controversial Brett Kavanaugh Letter, Speaks Out about Her Allegation of Sexual Assault." *Washington Post,* September 12, 2018. https://www.washingtonpost.com/.

Brown, Rita Mae. (1972) 1975. "The Shape of Things to Come." In *Lesbianism and the Women's Movement,* edited by Nancy Myron and Charlotte Bunch, 69–77. Baltimore: Diana Press.

Brown, Wendy. 1989. Review of *Feminism Unmodified: Discourses on Life and Law,* by Catharine A. MacKinnon (1987). *Political Theory* 17 (3): 489–92.

Brown, Wendy. 2009. *Edgework: Critical Essays on Knowledge and Politics.* Princeton, N.J.: Princeton University Press.

Brownmiller, Susan. 1973. "Is Porn Liberating?" *Boston Globe,* September 11, 1973.

Brownmiller, Susan. 1975. *Against Our Will: Men, Women, and Rape.* New York: Simon & Schuster.

Brownmiller, Susan. 1979. Remarks in "Panel Discussion: Effects of Violent Pornography." *New York University Review of Law and Social Change* 8:225–45.

Brownmiller, Susan. 1980. "Let's Put Pornography Back in the Closet." In Lederer 1980, 252–55.

Brownmiller, Susan. 1999. *In Our Time: Memoir of a Revolution.* New York: Dial Press.

Bruck, Connie. 2019. "Alan Dershowtiz, Devil's Advocate." *New Yorker,* July 29, 2019. https://www.newyorker.com/.

Buckley, William F. 1991. "Please, Libertarians Disunite." *Sun Journal,* September 30, 1991.

Bumiller, Kristin. 2008. *In an Abusive State: How Neoliberalism Appropriated the Feminist Movement against Sexual Violence.* Durham, N.C.: Duke University Press.

Bunch, Charlotte. 1980. "Lesbianism and Erotica in Pornographic America." In Lederer 1980, 91–94.

Butler, Judith. 1982. "Politics, Pleasure, Pain: The Controversy

Continues; Diary of a Conference on Sexuality." *Gay Community News,* December 4, 1982.

Butler, Judith. 2011. "Bodies in Alliance: Gender Theorist Judith Butler on the Occupy and SlutWalk Movements." Interview with Kyle Bella. Truthout, December 15, 2011. https://truthout.org/.

Butler, Judith. 2016. *Notes toward a Performative Theory of Assembly.* Cambridge, Mass.: Harvard University Press.

Caffrey, Raymond T. 1985. "*Lady Chatterley's Lover*: The Grove Press Publication of the Unexpurgated Text." *Syracuse University Library Associates Courier* 20 (1): 49–79.

Calderon, Nikki, and Derek Wakefield. 2014. "A Resolution to Mandate Warnings for Triggering Content in Academic Settings." Associated Students Senate, University of California, Santa Barbara, February 25, 2014. https://www.as.ucsb.edu/senate/resolutions/a-resolution-to -mandate-warnings-for-triggering-content-in-academic-settings/.

Califia, Pat. (1980) 1994a. "The Age of Consent: The Great Kiddy Porn Scare of '77." In Califia 1994d, 39–52.

Califia, Pat. (1980) 1994b. "The Aftermath of the Great Kiddy Porn Scare of '77." In Califia 1994d, 53–70.

Califia, Pat. (1982) 1994c. "Public Sex." In Califia 1994d, 71–82.

Califia, Pat. 1980a. "Among Us, Against Us—The New Puritans." *Advocate* 290:14.

Califia, Pat. 1980b. *Sapphistry: The Book of Lesbian Sexuality.* Tallahassee, Fla.: Naiad Press.

Califia, Pat. 1981a. "A Personal View of the History of the Lesbian S/M Community and Movement in San Francisco." In *Coming to Power: Writings and Graphics on Lesbian S-M,* edited by Samois, 245–86. Boston: Alyson.

Califia, Pat. 1981b. "Feminism and Sadomasochism." *Heresies* 3 (4): 30–36.

Califia, Pat. 1983. "Letter to the Editor," in "Notes and Letters." *Feminist Studies* 9 (3): 594–97.

Califia, Pat. 1988. *Macho Sluts.* Boston: Alyson.

Califia, Pat. 1994d. *Public Sex: The Culture of Radical Sex.* Pittsburgh: Cleis Press.

Campbell, Alexia Fernandez. 2019. "McDonalds Workers Are Striking and Suing the Company—In the Same Week." Vox, May 21, 2019. https:// www.vox.com/.

Caringella, Susan. 2009. *Addressing Rape Reform in Law and Practice.* New York: Columbia University Press.

Carmon, Irin. 2020. "The Weinstein Verdict Is Radical." Cut, February 24, 2020. https://www.thecut.com/.

Carr, Joetta. 2013. "The SlutWalk Movement: A Study in Transnational Feminist Activism." *Journal of Feminist Scholarship* 4 (4): 24–38.

CBS News. 2017. "More than 12M 'Me Too' Facebook Posts, Comments, Reactions in 24 hours." CBS News, October 17, 2017. https://www.cbsnews.com/.

Chancer, Lynn S. 1998. *Reconcilable Differences: Confronting Beauty, Pornography, and the Future of Feminism.* Berkeley: University of California Press.

Chapkis, Wendy. 1997. *Live Sex Acts: Women Performing Erotic Labor.* New York: Routledge.

Charen, Mona. 2018. "What Is the Real Message of #MeToo?" *Jewish World Review,* January 18, 2018. http://www.jewishworldreview.com/.

Chen, Ching-In, Jai Dulani, and Leah Lakshmi Piepzna-Samarasinha, eds. 2011. *The Revolution Starts at Home: Confronting Intimate Violence within Activist Communities.* Boston: South End Press.

Chevigny, Paul. 1979. Remarks in "Panel Discussion: Effects of Violent Pornography." *New York University Review of Law and Social Change* 8:225–45.

Coalition for a Feminist Sexuality. 1983. "Leaflet," in "Notes and Letters." *Feminist Studies* 9 (1): 180–82.

Cohen, Larry. 1977. "SWA Votes to Permit Pornography." *Collegian,* February 16, 1977.

Collins, Patricia Hill. 1990. *Black Feminist Thought: Knowledge, Consciousness and the Politics of Empowerment.* London: Unwin Hyman.

Collins, Patricia Hill. 1993. "Pornography and Black Women's Bodies." In *Making Violence Sexy: Feminist Views on Pornography,* edited by Diana E. H. Russell, 97–103. New York: Teachers College.

Collins, Patricia Hill. 2000. *Black Feminist Thought: Knowledge, Consciousness and the Politics of Empowerment.* 2nd ed. New York: Routledge.

Combahee River Collective. 2014. "A Black Feminist Statement." *Women's Studies* 42:271–80.

Comstock, Anthony. 1883. *Traps for the Young.* New York: Funk & Wagnalls.

Conway, Rosemary. 1976a. "Central Defeats Porno Movie." *Collegian,* November 30, 1976.

Conway, Rosemary. 1976b. "Central Govn't Debates Movies Guarantee." *Collegian,* December 7, 1976.

Cooper, Anna Julia. 1892. *A Voice from the South.* Xenia, Ohio: Aldine.

Cooper, Brittney. 2016. "Intersectionality." In *The Oxford Handbook of Feminist Theory,* edited by Lisa Disch and Mary Hawkesworth, 385–406. Oxford: Oxford University Press.

Corbman, Rachel. 2015. "The Scholars and the Feminists: The Barnard Sex Conference and the History of the Institutionalization of Feminism." *Feminist Formations* 27 (3): 49–80.

Cornell, Drucilla. 1990. "Sexual Difference, the Feminine, and Equivalency: A Critique of MacKinnon's *Toward a Feminist Theory of the State.*" *Yale Law Journal* 100 (7): 2247–75.

Cornell, Drucilla. 2000. *Feminism and Pornography.* Oxford: Oxford University Press.

Corrigan, Rose. 2013. *Up Against a Wall: Rape Reform and the Failure of Success.* New York: New York University Press.

Crawford, Bridget. 2011. "An Open Letter from Black Women to the Slut-Walk." Feminist Law Professors, September 24, 2011. https://www.feministlawprofessors.com/.

Crenshaw, Kimberlé Williams. 1989. "Demarginalizing the Intersection of Race and Sex: A Black Feminist Critique of Antidiscrimination Doctrine, Feminist Theory, and Antiracist Politics." *University of Chicago Legal Forum* 1989 (article 8): 139–67.

Crenshaw, Kimberlé Williams. 1991. "Mapping the Margins: Intersectionality, Identity Politics, and Violence against Women of Color." *Stanford Law Review* 43 (6): 1241–99.

Crenshaw, Kimberlé Williams. 1995. "Comments of an Outsider on the First Amendment." In Lederer and Delgado 1995, 169–75.

Crenshaw, Kimberlé Williams. 2012. "From Private Violence to Mass Incarceration: Thinking Intersectionally about Women, Race, and Social Control." *UCLA Law Review* 59 (6): 1419–72.

Critical Resistance and Incite! 2003. "Resistance-INCITE! Statement on Gender Violence and the Prison-Industrial Complex in the United States." *Social Justice* 30 (3): 141–50.

Daily Mail. 2011. "Scantily-Clad 'Slutwalk' Women March on New York after Police Tell Them to 'Cover Up' to Avoid Rape." *Daily Mail,* October 2, 2011. https://www.dailymail.co.uk/.

Davis, Angela. 1981. *Women, Race, and Class.* New York: Vintage Books.

De Grazia, Edward. 1969. *Censorship Landmarks.* New York: R. R. Bowker.

De Grazia, Edward. 1992. *Girls Lean Back Everywhere: The Law of Obscenity and the Assault on Genius.* New York: Random House.

DeJean, Joan E. 2002. *The Reinvention of Obscenity: Sex, Lies, and Tabloids in Early Modern France.* Chicago: University of Chicago Press.

Delaney, C. F., ed. 1994. *The Liberalism-Communitarianism Debate.* Lanham, Md.: Rowman & Littlefield.

Delgado, Richard, and Jean Stefancic. 1992. "Pornography and Harm to Women: 'No Empirical Evidence?' " *Ohio State Law Journal* 53 (4): 1037–56.

Dershowitz, Alan M. 1982. *The Best Defense.* New York: Random House.

Dershowitz, Alan M. 2002. *Shouting Fire: Civil Liberties in a Turbulent Age.* Boston: Little, Brown.

Devlin, Patrick. 1965. *The Enforcement of Morals.* Oxford: Oxford University Press.

Diamant, Anita. 1981. "Porn Again: An Old Debate, New Feminist Theory, and the Same Damned Questions." *Boston Phoenix,* June 2, 1981.

Diamba, Jessy. 2014. "A.S. Resolution Policy Aims to Protect Students from PTSD Triggers." *Daily Nexus,* University of California, Santa Barbara, March 7, 2014. https://dailynexus.com/.

Dines, Gail, and Wendy J. Murphy. 2011. "SlutWalk Is Not Sexual Liberation." *Guardian,* May 8, 2011. https://www.theguardian.com/.

Dixon, Ejeris, and Leah Lakshmi Piepzna-Samarasinha, eds. 2020. *Beyond Survival: Strategies and Stories from the Transformative Justice Movement.* Chico, Calif.: AK Press.

Douglass, Carole Anne, and Alice Henry. 1982. "Towards a Politics of Sexuality." *off our backs* 12 (6): 2–4, 20–21.

Dow, B., and J. Wood. 2014. "Repeating History and Learning from It: What Can Slutwalks Teach Us about Feminism?" *Women's Studies in Communication* 37:22–43.

Downs, Donald Alexander. 1989. *The New Politics of Pornography.* Chicago: University of Chicago Press.

Duggan, Lisa, and Nan D. Hunter. 2006. *Sex War: Sexual Dissent and Political Culture.* 10th anniversary ed. New York: Routledge.

Duggan, Lisa, and Ann Snitow. 1984. "Porn Law Is about Images, Not Power." *Newsday,* September 26, 1984.

Dworkin, Andrea. (1981) 1991. *Pornography: Men Possessing Women.* New York: Plume.

Dworkin, Andrea. 1979. "Pornography: The New Terrorism." *New York University Review of Law and Social Change* 8:215–18.

Dworkin, Andrea. 1979. Remarks in "Panel Discussion: Effects of Violent

Pornography." *New York University Review of Law and Social Change* 8:225–45.

Dworkin, Andrea. 1987. *Intercourse.* New York: Free Press.

Dworkin, Andrea. 1993a. *Letters from a War Zone.* Brooklyn, N.Y.: Lawrence Hill.

Dworkin, Andrea. 1995. "Fighting Talk." Interview with Michael Moorcock. *New Statesman and Society,* April 21, 1995.

Dworkin, Andrea. 2019. *Last Days at Hot Slit: The Radical Feminism of Andrea Dworkin.* Edited by Johanna Fateman and Amy Scholder. Pasadena, Calif.: Semiotext(e).

Dworkin, Andrea, and Catherine A. MacKinnon. 1985. *The Reasons Why: Essays on the New Civil Rights Law Recognizing Pornography as Sex Discrimination.* Minneapolis: Pornography Resource Centre.

Dworkin, Andrea, and Catharine A. MacKinnon. 1988. *Pornography and Civil Rights: A New Day for Women's Equality.* Minneapolis: Organizing against Pornography.

Dworkin, Andrea, Gloria Jacobs, Marcia Ann Gillespie, Barbara Findlen, Marilyn French, and Ntozake Shange. 1994. "Where Do We Stand on Pornography?" *Ms.* 4 (4): 32–41.

Dworkin, Ronald. 1978. *Taking Rights Seriously.* Cambridge, Mass.: Harvard University Press.

Dworkin, Ronald. 1981. "Do We Have a Right to Pornography?" *Oxford Journal of Legal Studies* 1 (2): 177–212.

Dworkin, Ronald. 1985. *A Matter of Principle.* Cambridge, Mass.: Harvard University Press.

Dworkin, Ronald. 1991a. "Liberty and Pornography." *New York Review of Books* 38 (4): 12–15.

Dworkin, Ronald. 1991b. "Two Concepts of Liberty." In *Isaiah Berlin: A Celebration,* edited by Edna and Avishai Margalit, 100–109. London: Hogarth Press.

Dworkin, Ronald. 1992. "The Coming Battles over Free Speech." *New York Review of Books* 39 (11): 55–64.

Dworkin, Ronald. 1993b. "Women and Pornography." *New York Review of Books* 40 (17): 36–42.

Dworkin, Ronald. 1994. "Pornography: An Exchange." *New York Review of Books* 41 (5): 36–42.

Dyzenhaus, David. 1992. "John Stuart Mill and the Harm of Pornography." *Ethics* 102 (3): 534–51.

Dyzenhaus, David. 1994. "Pornography and Public Reason." *Canadian Journal of Law and Jurisprudence* 7:261–81.

Eaton, Anne W. 2007. "A Sensible Antiporn Feminism." *Ethics* 117 (4): 674–715.

Echols, Alice. 1989. *Daring to Be Bad: Radical Feminism in America, 1967–1975.* Minneapolis: University of Minnesota Press.

Ellenbogen, Phillip. 2009. "Beyond the Border: A Comparative Look at Prison Rape in the United States and Canada." *Columbia Journal of Law and Social Problems* 42 (3): 335–72.

Ellis, Kate, Beth Jaker, and Nan D. Hunter, eds. 1986. *Caught Looking: Feminism, Pornography, and Censorship.* East Haven, Conn.: Longriver Books.

Ellis, Richard. 1988. "Disseminating Desire: Grove Press and the 'End[s] of Obscenity.'" In *Perspectives on Pornography: Sexuality in Film and Literature,* edited by Gary Day and Clive Bloom, 26–43. New York: St. Martin's Press.

Elshtain, Jean Bethke. 1981. *Public Man, Private Woman: Women in Social and Political Thought.* Princeton, N.J.: Princeton University Press.

English, Deirdre. 1987. "Did Porn Destroy Pompeii?" *Mother Jones* 12 (6): 49–50.

English, Deirdre, Amber Hollibaugh, and Gayle Rubin. 1982. "Talking Sex: A Conversation on Sexuality and Feminism." *Feminist Review* 11:40–52.

Fahringer, Herald Price. 1979. "'If the Trumpet Sounds an Uncertain Note . . .'" *New York University Review of Law and Social Change* 8:251–53.

Fahs, Breanne. 2014. "'Freedom To' and 'Freedom From': A New Vision for Sex Positive Politics." *Sexualities* 17 (3): 267–90.

Farrow, Ronan. 2017. "From Aggressive Overtures to Sexual Assault: Harvey Weinstein's Accusers Tell Their Stories." *New Yorker,* October 10, 2017. https://www.newyorker.com/.

Fasteau, Brenda Feigen. 1979. Remarks in "Panel Discussion: Effects of Violent Pornography." *New York University Review of Law and Social Change* 8:225–45.

Fateman, Johanna. 2019. Introduction to *Last Days at Hot Slit: The Radical Feminism of Andrea Dworkin,* by Andrea Dworkin, edited by Johanna Fateman and Amy Scholder, 9–42. Pasadena, Calif.: Semiotext(e).

Feinberg, Joel. 1984. *The Moral Limits of the Criminal Law.* 4 vols. Oxford: Oxford University Press.

Feminist Studies Editors. 1983. "Apology," in "Notes and Letters." *Feminist Studies* 9 (3): 589.

Ferguson, Ann. 1984. "Sex War: The Debate between Radical and Libertarian Feminists." *Signs* 10 (1): 106–12.

Flaherty, Colleen. 2014. "Trigger Unhappy." *Inside Higher Ed,* April 14, 2014. https://www.insidehighered.com/.

Foucault, Michel. 1977. *Discipline and Punish: The Birth of the Prison.* Translated by Alan Sheridan. New York: Vintage Books.

Foucault, Michel. 1984. *The Foucault Reader.* Edited by Paul Rabinow. New York: Pantheon.

France, Marie. 1984. "Sadomasochism and Feminism." *Feminist Review* 16:35–42.

French, David. 2018. "The Great Due Process Revival." *National Review,* February 25, 2018. https://www.nationalreview.com/.

Friedman, Deb. "Feminist Perspectives on Pornography." 1979. *off our backs* 9 (1): 2–3, 30.

Gerhard, Jane F. 2001. *Desiring Revolution: Second-Wave Feminism and the Rewriting of American Sexual Thought, 1920 to 1982.* New York: Columbia University Press.

Gessen, Masha. 2017. "Sex, Consent, and the Dangers of 'Misplaced Scale.'" *New Yorker,* November 27, 2017. https://www.newyorker.com/.

Glass, Loren. 2013. *Counterculture Colophon: Grove Press, the "Evergreen Review," and the Incorporation of the Avant-Garde.* Stanford, Calif.: Stanford University Press.

Goldberg, Jonah. 2014. "The Peculiar Madness of Trigger Warnings." *Los Angeles Times,* May 19, 2014.

Gontarski, S. E. 1998. "Modernism, Censorship, and the Politics of Publishing: The Grove Press Legacy." Lecture delivered at the University of North Carolina, Chapel Hill, April 23, 1998.

Gottschalk, Marie. 2006. *The Prison and the Gallows: The Politics of Mass Incarceration in America.* Cambridge: Cambridge University Press.

Grant, Judith. 2006. "Andrea Dworkin and the Social Construction of Gender." *Signs* 31 (4): 967–93.

Grove Press, Inc. v. Christenberry. 1960. 175 F. Supp. 488 (S.D.Y.N. 1959), aff'd, 276 F.2d 433 (2d Cir. 1960).

Grove Press v. Gerstein. 1964. 378 U.S. 577 (1964).

Gruson, Lindsay. 1984. "Pornography Bill Is Issue in Suffolk." *New York Times,* November 13, 1984. https://www.nytimes.com/.

Halberstam, Jack. 2017. "Trigger Happy: From Content Warning to Censorship." *Signs* 42:535–42.

Hamilton, Amy. 1993. "Sex Wars." *off our backs* 23 (8): 3.

Hancock, Ange-Marie. 2016. *Intersectionality: An Intellectual History.* Oxford: Oxford University Press.

Hannon, Gerald. 1978. "Pornography: The New Terrorism." *Body Politic* 45:11–13.

Hartz, Louis. 1955. *The Liberal Tradition in America: An Interpretation of American Political Thought since the Revolution.* New York: Harcourt.

Heath, Melaine, Julie Gouweloos, and Jessica Braimoh. 2016. "Judging Women's Sexual Agency: Contemporary Sex Wars in the Legal Terrain of Prostitution and Polygamy." *Signs* 42 (1): 199–225.

Hefner, Hugh. 1963. "The Playboy Philosophy: Part Seven." *Playboy Magazine,* June 1963, 69–79.

Heiner, B., and S. Tyson. 2017. "Feminism and the Carceral State: Gender-Responsive Justice, Community Accountability, and the Epistemology of Antiviolence." *Feminist Philosophy Quarterly* 3 (1): Article 3.

Herman, Barbara. 1993. "Could It Be Worth Thinking about Kant on Sex and Marriage?" In *A Mind of One's Own: Feminist Essays on Reason and Objectivity,* edited by Louise M. Antony and Charlotte E. Witt, 53–72. Boulder, Colo.: Westview.

Hernroth-Roghtstein, Annika. 2017. "#MeToo and Trial By Mob." *National Review,* October 20, 2017. https://www.nationalreview.com/.

Hoffman, Barbara. 1976. "SW Must Have Sex, Race Programs." *Collegian,* December 1, 1976.

Holland, Sharon P. 2011. "The 'Beached Whale.'" *GLQ* 17 (1): 89–95.

Hollibaugh, Amber L. 2000. *My Dangerous Desires: A Queer Girl Dreaming Her Way Home.* Durham, N.C.: Duke University Press.

hooks, bell. 1984. *Feminist Theory: From Margin to Center.* Brooklyn: South End Press.

Horowitz, Helen Lefkowitz. 2002. *Rereading Sex: Battles over Sexual Knowledge and Suppression in Nineteenth-Century America.* New York: Knopf.

Hunter, Nan, and Sylvia Law. 1987. "Brief Amici Curiae of Feminist Anti-censorship Taskforce, et al., in *American Booksellers v. Hudnut.*" *University of Michigan Journal of Law Reform* 21:69–136.

James, Selma. 2011. "My Placard Read 'Pensioner Slut' and I Was Proud of It." *Guardian,* June 19, 2011. https://www.theguardian.com/.

Jarvie, Jenna. 2014. "Trigger Happy." *New Republic,* March 3, 2014. https://newrepublic.com/.

Jarvis, Heather. 2011. "Slut-Shaming Begone: An Interview with Heather Jarvis, Cofounder of SlutWalk." Conducted by A. Mistry. Alternet, May

20, 2011. Available at http://web.colby.edu/social-movements/wm
-experience-of-activists/.

Johnson, Kai, Tanika Lynch, Elizabeth Monroe, and Tracey Wang. 2015.
"Our Identities Matter in Core Classrooms." *Columbia Spectator,* April
30, 2015. https://www.columbiaspectator.com/.

Johnson, Kjerstin. 2010. "Douchebag Decree: Oh, Susannah Breslin . . ."
Bitch Media, April 15, 2010. https://www.bitchmedia.org/.

Kagan, Elena. 1995. "Regulation and Hate Speech and Pornography after
R.A.V." In Lederer and Delgado 1995, 202–7.

Kaiser, David, and Lovisa Stannow. 2013. "The Shame of Our Prisons:
New Evidence." *New York Review of Books,* October 24, 2013 https://
www.nybooks.com/.

Kakutani, Michiko. 1993. "Pornography, the Constitution and a Fight
Thereof." *New York Times,* October 29, 1993. https://www.nytimes
.com/.

Kaminer, Wendy. 1980a. "Pornography and the First Amendment: Prior
Restraints and Private Action." In Lederer 1980, 239–46.

Kaminer, Wendy. 1980b. "A Woman's Guide to Pornography and the
Law." *Nation,* June 1980.

Kaminer, Wendy. 1992. "Feminists against the First Amendment." *Atlantic,* November 1992.

Kantor, Jodi, and Rachel Abrams. 2017. "Gwyneth Paltrow, Angelina Jolie,
and Others Say Weinstein Harassed Them." *New York Times,* October
10, 2017. https://www.nytimes.com/.

Kantor, Jodi, and Megan Twohey. 2017. "Harvey Weinstein Paid Off
Sexual Harassment Accusers for Decades." *New York Times,* October 5,
2017. https://www.nytimes.com/.

Kapur, Ratna. 2012. "Pink Chaddis and SlutWalk Couture: The Postcolonial Politics of Feminism Lite." *Feminist Legal Studies* 20 (1): 1–20.

Katz, Leanne. 1993. "Introduction: Women, Censorship, and 'Pornography.'" *New York Law School Law Review* 1:9–18.

Kelly, E. 2010–11. "Philly Stands Up: Inside the Politics and Poetics of
Transformative Justice and Community Accountability in Sexual Assault
Situations." *Social Justice* 37 (4): 44–57.

Khan, Ummni. 2014. *Vicarious Kinks: S/M in the Socio-legal Imaginary.*
Toronto: University of Toronto Press.

Kim, Mimi E. 2015. "Dancing the Carceral Creep: The Anti–Domestic
Violence Movement and the Paradoxical Pursuit of Criminalization, 1973–1986." Google Scholar. https://escholarship.org/content/
qt804227k6/qt804227k6.pdf.

King, Deborah. 1988. "Multiple Jeopardy, Multiple Consciousness: The Context of a Black Feminist Ideology." *Signs* 14 (1): 42–72.

Kirkpatrick, Jennet. 2010. "Introduction: Selling Out? Solidarity and Choice in the American Feminist Movement." *Perspectives on Politics* 8 (1): 241–45.

Kirschner, Molly. 2011. "A 17-Year-Old Does SlutWalk." *Ms.,* October 4, 2011. https://msmagazine.com/.

Klemesrud, Judy. 1978. "Women, Pornography, and Free Speech: A Fierce Debate at NYU." *New York Times,* December 4, 1978. https://www .nytimes.com/.

Koedt, Anne. 1971. "Lesbianism and Feminism." In *Notes from the Third Year: Women's Liberation,* single-issue magazine, 84–89. New York: New York Radical Feminists.

Kraus, Barbara. 1979. "Speech, Equality, and Harm: Feminist Legal Perspectives on Pornography and Hate Propaganda." *off our backs* 23 (4): 4–5.

Laden, Anthony S. 2003. "Radical Liberals, Reasonable Feminists: Reason, Power and Objectivity in MacKinnon and Rawls." *Journal of Political Philosophy* 11 (2): 133–52.

Ladenson, Elisabeth. 2006. *Dirt for Art's Sake: Books on Trial from "Madame Bovary" to "Lolita."* Ithaca, N.Y.: Cornell University Press.

Lancaster, Roger N. 2011. *Sex Panic and the Punitive State.* Berkeley: University of California Press.

Langton, Rae. 1990. "Whose Right? Ronald Dworkin, Women and Pornographers." *Philosophy and Public Affairs* 19 (4): 311–59.

Langton, Rae. 1993. "Speech Acts and Unspeakable Acts." *Philosophy and Public Affairs* 22 (4): 293–330.

Langton, Rae. 1999. "Pornography: A Liberal's Unfinished Business." *Canadian Journal of Law and Jurisprudence* 12:109–33.

Larson, Jane E. 1993. "Women Understand So Little, They Call My Good Nature 'Deceit': A Feminist Rethinking of Seduction." *Columbia Law Review* 93 (2): 374–472.

Law, Sylvia. 1979. "Panel Discussion: Effects of Violent Pornography." *New York University Review of Law and Social Change* 8:225–45.

Lawrence, D. H. (1930) 2004. "Pornography and Obscenity." In *Late Essays and Articles,* edited by James T. Boulton, 233–53. Cambridge: Cambridge University Press.

Leach, Brittany. 2013. "Slutwalk and Sovereignty: Transnational Protest as Emergent Global Democracy." Paper presented at American Political

Science Association annual meeting, Chicago, August 29–September 1, 2013. https://ssrn.com/abstract=2300699.

Lederer, Laura. 1980a. "Women Have Seized the Executive Offices of Grove Press Because . . ." In Lederer 1980, 267–71.

Lederer, Laura, ed. 1980b. *Take Back the Night: Women on Pornography.* New York: William Morrow.

Lederer, Laura, and Richard Delgado, eds. 1995. *The Price We Pay: The Case against Racist Speech, Hate Propaganda, and Pornography.* New York: Hill & Wang.

Lee, Lila. 2000. "Fact's Fantasies and Feminism's Future: An Analysis of the Fact Brief's Treatment of Pornography Victims." *Chicago-Kent Law Review* 75 (3): 785–804.

Leidholdt, Dorchen. 1995. "Pornography in the Workplace: Sexual Harassment Litigation under Title VII." In Lederer and Delgado 1995, 216–32.

Leidholdt, Dorchen, and Janice G. Raymond. 1990. *The Sexual Liberals and the Attack on Feminism.* New York: Pergamon.

Lerman, Lisa. 1979. "Violent Pornography: Degradation of Women versus Right of Free Speech: Preface." *New York University Review of Law and Social Change* 8:181–85.

Lesbians of Colour. 1987. "Racism in Pornography." In *Good Girls/Bad Girls: Sex Trade Workers and Feminists Face to Face,* edited by Laurie Bell, 58–66. Toronto: Seal Press.

Lewis, Felice Flanery. 1976. *Literature, Obscenity, and the Law.* Carbondale: Southern Illinois University Press.

Lim, Jason, and Alexandra Fanghanel. 2013. "'Hijabs, Hoodies, and Hotpants': Negotiating the 'Slut' in SlutWalk." *Geoforum* 48:207–15.

Linden, Robin Ruth, Darlene Pagano, Diana E. H. Russell, and Susan Leigh Star, eds. 1982. *Against Sadomasochism: A Radical Feminist Analysis.* San Francisco: Frog in the Well.

Lipschutz, Barbara. 1979. "Cathexis: A Preliminary Investigation into the Nature of S-M." In *What Color Is Your Handkerchief? A Lesbian S/M Sexuality Reader,* edited by Samois, 8–11. Berkeley, Calif.: Samois.

London, Ephraim. 1979a. Remarks in "Panel Discussion: Effects of Violent Pornography."

Longino, Helen E. 1980. "Pornography, Oppression, and Freedom: A Closer Look." In Lederer 1980, 40–54.

Lorde, Audre. (1978) 1980. "The Uses of the Erotic: The Erotic as Power." In Lederer 1980, 295–300.

Lorde, Audre. 1982. *Zami: A New Spelling of My Name.* New York: Crossing Press.

Lorde, Audre. 1984. *Sister Outsider.* New York: Ten Speed Press.

Los Angeles Times Editorial Board. 2014. "Warning: College Students, This Editorial May Upset You." *Los Angeles Times,* March 31, 2014. https://www.latimes.com/.

Love, Heather. 2011. "Introduction." *GLQ* 17 (1): 1–14.

Lukianoff, Greg, and Jonathan Haidt. 2015. "The Coddling of the American Mind." *Atlantic,* September 2015. https://www.theatlantic.com/.

MacKinnon, Catharine A. 1979. *Sexual Harassment of Working Women.* New Haven, Conn.: Yale University Press.

MacKinnon, Catharine A. (1981) 1987. "Sex and Violence: A Perspective." In MacKinnon 1987a, 85–92.

MacKinnon, Catharine A. (1985) 1987. "Francis Biddle's Sister: Pornography, Civil Rights, and Speech." In MacKinnon 1987a, 163–97.

MacKinnon, Catharine A. 1983a. "Feminism, Marxism, Method and the State: Toward Feminist Jurisprudence." *Signs* 8 (4): 635–58.

MacKinnon, Catharine A. 1983b. "Not a Moral Issue." *Yale Law and Policy Review* 2:321–45.

MacKinnon, Catharine A. 1985. "Pornography, Civil Rights, and Speech." *Harvard Civil Rights–Civil Liberties Law Review* 20:1–70.

MacKinnon, Catharine A. 1987a. *Feminism Unmodified: Discourses on Life and Law.* Cambridge, Mass.: Harvard University Press.

MacKinnon, Catharine A. 1987b. "On Collaboration." In MacKinnon 1987a, 198–205.

MacKinnon, Catharine A. 1989. *Toward a Feminist Theory of the State.* Cambridge, Mass.: Harvard University Press.

MacKinnon, Catharine A. 1993. *Only Words.* Cambridge, Mass.: Harvard University Press.

MacKinnon, Catharine A. (1993) 1995. "Speech, Equality, and Harm: The Case against Pornography." In Lederer and Delgado 1995, 301–14.

MacKinnon, Catharine A. 1997. "The Roar on the Other Side of the Silence." In MacKinnon and Dworkin 1997, 3–24.

MacKinnon, Catharine A. 2001. "'The Case' Responds." *American Political Science Association* (3): 709–11.

MacKinnon, Catharine A. 2006. *Are Women Human? And Other International Dialogues.* Cambridge, Mass.: Harvard University Press.

MacKinnon, Catharine A., and Andrea Dworkin. 1997. *In Harm's Way: The Pornography Civil Rights Hearings.* Cambridge, Mass.: Harvard University Press.

MacKinnon, Catharine A., and Durba Mitra. 2018. "Ask a Feminist:

Sexual Harassment in the Age of #MeToo." Audio conversation. *Signs,* June 4, 2018. http://signsjournal.org/mackinnon-metoo/.

Mallory, Christy, Amira Hasenbush, and Brad Sears. 2015. "Discrimination and Harassment by Law Enforcement Officers in the LGBT Community." eScholarship, University of California, Williams Institute. https://escholarship.org/uc/item/5663q0w1.

McCormack, Thelma. 1985. "Feminism and the First Amendment." *Justice Quarterly* 2 (2): 271–82.

McElroy, Wendy. 1982. *Freedom, Feminism, and the State: An Overview of Individualist Feminism.* Washington, D.C.: Cato Institute.

McElroy, Wendy. 1995. *XXX: A Woman's Right to Pornography.* New York: St. Martin's Press.

McGlynn, Clare, and Ian Ward. 2009. "Pornography, Pragmatism, and Proscription." *Journal of Law and Society* 36 (3): 327–51.

Meese Commission (Attorney General's Commission on Pornography). 1986. *Final Report of the Attorney General's Commission on Pornography.* Nashville, Tenn.: Rutledge Hill Press.

Merkin, Daphne. 2018. "Publicly, We Say #MeToo. Privately, We Have Misgivings." *New York Times,* January 5, 2018. https://www.nytimes.com/.

Michelman, Frank I. 1988–89. "Conceptions of Democracy in American Constitutional Argument: The Case of Pornography Regulation." *Tennessee Law Review* 56:291–313.

Michelman, Frank I. 1995. "Civil Liberties, Silencing, and Subordination." In Lederer and Delgado 1995, 272–76.

Mill, John Stuart. (1869) 1989. *"On Liberty" and Other Writings.* Edited by Stefan Collini. Cambridge: Cambridge University Press.

Miller, Michael E. "Columbia Students Claim Greek Mythology Needs a Trigger Warning." *Washington Post,* May 14, 2015. https://www.washingtonpost.com/.

Miller v. California. 1973. 413 U.S. 15.

Miller-Young, Mireille. 2014. *A Taste for Brown Sugar: Black Women in Pornography.* Durham, N.C.: Duke University Press.

Miriam, K. 2012. Feminism, Neoliberalism, and SlutWalk. *Feminist Studies* 38 (1): 262–66.

Mitra, Durba. 2012. "Critical Perspectives on SlutWalks in India." *Feminist Studies* 38 (1): 254–61.

Moira, Fran. 1982a. "Politically Correct, Politically Incorrect Sexuality." *off our backs* 12 (6): 22–23.

Moira, Fran. 1982b. "Lesbian Sex Mafia ['l s/m'] Speakout." *off our backs* 12 (6): 22–24.

Moira, Fran. 1982c. "Barnard Finale." *off our backs* 12 (6): 24.

Moira, Fran. 1982d. "Response." *off our backs* 12 (7): 23, 26.

Moraga, Cherríe. 1982. Transcript of audio recording of the Lesbian Sex Mafia Speakout on Politically Incorrect Sex, New York, April 25, 1982. Original recording preserved in the Lesbian Herstory Archives (call number SPW 1532-33).

Moraga, Cherríe. 1982. "Barnard Sexuality Conference: Played between White Hands." *off our backs* 12 (7): 23, 26.

Moraga, Cherríe, and Gloria Anzaldúa, eds. 1981. *This Bridge Called My Back: Writings by Radical Women of Color.* Latham, N.Y.: Kitchen Table: Women of Color Press.

Moran, Rachel. 2015. *Paid For: My Journey through Prostitution.* New York: Norton.

Morgan, Robin. 1977. *Going Too Far: The Personal Chronicle of a Feminist.* New York: Random House.

Morgan, Robin. 1980. "Theory and Practice: Pornography and Rape." In Lederer 1980, 134–40.

Morgan, Robin. 1995. "Eroticizing Violence." Letter to the editor. *New York Times Book Review,* February 19, 1995, 39. https://timesmachine.nytimes.com/timesmachine/1995/02/19/667395.html.

Morgan, Robin. 2001. *Saturday's Child: A Memoir.* New York: Norton.

Myron, Nancy, and Charlotte Bunch. 1975. *Lesbianism and the Women's Movement.* Baltimore: Diana Press.

Neier, Aryeh. 1980. "Expurgating the First Amendment." *Nation,* June 21, 1980.

New York Times. 1984. "Minneapolis Mayor Vetoes Plan Defining Pornography as Sex Bias." *New York Times,* January 6, 1984. https://www.nytimes.com/.

Nussbaum, Martha Craven. 1999. *Sex and Social Justice.* Oxford: Oxford University Press.

O'Connor, Daniel and Neil Ortenberg, dir. 2007. *Obscene: A Portrait of Barney Rossett and Grove Press.* New York: Arthouse Films.

Okin, Susan Moller. 1979. *Women in Western Political Thought.* Princeton, N.J.: Princeton University Press.

Okin, Susan Moller. 1989. *Justice, Gender, and the Family.* New York: Basic Books.

Orlando, Lisa. 1982. "Lust at Last! or, Spandex Invades the Academy." *Gay Community News,* May 15, 1982.

Pateman, Carole. 1979. *The Problem of Political Obligation: A Critical Analysis of Liberal Theory.* Chichester, U.K.: Wiley.

Pateman, Carole. 1980. "Women and Consent." *Political Theory* 8 (2): 149–68.

Pateman, Carole. 1988. *The Sexual Contract.* Stanford, Calif.: Stanford University Press.

Pateman, Carole. 1989a. "'God Hath Ordained to Man and Helper': Hobbes, Patriarchy, and Conjugal Right." *British Journal of Political Science* 19 (4): 445–63.

Pateman, Carole. 1989b. "Feminist Critiques of the Public/Private Dichotomy." In *The Disorder of Women,* 118–40. Cambridge: Polity Press.

Pateman, Carole. 1990. "Sex and Power." Review of *Feminism Unmodified: Discourses on Life and Law,* by Catharine MacKinnon (1987). *Ethics* 100 (2): 398–407.

Patterson, Jennifer, ed. 2016. *Queering Sexual Violence: Radical Voices from within the Anti-violence Movement.* Riverdale, N.Y.: Riverdale Avenue Books.

Peligri, Justin. 2014. "Why We Need Trigger Warnings on Syllabi." *GW Hatchet,* George Washington University, April 16, 2014. https://www.gwhatchet.com/.

Pollard, Deana. 1990. "Regulating Violent Pornography." *Vanderbilt Law Review* 43:125–59.

Portillo, Tina. 1991. "I Get Real: Celebrating My Sadomasochistic Soul." In *Leatherfolk: Radical Sex, People, Politics, and Practice,* edited by Mark Thompson, 49–55. Boston: Alyson.

Rabban, David M. 1997. *Free Speech in Its Forgotten Years, 1870–1920.* Cambridge: Cambridge University Press.

Radicalesbians. (1970) 1971. "The Woman-Identified Woman." In *Notes from the Third Year: Women's Liberation,* single-issue magazine, 81–87. New York: New York Radical Feminists.

Redlich, Dean Norman. 1979. "Panel Discussion: Regulation of Pornography." *New York University Review of Law and Social Change* 8:281–300.

Reisman, Judith. 1978. "An Interview with Judith Reisman." *WAVPM NewsPage* 2 (3).

Reisman, Judith. 2010. *Sexual Sabotage: How One Mad Scientist Unleashed a Plague of Corruption and Contagion on America.* New York: WorldNetDaily Books.

Rembar, Charles. 1968. *The End of Obscenity: The Trials of "Lady Chatterley," "Tropic of Cancer," and "Fanny Hill."* New York: Random House.

Rich, Adrienne. 1980a. Afterword to Lederer 1980, 313–20.

Rich, Adrienne. 1980b. "Compulsory Heterosexuality and Lesbian Existence." *Signs* 5 (4): 631–60.

Rich, Adrienne. 1986. *Blood, Bread, and Poetry: Selected Prose, 1979–1985*. New York: Norton.

Richards, David. 1979. Remarks in "Panel Discussion: Effects of Violent Pornography." *New York University Review of Law and Social Change* 8:225–45.

Richie, B. E. 2012. *Arrested Justice: Black Women, Violence and America's Prison Nation*. New York: New York University Press.

Rorty, Richard. 1990. "Feminism and Pragmatism." Lecture delivered at the University of Michigan, December 7, 1990.

Rosen, Ruth. 2000. *The World Split Open: How the Modern Women's Movement Changed America*. New York: Viking.

Roth, Benita. 2004. *Separate Roads to Feminism: Black, Chicana, and White Feminist Movements in America's Second Wave*. Cambridge: Cambridge University Press.

Roth v. United States. 1957. 354 U.S. 476 (1957).

Rubin, Gayle. 1969. "Woman as Nigger." In *Masculine/Feminine: Reading in Sexual Mythology and the Liberation of Women,* edited by Betty Roszak, 231–41. New York: Harper & Row.

Rubin, Gayle. 1975. "The Traffic in Women: Notes on the Political Economy of Sex." In *The Second Wave: A Reader in Feminist Theory,* edited by Linda Nicholson, 27–62. New York: Routledge.

Rubin, Gayle. 1979. "Sexual Politics, the New Right, and the Sexual Fringe." In *What Color Is Your Handkerchief? A Lesbian S/M Sexuality Reader,* edited by Samois, 28–35. Berkeley, Calif.: Samois.

Rubin, Gayle. 1983. "Letters to the Editors." *Feminist Studies* 9 (3): 598–601.

Rubin, Gayle. 1984. "Thinking Sex: Notes for a Radical Theory of the Politics of Sexuality." In *Pleasure and Danger: Exploring Female Sexuality,* edited by Carole S. Vance, 267–319. Boston: Routledge & K. Paul.

Rubin, Gayle. 1991. "The Catacombs: A Temple of the Butthole." In *Leatherfolk: Radical Sex, People, Politics, and Practice,* edited by Mark Thompson, 119–41. Boston: Alyson.

Rubin, Gayle. 1993. "Afterword to 'Thinking Sex: Notes for a Radical Theory of the Politics of Sexuality.'" In *American Feminist Thought at Century's End: A Reader,* edited by Linda Kauffman, 3–64. Cambridge, Mass.: Blackwell.

Rubin, Gayle. 1997–98. "Revisioning Ann Arbor's Radical Past: An Interview with Gayle S. Rubin." Conducted by Karen Miller. In "Unequal Exchange: Gender and Economies of Power," special issue, *Michigan Feminist Studies* 12.

Rubin, Gayle. 2004. "Samois." In *Encyclopedia of Lesbian, Gay, Bisexual, and Transgender History in America,* edited by Mark Stein, 3:67–69. New York: Scribner.

Rubin, Gayle. 2011a. "Blood under the Bridge: Reflections on 'Thinking Sex.'" *GLQ* 17 (1): 15–48.

Rubin, Gayle. 2011b. *Deviations: A Gayle Rubin Reader.* Durham, N.C.: Duke University Press.

Russell, Diana. 1977. "On Pornography: Two Feminists' Perspectives." *Chrysalis* 4:11–17.

Russell, Diana E. H. 1982. "Sadomasochism: A Contra-feminist Activity." In Linden et al. 1982, 176–83.

Russell, Diana E. H., ed. 1993. *Making Violence Sexy: Feminist Views on Pornography.* New York: Teachers College.

Russo, Ann. 2018. *Feminist Accountability: Disrupting Violence and Transforming Power.* New York: New York University Press.

Ryan, Alan. 2012. "Liberalism." In *A Companion to Contemporary Philosophy,* edited by Robert E. Goodin, Philip Pettit, and Thomas Pogge, 360–82. West Sussex, U.K.: Wiley-Blackwell.

Safronova, Valeryia. 2018. "Catherine Deneuve and Others Denounce the #MeToo Movement." *New York Times,* January 9, 2018. https://www.nytimes.com/.

Sainato, Michael. 2018. "'It Was Like Hell': California Hotel Workers Break Their Silence on Abuse." *Guardian,* October 26, 2018. https://www.theguardian.com/.

Samois, ed. 1979. *What Color Is Your Handkerchief? A Lesbian S/M Sexuality Reader.* Berkeley, Calif.: Samois.

Samois, ed. 1981. *Coming to Power: Writings and Graphics on Lesbian S-M.* Boston: Alyson.

Samois, ed. 1982. *Coming to Power: Writings and Graphics on Lesbian S-M.* 2nd rev. ed. Boston: Alyson.

Sandoval, Chela. 1991. "U.S. Third World Feminism: The Theory and Method of Oppositional Consciousness in the Postmodern World." *Genders* 10 (1): 1–23.

Schaeffer, Denise. 2001. "Feminism and Liberalism Reconsidered: The Case of Catharine MacKinnon." *American Political Science Review* 95 (3): 699–708.

Schauer, Frederick. 1995. "Uncoupling Free Speech." In Lederer and Delgado 1995, 259–65.

Schlafly, Phyllis, ed. 1987. *Pornography's Victims.* Alton, Ill.: Pere Marquette Press.

Schrim, Janet. 1979. "A Proud and Emotional Statement." In *What Color Is Your Handkerchief? A Lesbian S/M Sexuality Reader,* edited by Samois, 23–25. Berkeley, Calif.: Samois.

Schroeder, Jeanne. 1992. "The Taming of the Shrew: The Liberal Attempt to Mainstream Radical Feminist Theory." *Yale Journal of Law and Feminism* 5:123–80.

Schroeder, Theodore. 1911. *"Obscene" Literature and Constitutional Law: A Forensic Defense of Freedom of the Press.* New York: privately printed.

Scoccia, Danny. 1996. "Can Liberals Support a Ban on Violent Pornography?" *Ethics* 106 (4): 776–99.

Sedgwick, Eve. 1993. *Tendencies.* Durham, N.C.: Duke University Press.

Shimizu, Celine Parreñas. 2007. *The Hypersexuality of Race: Performing Asian/American Women on Screen and Scene.* Durham, N.C.: Duke University Press.

Shklar, Judith N. 1998. "The Liberalism of Fear." In *Political Thought and Political Thinkers,* 3–21. Chicago: University of Chicago Press.

Showden, Carisa. 2011. *Choices Women Make: Agency in Domestic Violence, Assisted Reproduction, and Sex Work.* Minneapolis: University of Minnesota Press.

Sigel, Lisa. 1999. "Pat Califia." *Significant Contemporary American Feminists: A Biographical Sourcebook,* edited by Jennifer Scanlon. Westport, Conn.: Greenwood Press.

Simon, Jonathan. 2007. *Governing through Crime: How the War on Crime Transformed American Democracy and Created a Culture of Fear.* Oxford: Oxford University Press.

Sims, Karen, and Rose Mason with Darlene Pagano. 1982. "Racism and Sadomasochism: A Conversation with Two Black Lesbians." In *Against Sadomasochism: A Radical Feminist Analysis,* edited by Robin Ruth Linden, Darlene Pagano, Diana E. H. Russell, and Susan Leigh Star, 99–105. San Francisco: Frog in the Well.

Smith, Barbara. 1983. *Home Girls: A Black Feminist Anthology.* Latham, N.Y.: Kitchen Table: Woman of Color Press.

Smith, Barbara, and Akasha Gloria Hull, eds. 1982. *All the Women Are White, All the Blacks Are Men, but Some of Us Are Brave: Black Women's Studies.* New York: Feminist Press.

Smith, Marjorie. 1979. Remarks in "Panel Discussion: Effects of Violent Pornography." *New York University Review of Law and Social Change* 8:225–45.

Smith, Rogers. 1993. "Beyond Tocqueville, Myrdal, and Hartz: The

Multiple Traditions in America." *American Political Science Review* 87 (3): 549–66.

Snitow, Ann. 1986. "Retrenchment versus Transformation: The Politics of the Antipornography Movement." In *Caught Looking*, edited by Kate Ellis, Beth Jaker, and Nan D. Hunter, 10–17. East Haven, Conn.: Longriver Books.

"Speech, Equality, and Harm: Feminist Legal Perspectives on Pornography and Hate Propaganda." 1993. *off our backs* 4 (4).

Stansell, Christine. 2010. *The Feminist Promise: 1792 to the Present.* New York: Modern Library.

Steinem, Gloria. 1980. "Erotica and Pornography: A Clear and Present Difference." In Lederer 1980, 35–39.

Strossen, Nadine. 1987. "The Convergence of Feminist and Civil Liberties Principles in the Pornography Debate." *New York University Law Review* 62:201–35.

Strossen, Nadine. 1993. "A Feminist Critique of 'the' Feminist Critique of Pornography." *Virginia Law Review* 79:1099–190.

Strossen, Nadine. 1995. *Defending Pornography: Free Speech, Sex, and the Fight for Women's Rights.* New York: Scribner.

Strossen, Nadine. 1996. "Hate Speech and Pornography: Do We Have to Choose between Freedom of Speech and Equality?" *Case Western Reserve Law Review* 46:449–78.

Strub, Whitney. 2011. *Perversion for Profit: The Politics of Pornography and the Rise of the New Right.* New York: Columbia University Press.

Sunstein, Cass. 1986. "Pornography and the First Amendment." *Duke Law Journal* 35 (4): 589–627.

Sunstein, Cass. 1988. "Feminism and Legal Theory." *Harvard Law Review* 101 (4): 826–48.

Sunstein, Cass. 1992. "Neutrality in Constitutional Law (with Special Reference to Pornography, Abortion, and Surrogacy)." *Columbia Law Review* 92 (1): 1–52.

Sunstein, Cass. 1993. *The Partial Constitution.* Cambridge, Mass.: Harvard University Press.

Sunstein, Cass. 1995. "Words, Conduct, and Caste." In Lederer and Delgado 1995, 266–71.

Szakowski, Anastasia. 2011. "This Sunday: Wear Your Slut Pride at Slut-Walk." Shameless, March 29, 2011. https://shamelessmag.com/.

Taylor, Keeanga-Yamahtta. 2017. *How We Get Free: Black Feminism and the Combahee River Collective.* Chicago: Haymarket Books.

Taylor, Verta, and Leila J. Rupp. 1998. "Women's Culture and Lesbian Feminist Activism: A Reconsideration of Cultural Feminism." *Signs* 19 (1): 32–61.

Teish, Luisah. 1980. "A Quiet Subversion." In Lederer 1980, 115–18.

Terwiel, Anna. 2019. "What is Carceral Feminism?" *Political Theory* 48 (4): 421–42.

Truth, Sojourner. "Ain't I a Woman?" In *Anti-slavery Bugle* (New-Lisbon, Ohio), speech transcribed by Marius Robinson, June 21, 1851. In *Chronicling America: Historic American Newspapers.* Washington, D.C.: Library of Congress.

Tuerkheimer, Deborah. 2014. "Slutwalking in the Shadow of the Law." *Minnesota Law Review* 98:1453–511.

Tuerkheimer, Deborah. 2020. "I Spend Hours Talking to Victims. These Verdicts Will Give Them Hope." *New York Times,* February 24, 2020. https://www.nytimes.com/.

Valenti, Jessica. 2011. "SlutWalks and the Future of Feminism." *Washington Post,* June 3, 2011. https://www.washingtonpost.com/.

Vance, Carole. 1982. *Diary of a Conference on Sexuality.* Conference program. New York: Barnard College Women's Center.

Vance, Carole. 1993a. "More Danger, More Pleasure: A Decade after the Barnard Sexuality Conference." *New York Law School Law Review* 38:289–315.

Vance, Carole. 1993b. "Negotiating Sex and Gender in the Attorney General's Commission on Pornography." In *Sex Exposed: Sexuality and the Pornography Debate,* edited by Lynne Segal and Mary McIntosh, 29–49. New Brunswick, N.J.: Rutgers University Press.

Vance, Carole. 2010. "Thinking Trafficking, Thinking Sex." *GLQ* 17 (1): 135–43.

Vance, Carole S., ed. 1984. *Pleasure and Danger: Exploring Female Sexuality.* Boston: Routledge & K. Paul.

Vance, Carole, et al. 1983. "Barnard Conference Letter of Complaint," in "Notes and Letters." *Feminist Studies* 9 (1): 177–80.

Vance, Carole, and Ann Snitow. 1984. "Toward a Conversation about Sex in Feminism: A Modest Proposal." *Signs* 10 (1): 126–35.

Walker, Alice. 1980. "Coming Apart." In Lederer 1980, 95–104.

Walker, Alice. 1981. "Porn." In *You Can't Keep a Good Woman Down: Stories,* 77–84. Orlando, Fla.: Harcourt.

Walker, Alice. 1982. "A Letter of the Times, or Should This Sado-Masochism Be Saved?" Linden et al. 1982, 205–9.

Wallsgrove, Ruth. 1985. "Feminist Anti-censorship Taskforce: The Case against Indianapolis." *off our backs* 15 (6): 12–13.

Walters, Suzanna Danuta, ed. 2016. "Pleasure and Danger: Sexual Freedom and Feminism in the Twenty-First Century." Special issue, *Signs* 42 (1).

Walzer, Michael. 1990. "The Communitarian Critique of Liberalism." *Political Theory* 18 (1): 6–23.

Warner, Alex Ellis. 2012. "'Where Angels Fear to Tread': Feminism, Sex, and the Problem of SM, 1969–1993." PhD diss., Rutgers University.

Watson, Lori. 2007. "Pornography and Public Reason." *Social Theory and Practice* 33 (3): 467–88.

Way, Katie. 2018. "I Went on a Date with Aziz Ansari. It Turned Into the Worst Night of My Life." Babe, January 13, 2018. https://babe.net/.

Weiss, Bari. 2018. "Aziz Ansari Is Guilty. Of Not Being a Mind Reader." *New York Times,* January 15, 2018. https://www.nytimes.com/.

Weymouth, T., and Society of Janus. 1999. *Society of Janus: 25 Years.* Rev. ed. Prepared for SOJ 25. San Francisco: Society of Janus. http://www.hawkeegn.com/bdsm/janhis.pdf.

Whalley, Elizabeth, and Colleen Hackett. 2017. "Carceral Feminisms: The Abolitionist Project and Undoing Dominant Feminisms." *Contemporary Justice Review* 20 (4): 456–73.

Whisnant, Rebecca. 2016. "Our Blood: Andrea Dworkin on Race, Privilege, and Women's Common Condition." *Women's Studies International Forum* 58:68–76.

White, Gillian B. 2017. "The Glaring Blind Spot of the 'Me Too' Movement." *Atlantic,* November 22, 2017. https://www.theatlantic.com/.

Wilhelm, Heather. 2018. "#MeToo's Awkward Side Effects." *National Review,* February 7, 2018. https://www.nationalreview.com/.

Willis, Ellen. 1977. "Sexual Counterrevolution 1." *Rolling Stone,* March 24, 1977.

Willis, Ellen. 2014. *The Essential Ellen Willis.* Edited by Nona Willis Aronowitz. Minneapolis: University of Minnesota Press.

Wilson, Elizabeth. 1983. "The Context of 'Between Pleasure and Danger': The Barnard Conference on Sexuality." *Feminist Review* 13:35–41.

Wilson, Yolanda. 2018. "Why Black Women's Experiences of #MeToo Are Different." *Louisiana Weekly,* June 18, 2018. http://www.louisianaweekly.com/.

Witherell, Mary. 1982. "Futter Cites Inaccurate Portrayal for Confiscation." *Barnard Bulletin,* May 12, 1982.

Wythe, Philip. 2014. "Trigger Warnings Needed in Classroom." *Daily*

Targum, Rutgers University, February 18, 2014. https://www.daily targum.com/.

Young, Iris Marion. 2003. "The Logic of Masculinist Protection: Reflections on the Current Security State." *Signs* 29 (1): 1–25.

Zinn, Maxine Baca. 1986. "The Costs of Exclusionary Practices in Women's Studies." *Signs* 11 (2): 290–303.

Index

Lorna N. Bracewell is assistant professor of political science at Flagler College.